Between Desire and Reason

Between Desire and Reason

Rights Discourse at the Crossroads

Fernando Simón-Yarza

ROWMAN & LITTLEFIELD
INTERNATIONAL

London • New York

Published by Rowman & Littlefield International Ltd
6 Tinworth Street, London, SE11 5AL, UK
www.rowmaninternational.com

Rowman & Littlefield International Ltd. is an affiliate of Rowman & Littlefield
4501 Forbes Boulevard, Suite 200, Lanham, Maryland 20706, USA
With additional offices in Boulder, New York, Toronto (Canada), and Plymouth (UK)
www.rowman.com

Copyright © Fernando Simón-Yarza, 2020

This work is a slightly modified version of a book that appeared under the title *Entre el deseo y la razón. Los derechos humanos en la encrucijada*, © Centro de Estudios Políticos y Constitucionales.

All rights reserved. No part of this book may be reproduced in any form or by any electronic or mechanical means, including information storage and retrieval systems, without written permission from the publisher, except by a reviewer who may quote passages in a review.

British Library Cataloguing in Publication Data
A catalogue record for this book is available from the British Library

ISBN: HB 978-1-78661-440-7 | PBK 978-1-5381-4809-9

Library of Congress Cataloging-in-Publication Data Available

ISBN: 978-1-78661-440-7 (cloth)
ISBN: 978-1-5381-4809-9 (pbk)
ISBN: 978-1-78661-441-4 (electronic)

To Ángel J. Gómez Montoro, with gratitude and admiration

Bonum hominis est secundum rationem esse

Thomas Aquinas

* * *

Trahit sua quemque voluptas

Virgil

Contents

Presentation ... xv

Preface: A possible framework for understanding ... 1
   1. Teleology, reality principle and desire principle ... 1
   2. "Ateleological" liberalism and conservatism ... 3
   3. The liberal-ateleological interpretation of rights
      and the desire principle ... 5
   4. Outline ... 5

PART I: GOOD AND REASON IN TWO CLASSICAL POLITICAL TRADITIONS ... 9

1   The Aristotelian-Thomistic tradition ... 11
   1. Introduction ... 11
   2. Human teleology in the classical theory of moral
      natural law ... 12
      2.1. The end: Life according to reason ... 12
      2.2. The limit ... 14
      2.3. Universality of the principles and contingency of their
          recognition ... 15
      2.4. The historicity of understanding and the
          value of tradition ... 16
   3. From ethics to politics ... 17
      3.1. Common good ... 17
      3.2. The law ... 20
          (a) Law and common good ... 20
          (b) Positive law and natural law ... 22
      3.3. The limit of government and law ... 23

	4. Appendix. The reappearance of the antithesis *physis/nomos* in modernity	25
	4.1. A return to Glaucon: Thomas Hobbes	26
	4.2. Antiteleological radicalism in Jean-Jacques Rousseau	27
2	**Immanuel Kant**	**35**
	1. Introduction	35
	2. Reason and good in Kant's moral philosophy	35
	2.1. Matter and form in moral action	36
	2.2. Law, will, and good	38
	2.3. Happiness, good, and *summum bonum*	38
	2.4. Doctrine of virtue	39
	3. Reason and good in Kant's political philosophy	40
	3.1. The originary contract	40
	3.2. Law and morals	42
	(a) The external coercion of law	42
	(b) State and virtue	42
	(c) Legal duties to oneself?	43
	3.3. The ideal state	45
	4. Conclusion: The right to freedom in Kant	47

PART II: ANTIPERFECTIONIST LIBERALISM — 53

3	**"Free and equals": John Rawls's political philosophy**	**55**
	1. Introduction	55
	2. The good in the "original position"	56
	2.1. "Good" versus "contingent conceptions of the good"	58
	2.2. The partiality of primary goods	60
	3. Political liberalism	61
	3.1. Fundamental modifications	61
	3.2. Political not metaphysical?	63
	(a) Philosophical neutrality and religious neutrality	63
	(b) Rawlsian public reason	64
	(c) Philosophical neutrality and conflict of liberties	65
	4. Full theory of the good and Rawlsian liberties	66
	4.1. Goodness as rationality	66
	4.2. An "ateleological teleology"	68
4	**"Equal concern and respect": Ronald Dworkin's philosophy of rights**	**73**
	1. Introduction	73
	2. Clarifying political liberalism	73
	2.1. The principles behind the contract	73

2.2. Political liberalism in *A Matter of Principle*	75
2.3. The *Tanner lectures*	77
(a) Ethical liberalism	77
(b) Critical remarks	80
3. "Rights as trumps"	81
4. Critique of ethical realism and theory of moral truth	83
4.1. Moral truth as responsibility	83
4.2. Critical remarks	85

5 Goods and processes: Jürgen Habermas's ethical-political project   91

1. Introduction	91
2. "Discourse ethics"	92
3. Critical remarks on discourse ethics	94
3.1. The "postmetaphysical age" and the problem of the good	94
3.2. "Ateleological teleology" in Habermas's proceduralism	96
3.3. The reformulation of the "categorical imperative"	98
3.4. Real discourses	98
4. The value of Habermas's project: A criterion of public reason	100
4.1. An impartial criterion	100
4.2. An eminently procedural criterion	102

PART III: THE DEHUMANIZATION OF HUMAN RIGHTS   107

6 Mutual disinterest and civil liberties   109

1. Introduction	109
2. Liberal tolerance as indifference	110
2.1. Precarious recognition	110
2.2. Indifference calls to indifference	112
2.3. Ethical indifference and deterioration of justice	113
2.4. Indifference and cultural paternalism in Ronald Dworkin	114
2.5. Indifference and rights talk	115
3. Human rights and liberation of the libido in jurisprudence	116
3.1. The expansion of the right to privacy	116
3.2. Dialectic of liberal tolerance: The restriction of conscientious objection	121
4. Impossible neutrality and social policies	122

| 7 | Desireless life and undesirable life | 129 |

1. Introduction — 129
2. Desireless life — 130
   - 2.1. Subjective intrinsic values: Dworkin on the *nasciturus* — 131
   - 2.2. Critical remarks on Dworkin's position — 134
     - (a) A misunderstanding? — 134
     - (b) A contradictory theory of value — 135
     - (c) On the classical concept of person — 136
   - 2.3. The most consistent liberal: Singer on the *nasciturus* — 137
   - 2.4. The background problem — 140
     - (a) From ateleological liberalism to preference utilitarianism — 140
     - (b) An empiricist theory of the person — 141
3. Undesirable life — 142
   - 3.1. Assisted suicide in rights jurisprudence — 143
   - 3.2. The superfluous principle — 144
   - 3.3. Antiperfectionist liberalism and the defense of a right to assisted suicide — 145
   - 3.4. Conclusion: Euthanasia, dignified death, and therapeutic obstinacy — 147

8 Playing God? Promethean desires — 153

1. Introduction — 153
2. The thesis of antiperfectionist liberalism — 154
3. The "internal critique" — 155
4. Habermas's critique and the liberal response — 157
   - 4.1. Habermas against the reification of the human being — 157
   - 4.2. Replies to Habermas's standpoint — 158
5. The "external critique" and the liberal reply — 160
   - 5.1. Begotten or made? — 160
   - 5.2. Moral repugnance or physiological reaction? — 162
   - 5.3. Gift or mastery? — 163
6. Reflective equilibrium: Toward another way of thinking — 165

PART IV: CONSTRUCTIVE PROPOSALS — 171

9 Teleology of civil liberties — 173

1. Introduction — 173
2. The *end* of liberties: Basic goods — 174

    3. The *limit* of liberties: A "right to do wrong"?   180
        3.1. The Dworkin/Waldron thesis   180
        3.2. Finnis/George's critique: "Claim-rights" versus "liberty-rights"   181
        3.3. Other contributions to the debate   183
        3.4. Three kinds of claim-rights to do wrong   184
            (a) Prudential reasons   184
            (b) Strictly private questions   185
            (c) Absence of "public reasons"   186

10 Perfectionist liberalism and restriction of the rights discourse   191
    1. Introduction   191
    2. "Perfectionist liberalism" and "personal autonomy" in Joseph Raz   191
    3. Deliberative democracy and restriction of the rights discourse   194
        3.1. The meaning of constitutional rights in the context of discourse theory   195
        3.2. The expansion of rights: An approach to the problem   196
        3.3. The debate upon the expansion of rights: Revision of the arguments in favor of judicial activism   197
        3.4. Conclusion   201

Bibliography   205

Index of names   217

About the author   221

Presentation

I started to write this book in the academic year 2014–2015, during a research stay in the *James Madison Program in American Ideals and Institutions*, at Princeton University. The intellectual atmosphere of the program and the environment provided for by the beautiful Princeton campus constituted an extraordinary opportunity to induct myself into the philosophical traditions discussed in this book, especially the Platonic dialogues and the Aristotelian and Thomistic *corpus*.

I am firmly convinced that despite—or precisely because of—their being classical themes, the issues addressed in these pages are of great relevance to our times. An awareness is growing that the times we are living through reveal symptoms of dehumanization and that, as is sometimes said, there is a "crisis of values" beginning in education and permeating our social and political institutions. With this research, I have dedicated my best efforts to getting to the roots of some of these problems. Though it would be presumptuous to claim to have achieved my goal, it would also be dishonest to deny the purpose itself. I can but humbly hope for benevolence on the part of the reader in assessing my reasons.

I am deeply grateful to the director of the James Madison Program, the Princeton MacCormick Professor of Jurisprudence, Robert P. George, for receiving me as a visiting fellow. Not by chance, one of the reasons that led me to the James Madison Program was my admiration for the work of John Finnis and Robert P. George in the field of legal philosophy.

Among the authors who have influenced my project, I would also want to mention German philosopher Robert Spaemann, who has been one of the main sources of inspiration for these pages. Other authors occupying a similarly privileged position include Hans-Georg Gadamer, Alasdair MacIntyre, Charles Taylor, and Michael Sandel, whose remarks on the importance of tradition and the historicity of understanding have been very useful in my research; Joachim Hruschka and Sharon Byrd, authors of an excellent commentary on the Kantian doctrine of the Right; Ernst-Wolfgang Böckenförde, Martin Kriele, and Martin Rhonheimer, strong advocates of constitutional democracy and, at the same time, of the moral presuppositions necessary to preserve it; and Joseph Raz, whose "perfectionist liberalism" contains suggestive and valuable insights for our times.

My gratitude also extends to other colleagues and friends from the Program at Princeton to whom I had the opportunity to present my project at a germinal stage and whose remarks have been an invaluable help. I would like to mention specifically here Luis Téllez, David Oakley, Robert Koons, Gerard Bradley, Bradford Wilson, Sherif Girgis, Dominic Burbidge, and Danilo Petranovich. I am also indebted to professors Alejandro Vigo, Patricio Fernández, and José María Torralba, deep Kant scholars who have given me helpful suggestions and orientations for a careful and accurate reading of their works. I am especially grateful to Dominic Burbidge and the other members of the *Programme for the Foundations of Law and Constitutional Democracy* at the University of Oxford for the opportunity they gave me to expose some ideas related to the expansion of the rights discourse during an international seminar held at St. John College. I am indebted to Montserrat Herrero and the other members of the Research Seminar in Political Philosophy of the Institute for Culture and Society at the University of Navarra for several critical remarks on an early draft of the project. As they may notice, some of their insights led me to rectify part of my initial scheme. I am also grateful to Rafael Domingo, Miguel Martí, Miquel Solans, and Josep Maria Castellà for their reading of the final draft and further suggestions as well as for their ongoing encouragement during the whole project.

A very special mention should go to José Juan Moreso, Philosophy Professor at the University Pompeu Fabra in Barcelona, for his careful reading of an advanced draft of the book and for his thoughtful suggestions. Apart from helping me to improve the text, his remarks—coming from someone who belongs to a different philosophical tradition—oblige me to continue interrogating myself about my own positions and reflecting upon the points of agreement and convergence among the different authors treated in the book. Besides, they marked the beginning of an affable friendship and a sincere and fruitful academic conversation.

Finally, I must address a very special recognition of gratitude to Professor Ángel J. Gómez Montoro, a person with an uncommon ability to see the facts from a broad perspective and whose intelligence and prudence have guided me since I started my doctoral thesis many years ago. And above all, as always, I give thanks to my beloved parents and to God.

* * *

The cover picture (William Blake's *The Judgment of Solomon*, ca. 1799-1800) dramatically represents the biblical scene recounted in the *First Book of the*

Kings (3,16-18). There is a remarkable parallelism between the attitude of each of the two women, on the one hand, and modern liberalism and the classical conception of justice, on the other. We can compare the willingness to divide the indivisible with the genuine care for the human good; and we can see the contrast between a degenerated equal-rights rhetoric at the expense of the human good, and the readiness to set aside one's interest for the sake of the human good.

Preface: A possible framework for understanding

In the past few decades, one of the main debates in the field of political philosophy has been held between those who uphold the political relevance of the question of the good life—human fulfillment or the human good—and those who maintain a strict separation between this question and political justice.* For the first group, civil liberties are just a *conditio sine qua non* for the human good, by virtue of which they can obtain their value. For the second, the problem of the good life or the human good is a private question, and political society should dedicate itself simply to ensuring an adequate distribution of liberties which allows every individual to pursue their own life project, whatever its content may be. This political agnosticism with respect to the "good life" allows us to speak of an "antiperfectionist" or "ateleological" liberalism, terms I will employ interchangeably throughout the book. It is true that these terms are rather equivocal and could be understood in different ways. Yet I think they may legitimately be deployed to express political agnosticism toward the meaning of a good life, and this is the sense in which I will use these categories. In effect, "ateleological" liberalism maintains that the fundamental political category not only is not the "good" but rather "freedom" or "liberty" regardless or independent of the content of the good.

1. TELEOLOGY, REALITY PRINCIPLE, AND DESIRE PRINCIPLE

I would like to start the book by developing a framework of understanding that, in my view, sheds light upon this debate. In 1979, in a brief essay prepared for the *Festschrift* in honor of the German historian and philosopher Golo Mann—son of the celebrated writer Thomas Mann—Professor Robert

Spaemann proposed a thesis which provides an important hermeneutic key to understanding the modern political dichotomy that ideologically splits liberals and conservatives. According to Spaemann, both liberalism and conservatism are political streams associated with the abandonment of a teleological conception of the human being.[1]

If a human good or *telos* determined by reason is denied, our nonrational inclinations—which constitute the basis of our behavior—cease to be unified by a rational end and they assume the role of guides for our actions. If there is not a rational measure by which our subjective inclinations are justified or assessed—an objective *telos*—these are stripped of any reference beyond the mere satisfaction of individual desires. Thus, individual subjectivity begins to oscillate between what Freud called the "pleasure principle" (*Lustprinzip*) and the "reality principle" (*Realitätsprinzip*).

In his *Formulations on the Two Principles of Mental Functioning*, an essay published in 1911, Freud speaks of these two impulses as the fundamental motivations of human behavior: "just as the pleasure-ego can do nothing but *wish*, work for a yield of pleasure, and avoid unpleasure, so the reality-ego need do nothing but strive for what is *useful* and guard itself against damage." Logically enough, the "pleasure principle" could also be labeled *desire principle*. In fact, both expressions accurately translate the original German term: *Lustprinzip*. In the following pages, I will preferentially speak of the "desire principle."

Strictly speaking, the desire principle takes priority over the reality principle, which only emerges in a second moment, as a consequence of the contradiction produced by reality: the substitution of the reality principle for the desire principle implies "no deposing" but "a safeguarding" of the desire principle. "A momentary pleasure, uncertain in its results, is given up, but only in order to gain along the new path an assured pleasure at a later time."[2] The reality principle appears "under the influence of the instinct of self-preservation."[3] The true motivation of the behavior is therefore the satisfaction of one's desires, and the function of the reality principle is—in the words of Adorno and Horkheimer—to "keep the drives within the limits set by self-preservation."[4]

The Freudian dichotomy that emerges when we reject the idea of a rational *telos* beyond the mere subjective preferences of the individual can also be explained through the classical threefold division of goods, as expounded by Thomas Aquinas:

> Now the end has the nature of good, and good is threefold: the useful (*utile*), the pleasurable (*delectabile*), and the virtuous or honorable (*honestum*). Two of these, namely, the pleasurable and the virtuous or honorable, have the nature of end because both are desirable for their own sake. That indeed is called virtuous which is good according to reason, and this has pleasure attached to it.[5]

The classical idea of the good life as a "virtuous life" represents the *bonum honestum* for all human beings, their true purpose whose value is attached neither to the pleasure that it provides nor to its utility to obtain another good. If we reject the idea of a virtuous life as the true "honest good" (*bonum honestum*) accessible to reason, we are left with two kinds of good: the "pleasurable good" (*bonum delectabile*) and the "useful good" (*bonum utile*). Among them, only the pleasurable good is desirable for its own sake. Hence, if the concept of *bonum honestum* is no longer recognized, the useful good becomes completely subordinated to the pleasurable good. It is exactly the same dichotomy as that suggested by Freud: "desire" or "pleasure principle" (*pleasurable good*) and "reality principle" (*useful good*, for the sake of a pleasurable good).

Pleasure and self-preservation are, undoubtedly, two basic anthropological tendencies. The perfectionist idea of a rational *telos*, of a life in accordance with reason, presents itself as an *end* that provides purpose or meaning to those impulses. Once reason is taken away from the realm of the ends, the *ego*-pleasure tends to expand infinitely. It is stopped only by the *ego*-reality, which represses desire for the sake of self-preservation and which is in turn necessary to continue holding desires.

2. "ATELEOLOGICAL" LIBERALISM AND CONSERVATISM

The Aristotelian tradition of political philosophy takes the human good seriously. It takes shape in a theory of the good ruler and a theory of natural law. The erosion of the public acceptance of a rational *telos* or "good life" gives rise to an opposition between two competing political positions that fight to assert, respectively, the two antagonistic principles emerging as behavioral guides from a non-teleological nature: the desire principle (*liberalism*) and the reality principle (*conservatism*). It should be noted that this suggestion does not entail that non-teleological liberalism always advocates the mere satisfaction of immediate whims. It does not postulate, and nor does it reject, long-term desires; it does not discard, and nor does it recommend, prudence in the selection of the means to satisfy such desires. It just rejects that there is a rational good, intersubjectively acceptable, which orients those desires (*end*) and sets boundaries to them (*limit*); and conversely, it affirms the freedom of the individual to realize those desires. Non-teleological conservatism, on the other hand, represents the reality principle, that is, the keeping of desires within the limits of society's self-preservation.

A paradigmatic example of the contrast between non-teleological conservatism and liberalism on ethical questions is offered, in my view, by the legal-philosophical debate that arose in the 1960s as a result of the lecture delivered by Patrick Devlin in 1958 at the British Academy. Leaving aside the particular question that produced the debate, Devlin defended the right of society to enforce public morality with a conservative argument in the non-teleological sense I have indicated, that is, an argument based on the *reality principle*. In his view, disregarding the truth claims of a moral judgment, "society may use the law to preserve morality in the same way as it uses it to safeguard anything else that is essential to its existence." It is important to note that Devlin did not support his claim with the trivial assertion that any society protects its own ideas but with the right of society to protect its own ideas as part of its "existence" or "moral integrity," disregarding the greater or lesser rationality of their content.[6] The limits placed on liberty to protect public morality are conceived not by reference to the human good of the citizens but to the integrity of the social system: "there must be toleration of the maximum individual freedom that is consistent with the integrity of society."[7] As can be seen, Devlin's argument was a conservative argument, exclusively grounded in the reality principle. At the other extreme of the debate—the desire principle—we could place the conception then defended by Ronald Dworkin,[8] to whom I will dedicate one of the chapters of this book.

In addition to what has been said, it is worth indicating that we should not expect an exact correspondence between the reality principle or the desire principle and the party which, at any particular time, calls itself either "conservative" or "liberal." It is not rare for the option for conservatism or progressivism to be attached to a circumstantial advantage of a class or an individual. With the goal of maximizing social welfare, for instance, some progressives have strongly invigorated the state's structure, which is also a conservative force of order. Seeing their interests jeopardized, many conservatives have demanded more laissez-faire and have defined themselves as libertarians. Similarly, so-called conservatives turn easily into liberals whenever new possibilities of satisfaction without actual risk for their possessions arise, and progressives easily become conservatives when social emancipation threatens their *status*. On environmental issues, for example, many so-called conservatives have embraced for decades the liberal principle of the expansion of desire, thus making their interest prevail over the interests of future generations. For their part, European social democrats have become conservatives in view of the rise of radical leftist movements, in some cases due to the fear of losing the benefits provided by the *status quo*. Finally, we can also see how radical leftist socialism (*desire principle*), once in power, easily turns into real conservative socialism (*reality principle*). The "moral hemiplegia" pointed out by Ortega y Gasset may be sustained in the abstract, but in real life the roles are frequently exchanged—as Ortega himself emphasized—for the sake of interest.[9]

3. THE LIBERAL-ATELEOLOGICAL INTERPRETATION OF RIGHTS AND THE DESIRE PRINCIPLE

The framework already sketched out also sheds light on understanding the debate between natural law theory and "antiperfectionist" liberalism with respect to the meaning of civil liberties. Antiperfectionist liberalism tends to consider them as entitlements which are justified as mere individual "choice." But the question that immediately arises is the following: where do the limits of liberties thus considered lie? Ateleological liberalism has offered the following answer: in the liberties of others. But we could further ask: what objective parameter can be used to resolve conflicts and settle disputes between the liberty preferences of some people and the liberty preferences of others? Facing this objection by Herbert L. A. Hart, John Rawls said that "a liberty is more or less significant depending on whether it is more or less essentially involved in, or is a more or less necessary institutional means to protect, the full and informed and effective exercise of the moral powers in one (or both) of the two fundamental cases [namely, the capacity for a conception of justice (1) and the capacity for a conception of the good (2)]."[10] Nevertheless, it seems that the importance that a liberty has for "the exercise of the capacity for a conception of the good" will depend on which particular conception of the good is at issue, and this takes us back to the preferences of the individual in question. I honestly think that a successful resolution of the collisions of liberties is impossible without a judgment about the different values of the various exercises of liberty at stake and about how worthy of legal protection they are.

4. OUTLINE

Throughout this book, I will go into the very substance of the debate on political "perfectionism" and "antiperfectionism." In part I (chapters 1 and 2), I will present a synthesis of the place that the human good identified by reason occupies in the Aristotelian-Thomistic and in the Kantian ethical-political tradition. As will be seen, the first of them expounds an unequivocal perfectionistic teleology and places the idea of the "common good" at the core of its political considerations. Kantian liberalism, for its part, shares some similarities with the Aristotelian-Thomistic tradition, notwithstanding significant differences too. With this exposition, I intend the reader to appreciate the contrast between those two understandings of "classical" philosophy, on the one hand, and contemporary antiperfectionist liberalism, on the other.

Antiperfectionist liberalism will be examined in part II of the book. First, I will summarize and criticize the political positions defended by John Rawls (chapter 3) and Ronald Dworkin (chapter 4), perhaps the main representatives of antiperfectionist liberalism in the English-speaking academy. A chapter will be dedicated to the ethical project developed by Jürgen Habermas, an author who has acquired an outstanding public importance in Europe. Though maintaining more nuanced positions than the Rawlsian and Dworkinian ones with regard to human teleology, Habermas has also postulated the irrelevance of the question of the good life in the field of political philosophy (chapter 5).

In part III, I will try to show how the complete overlook or disregard of the problem of the good life in the interpretation of the content of liberties ends up in a dehumanization of those liberties. I will use as reference fields the political disinterest regarding the human good of the citizens (chapter 6), the problem of abortion and euthanasia (chapter 7), and the defense made by relevant proponents of antiperfectionist liberalism of so-called liberal eugenics (chapter 8).

To conclude, part IV of the book will be dedicated to the formulation of some constructive proposals for a better understanding of rights in a pluralistic society. I will use for that purpose several valuable categories coined—or at least widely disseminated—by liberal authors, for example, Rawlsian "public reason" or Habermasian "deliberative democracy." I will start this last part by sketching a teleology of freedom's rights (chapter 9). Right after, I will refer to Joseph Raz's liberalism as a fruitful dialogue partner for the classical perfectionist tradition, and I will advocate for the restriction of the discourse of individual freedoms in favor of a stronger democratic deliberation (chapter 10).

As the reader will see, the different chapters of the book enjoy some internal independence. I have proceeded in this way to give a wide perspective of the problems discussed, a vision that should allow the reader to correlate the views of the authors and traditions discussed and contrast them with each other. The inevitable consequence is that the reader may easily omit the reading of a chapter with which they are more familiarized and go directly to others that they find more interesting. Overall, however, the discourse is guided by the hermeneutic principle already indicated: we always move between the classical "perfectionist" teleology, which confers on the human good a preeminent position in the political philosophy and in the interpretation of constitutional categories, including civil liberties, and the "desire principle," which ignores the human good in the interpretation of those liberties.

Another consequence of the number of traditions and authors examined, together with other factors such as the huge bibliography for each of them or the—deliberately moderate—length planned for the book, has been to eschew offering a detailed analysis of the secondary literature. In this vein, I focus on examining some works which have been particularly valuable for my own reading and understanding of the works discussed and that have somehow conditioned the debate. It goes without saying that a more careful study of each author would require a more exhaustive analysis upon the controversies on his works.

Finally, it is also worth noting that the study of the different authors is not confined to their political philosophy but includes references to their moral theories whenever that is useful for a better understanding of their political positions. Starting with the Aristotelian-Thomistic and the Kantian tradition, all the political and legal theories discussed in the book have underlying moral presuppositions, the understanding of which may be important. In the following pages, I have thus attempted to give a faithful account of the thought expounded by their authors, unraveling, if necessary, their moral theory.

NOTES

* Readers who are not familiar with the term 'perfectionism' may draw the wrong conclusion that Aristotle and the classical tradition are committed to something like utopianism or the perfectibility of man. Despite being an ambiguous label, the term "perfectionism" only purports to express the central role of the question of the good life in their political philosophy.

1. Robert Spaemann, "Zur Ontologie der Begriffe 'Rechts' und 'Links,'" in *Was die Wirklichkeit lehrt: Golo Mann zum 70. Geburtstag*, ed. H. Hentig and A. Nitschke (Frankfurt am Main: Fischer, 1979), pp. 141–52.

2. Sigmund Freud, "Formulations on the Two Principles of Mental Functioning," in *The Standard Edition of the Complete Psychological Works of Sigmund Freud*, XII, ed. J. Strachey and A. Freud (London: Hoghart Press, 1953), p. 223.

3. Sigmund Freud, *Jenseits des Lustprinzips* (1920), in *Gesammelte Werke*, XIII, 8th ed. (Frankfurt am Main: Fischer, 1976), p. 6.

4. Max Horkheimer and Theodor W. Adorno, *Dialectic of Enlightenment. Philosophical Fragments* (Stanford, CA: Stanford University Press, 2002), p. 168: "in its negotiations with the superego, the ego, the agency of social control within the individual, keeps the drives within the limits set by self-preservation."

5. "Bonum in tria dividitur: utile, delectabile et honestum. Quod duo, scilicet delectabile et honestum, habent rationem finis, quia utrumque est appetibile propter seipsum. Honestum autem dicitur, quod est bonum secundum rationem, quod quidem habet delectationem annexam" (*Comment. Nich. Eth.*, I, 5, § 58).

6. P. Devlin, *The Enforcement of Morals* (Oxford: Oxford University Press, 1965), p. 11.

7. Devlin, *Enforcement of Morals*, p. 16.

8. R. Dworkin, "Lord Devlin and the Enforcement of Morals," *Yale Law Review* 75 (1965–1966): 986–1005.

9. See Ortega y Gasset, *La rebelión de las masas* (Madrid: Espasa Calpe, 2005), p. 61.

10. John Rawls, *Political Liberalism*, exp. ed. (New York: Columbia University Press), VIII, § 9, pp. 335–36.

Part I

GOOD AND REASON IN TWO CLASSICAL POLITICAL TRADITIONS

Chapter 1

The Aristotelian-Thomistic tradition

1. INTRODUCTION

As indicated in my Introduction, I would like to dedicate the first part of the book to examining two "classical" traditions of moral and political philosophy. The first of them, which I will deal with in this chapter, begins with Plato's writings. Indeed, these are among the first to clearly postulate the overcoming of the antithesis—maintained by the Sophists—between human nature (*physis*) and political conventions (*nomos*). According to this antithesis, that which is "according to nature" (*kata physin*) would be to the benefit of the stronger, taking advantage of the rest of mankind and avoiding punishment; whereas, conversely, that which is according to the law would be merely conventional and unnatural.[1] Against this conception, Plato connects human laws and justice to a nature which precedes all conventions. This can be seen, for instance, in a famous fragment of the 10th Book of *The Laws*. Speaking through an Athenian citizen, Plato censures those who maintain that

> statesmanship in special . . . is a thing which has a little in common with nature, but is mainly a business of art; legislation, likewise, is altogether an affair not of nature, but of art, and its positions are unreal . . . ; they actually declare that . . . there is absolutely no such thing as a real and natural right, that mankind are eternally disputing about rights and altering them. . . . All these views, my friends, come from men who impress the young as wise, prose writers and poets who profess that indefeasible right means whatever a man can carry with the high hand. Hence our epidemics of youthful irreligion—as though there were no gods such as the law enjoins us to believe in—and hence the factions created by those who seek, on such grounds, to attract men to the "really and naturally right life," that is, the life of real domination over others, not of conventional service to them.[2]

This challenge to positivistic conventionalism, as well as the affirmation of what is "naturally just," was the basis upon which the classical philosophers founded what Isaiah Berlin called "the central tradition of Western political thought."[3] I will henceforth refer to it as "the classical tradition." It is a tradition completely guided by a "perfectionist" teleology based on the idea of the "good life" and on the "moral natural law." Its most elaborate and accomplished expression is probably to be found in the work of Thomas Aquinas, which will be discussed in detail in the following sections.

2. HUMAN TELEOLOGY IN THE CLASSICAL THEORY OF MORAL NATURAL LAW

Before fully entering into the classical conception of political philosophy, I will make some general remarks on the ethics underlying such political wisdom. Though discussing moral topics might seem like abandoning the field of political philosophy, the following exposition is necessary, in my view, to acquiring a sound view of the classical political tradition.

2.1. The end: Life according to reason

According to the classical tradition, reason indicates to man not only what "things" are but also what "good and evil" are. Insofar as reason knows what things are, we refer to it as theoretical reason; and insofar as it knows what should be done or avoided, we refer to it as practical reason.[4] While the object of theoretical reason is "the truth," the object of practical reason is "the good." Theoretical reason seeks what *is* without any purpose beyond the fact of knowing, while practical reason inquires about the desirable and the undesirable, about what ought to be done or avoided.

The inner disposition of man toward the rational good receives the name of virtue, and virtue is acquired by acting in accordance with the good determined by reason. To understand this, it is worth mentioning the basic Aristotelian distinction between *praxis* and *poiesis*. Aristotle speaks of *poiesis* to describe human action from the perspective of its aptitude to achieve certain external outcomes, that is, from the perspective of its suitability to produce goods which exist outside the agent. By contrast, he speaks of human action as *praxis* to describe it from the perspective of the imprint that action itself leaves on the acting subject.[5] This is, strictly speaking, the moral dimension or the moral meaning of human action. Every human action—including the production of external things, *poiesis*—is *praxis*, since it leaves an imprint on the agent; it seals a habit or disposition in his powers or capacities. Besides its external consequences, human action always has an immanent dimension:

it either corrupts or perfects the human being. The agent's perfection through his actions is what we call virtue.

Among the "cardinal" virtues, those that subordinate the sensitive part of the soul—libido or sensuality (*epithymia*), on the one hand, and spirit or aggressiveness (*thymos*), on the other[6]—to reason are the most basic ones. However, from a political point of view, justice and prudence have a special significance. Just as temperance and fortitude demand the subordination of the sensitive part of the soul to one's rational good, justice is the virtue that subordinates the will itself to the rational good owed to others, be it the rational good of one person or the rational good of the whole community.[7] In Ulpian's famous definition, justice is the disposition of the will to give each person his due ("his right thing," *ius suum*).[8] As regards prudence, it is the right disposition of one's practical understanding toward the good: the "right reason applied to practice" (*recta ratio agibilium*).[9]

The virtuous life, life in accordance with reason, constitutes the good life (*eu zen*) for human beings. The harmonious arrangement of their drives becomes a genuine "second nature."[10] They achieve what the Greek philosophers called *eudaimonia*, which is not a merely subjective state of pleasure. It is the true "fulfillment" of man, "human flourishing," or the "good life," which precisely consists in a life "in accordance with reason" (*kata logon*) and "in accordance with virtue" (*kat'areten*).[11] The perfection of a subject has, as Thomas Aquinas explains, a twofold dimension: on the one hand, it means his deepest "good" (*bonum, agathon*), since it is his worthily desired *end*; on the other, it means his true "beauty" (*pulchrum, kalon*), since it is his *form*, attractive to rational contemplation.[12]

The term *eudaimonia* designates the complete fulfillment of a human being in a virtuous life.[13] This flourishing cannot be understood as a simple transposition of an external pattern of behavior that would exclude the spontaneity of the agent. Far from it, as the rational integration of natural inclinations may adopt multiple forms and depends on innumerable factors,[14] among them the proper temperament, tastes, and abilities. This framework for creativity is obviously restrained—though also enriched—by the responsibilities and circumstances we face. Overall, however, human life could be compared to a work of art whose lines and shapes are not exhaustively preestablished by norms.

Finally, the virtuous life is conceived of in the classical tradition as the true autonomy of man since, living that way, he acts according to the superior part of his being: reason. The "upright person" (*spoudaios*)[15] does not stipulate the moral law but, by following its commandments, is ruled by reason and becomes, in a certain sense, "master of himself." It is not uncommon for the classics to encounter the objection that autonomy means self-legislation and that freedom is opposed to heteronomy. Against this, however, their exponents notice that human beings participate in a law that has validity independent of their will. The duty is not "invented" by reason but derives from the perception of good and evil through reason. To act in accordance with reason has nothing to do with heteronomy but consists precisely in being free.[16]

2.2. The limit

The teleological experience is not only the rational experience of human good but also of evil; not only the experience of the *end* but also of the *limit*. Indeed, the classical notion of *telos* conveys both meanings: "end" and "limit."[17] There exists, therefore, a profound unity between the affirmative and negative norms of practical reason, a unity which is grounded in the common basis of both and which manifests in all sorts of spheres of human fulfillment. The limit (*terminus*) lies where actions cease to be compatible with human fulfillment but rather frustrate it. Considering that the virtuous life adopts multiple forms depending on different contexts and temperaments, an action against virtue may also differ depending on the contexts and persons. Yet the classical tradition has long acknowledged the existence of acts that always and in every case (*semper et ad semper*)[18] thwart and pervert the rational good of man. As Aristotle says in a well-known passage of the *Nicomachean Ethics*,

> But not every action nor every passion admits of a mean; for some have names that already imply badness, e.g. spite, shamelessness, envy, and in the case of actions adultery, theft, murder; for all of these and suchlike things imply by their names that they are themselves bad, and not the excesses or deficiencies of them. It is not possible, then, ever to be right with regard to them; one must always be wrong.[19]

It is worth noting that the expression "natural law" is sometimes deployed with special reference to these limits, given the unconditional obligation that they express. Thus, while the positive dimension (*end*) of the human *telos* has a plural and open character and is dependent upon multiple circumstances, its negative dimension (*limit*) has the closed and unconditional character typical of a legal prohibition: "it is a negative precept that fixes the boundary (*terminus*) that man must not exceed in his moral actions."[20]

We should not disregard, in any case, that the obligation expressed by the limit is completely subordinated to the end. Bad actions are not bad due to their violation of the law, but, conversely, they violate the law due to their badness. And they are bad because they corrupt man, because they thwart his end of a life in accordance with reason.

2.3. Universality of the principles and contingency of their recognition

It is appropriate to dedicate a few words to tackling some difficulties and misunderstandings that have arisen from the teleological conception of human nature as a basis for ethics and a presupposition for politics. A common error lies in mistaking the universality of a principle's validity for the universality of its knowledge or recognition. As the classical tradition teaches, only the first principles of practical reason are universally known and cannot be obscured in the mind[21]—which does not mean that they are innate. That the good should be pursued (*bonum est faciendum et prosequendum*) does not require, of course, any demonstration, since it is the first principle of practical reason. The very apprehension of the good is attached to the knowledge that good is what should be pursued.[22] Subsequently, the so-called most common principles (*communissima*) are self-evident (*per se nota*) and do correspond to the objects of the basic inclinations of the human being: "knowledge is good," "friendship is good," "homeliness is good," "the union of the sexes is good," and so forth.

Beyond the first principles, however, there are controversies regarding what is good. The vulgar thesis of conventionalism consists in affirming that the lack of agreement on the content of the good shows the absence of truth in this matter. The historical success of this argument seems to contrast—as Leo Strauss said—with its poor philosophical merits.[23] Contradictory opinions with regard to the good do not prove the lack of existence of the good but— redundancy intended—the existence of contradictory opinions. The causes of these discrepancies are multiple—for example, the corruption of moral knowledge as a consequence of acting against virtue. Every virtue entails a participation of the human being in the rational good. Vice, by contrast, thwarts this participation and impairs perception of the good. In the words of Aristotle,

> The man that has been ruined by pleasure or pain forthwith fails to see any such principle—to see that for the sake of this or because of this he ought to choose and do whatever he chooses and does; for vice is destructive of the principle.[24]

Moral knowledge is a disposition, a habit; but only knowledge of first principles—what Thomas Aquinas calls "synderesis"[25]—remains indelibly printed in human nature. Beyond the most basic principles, errors in the reasoning process, lack of imagination, misperception,[26] immoral acts, and depravation of social customs disorient individuals with respect to their true good, clouding reason and judgment about what should be done.

2.4. The historicity of understanding and the value of tradition

Though everybody acknowledges the most general principles of practical reason, moral knowledge is maintained and developed through the generations by moral traditions. The accumulation of life experiences gives shape to rational practical discourses transformed through time into habits and customs. The popular acknowledgment of the *auctoritas* of the elders, as well as community practice, gives rise to moral and legal aphorisms and opinions which constitute "truthful opinion" (*endoxa*)[27] and deserve a higher respect than mere opinions (*doxa*). The rationality of these truthful opinions cannot be replaced by any political judgment coming from power structures, regardless of its democratic pedigree. For it is clear that centralized political judgments lack, for obvious reasons, the transparency and authenticity of immediate human relations.[28]

The rationality of the *endoxa* cannot be replaced even by theoretical speculation. Deeply aware of the historical condition of man, Hans-Georg Gadamer made an accurate and lucid criticism of what he called "the fundamental prejudice of the Enlightenment," namely, the "prejudice against prejudice itself, which deprives tradition of power."[29] By contrast, the "superiority of ancient ethics" lies in the fact that "it grounds the transition from ethics to politics, to the art of sound legislation, with a view on the indispensability of tradition."[30] Similarly, Julia Annas has characterized as a positive feature of ancient ethics the fact of beginning with moral experience and intuition in order to refine them critically, instead of undertaking the task of creating a "rational system" *a priori*, as happens in some modern ethical and political projects.[31]

In the face of anti-traditionalist prejudice, however, recognition of the historicity of understanding does not demand a descent into historicist relativism. As the founder of modern philosophical hermeneutics said, such a way out would be a false step. As with relativistic skepticism, radical historicism is nothing but the radicalization of the Enlightenment's anti-traditionalist prejudice, up to the point of making the Enlightenment tradition a victim of its own criticism.[32] Relativistic skepticism does not merely underline the historical conditioning of the Enlightenment, but it also deprives any historical tradition—including the Enlightened one—of any possibility of being universally true. This attitude closes the eyes to the basic human experience of the difference between ancient wisdom and unjustified prejudice, between the recognition of authority—which is a source of knowledge—and blind obedience. The experience of this distinction leads to the formation of a well-founded, critical conscience, a conscience awakened to reality. This is precisely the "dialectical" method used by Aristotle in his moral inquiry. It proceeds through a critical examination of the facts provided by one's experience and by the *endoxa*, unmasking contradictions in order to reach the conclusions of moral science.[33] These conclusions will necessarily have an imprecise and general nature, since nothing else can be expected from a general science of human conduct. Beyond the general principles and the absolute limits of action, all positive moral rules—give back what you borrowed, help the needy, and so forth—apply "as a general rule" (*hos epi to poly*) but not in every case.[34]

To conclude—and returning to the previous point—it is impossible to attain a truly critical mind simply through prejudice against every prejudice, seeking to overlook the historicity and finitude of the human person. By acting in such a way, we refuse to acknowledge what we have inherited and therefore to discern what is false in that heritage. Authority and tradition are, as Gadamer has said, a precondition for understanding.[35] On this basis, I think that modern hermeneutics has unmasked an adolescent mood at the heart of the Enlightened attempt to reach the adult age by thinking "independently." A mood that reminds us, by the way, of Socrates's warning not to turn young people into dialectics, since they like to destroy opinions received at home, without being able to replace them with the truth.[36] In short, it is necessary to develop a critical spirit, but that spirit cannot mature by means of a simple opposition to historical wisdom.

3. FROM ETHICS TO POLITICS

In line with classical ethics, classical political theory is a theory of good government and of natural law. As I have already indicated, its major premise is that man is by nature a social animal (*zoon politikon*). This entails that he can only lead a life sufficiently equipped for his own fulfillment—such is the meaning of the Aristotelian *autarkeia*—within a political community.[37] Thus, the purpose of the political community is not simply to ensure the survival of its citizens but, as Aristotle says at the beginning of his *Politics*, also to seek the integral fulfillment of man.[38] Though it comes into existence in order to ensure the satisfaction of the needs of life (*zen*), the *polis* continues to exist for the sake of the "good life" (*eu zen*) of its citizens. The satisfaction of basic needs is the first and most urgent of all public tasks and, at the same time, an essential prerequisite for complete human fulfillment, which can only be attained within society.[39]

3.1. Common good

In a certain sense, we can consider the last chapter of the Aristotelian *Nicomachean Ethics* as an introduction to the *Politics*, for there is an ineluctable interdependence between ethics and politics, between the private good and the common good, between personal virtue and public justice. According to Aristotle, "It is difficult to get from youth up a right training for excellence if one has not been brought up under right laws."[40] Similarly, Thomas Aquinas says that "men congregate in order to live well together, something which the individual man living alone could not attain."[41] In this sentence, we find the essence of the idea of the common good, an idea that was a turning point between the pre-Socratics and the classical tradition. True human flourishing cannot be attained individually but depends on certain political and social conditions that make it possible. Thus, the political community is necessary for human happiness: it is not possible to live a good life without being nourished by the education, customs and laws of a country or without reciprocal benefits resulting for the education, customs and laws of that country. As MacIntyre has stressed, we lived immersed in an institutionalized ensemble of "relationships of the kind of giving and receiving" without which practical reason cannot develop. This implies that "the making and sustaining of those relationships is inseparable from the development of those dispositions and activities through which each is directed toward becoming an independent practical reasoner."[42]

Let us insist that the virtuous life depends on a set of conditions that makes it possible. The participative nature of this common good—individual possession of which does not diminish but rather enhances its possession by others—lies in the core of the Platonic criticism of the Sophists. The latter conceived of the good as something individual and exclusive by definition; therefore, they considered the "so-called" common good as nothing but the individual interests of the ruler.[43]

The common good is indispensable for the well-being of the constituent parts, analogously to how the earth's mineral richness is indispensable for plants to flourish and be nourished. As long as the welfare of citizens depends on the common good, Aristotle says that the common good has a "greater and more complete" nature:

> For even if the end is the same for a single man and for a state, that of the state seems at all events something greater and more complete both to attain and to preserve; for though it is worthwhile to attain the end merely for one man, it is finer and more godlike to attain it for a nation or for city-states.[44]

This superiority of the common good over the merely individual good is exposed to misinterpretations and has in fact been misinterpreted on several occasions—both by its critics, to justify individualism, and by some apparent apologists, to justify an overly authoritarian zeal. To avoid such misunderstandings, some important remarks should be made:

(a) First, the political community lacks a "natural unity" and, therefore, a "natural good" independent from the good of its parts. Thomas Aquinas explicitly denies cities and homes the "unity of nature" (*unitas naturae*), merely assigning them a "unity according to order" (*secundum ordinem*).[45] The political community is not a big individual with its own existential attributes—as it is, for example, in Rousseau's writings—but a group of homes. Consequently, the good of the political community should not be opposed to the good of its parts but rather requires it. Following Aristotle's expression, the superiority of the common good is due to its "architectonic"[46] character: it underlies the good of all citizens. The citizens are only parts to the extent that they belong to that higher order (*secundum ordinem*) on whose adequate disposition the welfare of all the citizens depends. Unlike the home and the state, however, persons have an individual substantiality that may not be reduced to a reference to the whole and that sets boundaries to the demands of the whole. Political activity is not simple *poiesis*, consisting merely in "producing" value content in a technical way, but constitutes a moral *praxis* in itself. The ruler cannot behave in purely consequentialist terms, sacrificing the dignity of the person for the sake of a supposed "quantitative" perfection of the political body. Justice limits the scope of the ruler's action in his task of promoting the common good: "no man ought to injure a person unjustly, in order to promote the common good,"[47] declares Aquinas. *Telos* means not only "end" but also "limit." And the end does not justify the transgression of the limit, since the transgression of the limit would precisely frustrate the end. The end does not justify the means but excludes certain means.

(b) The relationship between virtuous life and political community is not limited to the fact that virtue cannot develop outside of the political community but works the other way around too: *justice in the political community cannot be preserved without virtue*. Just as the good of the whole results in the good of the parts, the good of the parts results in the good of the whole. Indeed, justice—the disposition of the will to give each person their due—may be "individual" or "general" depending on whether it refers to the good of an individual or to the good of the whole. Acting virtuously with regard to all the citizens is what pertains to "general justice."[48] Hence, when moral virtues decrease within society, social relationships diminish. For moral virtues are not purely private but have a "political" dimension, in the sense that "it is by reason of these virtues that man behaves himself well in the conduct of human affairs."[49] Notwithstanding this, it is true that general or legal justice pertains mainly to the ruler, who is in a stricter and more essential sense in charge of the whole group of citizens.[50]

Taking into account all the nuances and observations made in the previous paragraphs, I think we should not be afraid of asserting that the individual pertains to the community like a part to the whole. As for the reluctance of the individualistic mentality to admit this idea, we must be critical: life in accordance with reason is neither selfish nor indifferent toward the other.[51]

3.2. The law

Consistent with the previous considerations, the law is conceived by the classical tradition as a rule "directed to the common good."[52] Here too, teleology is the decisive point for the classics, the "first principle" of all practical affairs. The end of the law does not differ from the end of the whole community, that is, the integral human fulfillment of the citizens, their ability to lead a virtuous life.

(a) Law and common good

The law is an "extrinsic"[53] principle in human affairs, in the sense that it cannot produce virtue or human perfection on its own. Nevertheless, that is not an obstacle to affirming that it plays a very important role in human fulfillment. The fact that it is an extrinsic principle means it cannot create good will by itself. Yet law undeniably exerts a powerful influence, for good or for bad, in the education and customs of a country—all the more so given that, in modern states, laws heavily regulate the education of citizens. The thesis that moral perfection is a purely private issue contradicts the very practice and experience of institutions. Strictly speaking, the virtuous life and good laws are mutually conditioning factors, the first being the cause of the second and the second the cause of the first. If citizens lack virtues, it is impossible to assure the common good.[54] And conversely, the development of virtue requires just laws.[55]

It cannot be ignored, however, that the powers of government are limited, becoming more so as the size of the political community and pluralism among its members grow. In his efforts to define the *communitas perfecta*, Aristotle himself attempted to set boundaries on the population of the *polis*, having in mind that, as it grows, the increased distance between rulers and subjects debilitates government.[56] In line with this thought, we should note that the modern national state does not constitute a people tightly bound together—at least not in the sense envisaged by classical political philosophy—and that whenever it is presented as such an incarnation of a strong national spirit, dangerous fictions come to replace reason and reality.[57] However, the end of the political community is still in this case the common good, no matter that the powers of the public authorities regarding the complete fulfillment of the citizens are limited and—to a great extent—have to be placed at the service of the spontaneity of other political communities closer to the individual. As the political community grows, the capacity of its authorities to directly promote the human good decreases, but there always remains a responsibility to remove serious obstacles to human fulfillment. In particular, there always persists a responsibility to encourage small communities to carry out educational tasks, which, by definition, a great state could not assume without putting pluralism at risk.

The political conditions of modernity require classical political philosophy—mainly referred to as the proper exercise of politics—to be complemented with the political wisdom of constitutionalism, more focused on elucidating the fairest institutional structures for the political process: the *Quis iudicabit?*. The government has to be limited, but that is not to say that it should ignore the integral good of citizens, of present and future generations, as it legislates. It cannot overreach its powers, but neither can it cease to promote the integral good of the people while remaining within its boundaries. Approving a law that could lead society to moral depravation is, in this sense, a gravely unjust act. Notwithstanding how limited the functions of the public authorities are with regard to the common good, they are always called upon to advance it and never to impair it. In a modern and plural context, the promotion of the integral good of citizens mainly takes the form of assisting families and encouraging a social ecology that enables parents to fulfill their educational responsibilities, which in turn constitute the *bonum familiae* with which they contribute to the *bonum commune*.

The fact that the state cannot indiscriminately impose the integral good of the citizens, ignoring their customs and convictions, does not allow us to deny that the law must take that good into account. The classical tradition has no hesitation in affirming that the law takes into account persons and times. Once again, the *telos* of the government and the powers to carry out that *telos* have to be distinguished. Unlike some versions of rationalistic natural law theory, the classical tradition of political philosophy explicitly rejects the notion that the just law is an ideal and ahistorical pattern for the legislator, or that it can ignore the historical circumstances of time and place. Thomas Aquinas insists that the common good is complex and that practical reason—the virtue of prudence—always deals with particulars. Hence, practical judgment is by definition fallible and, in dealing with human issues, age and experience have an inestimable value. For "law should take account of many things, as to persons, as to matters, and as to times."[58] In several passages, Aquinas reiterates that laws cannot indiscriminately impose obligations, because men are imperfect and enforcing overburdensome conduct—even if it is good—would lead to worse results,[59] and society would be deprived of multiple benefits.[60] The legislator should only prohibit those moral evils that are especially obnoxious for political society, in particular those that lead to personal or social harm.[61] Law is "unable to forbid all that is contrary to virtue; and it suffices for it to prohibit whatever is destructive of human intercourse, while it treats other matters as though they were lawful, not by approving of them, but by not punishing them."[62]

Last, human fulfillment through virtue has nothing to do with stifling moralism, which would be incompatible with cultural development. A moralism that repressed human spontaneity would not contribute to human excellence and, in that sense, would not truly promote virtue. The classical concept of virtue (*areté*) points toward human excellence in a wide sense. An untrammeled zeal for the suppression of vice in society—let us consider, for instance, the social environment of Victorian England, whose moralism is censured by John Stuart Mill in his introductory chapter of *On liberty*—has habitually resulted in negative effects. It generates an atmosphere of uniformity and timorousness that impedes cultural development. This goes directly against the "common good," which "comprises many things" (*bonum autem commune constat ex multis*) and includes everything that happens to be "useful for human life."[63]

(b) Positive law and natural law

As we have just seen, the orientation of the law to the common good does not constitute a mere option for the legislator but pertains to the essence of law as its final cause. This means that the law is not a mere arbitrary decree but constitutes a rational "rule and measure." It is obvious that this does not prevent the legislator from enacting arbitrary and unjust laws. With good reason, however, the classical tradition does not consider these to be law in its fullest sense. The principles that regulate rational behavior are not arbitrarily invented but give shape to what the classical philosophers called natural law. Thomas Aquinas concludes that all the laws of the political community derive in a certain sense from natural law. Of course, this means not that every human law may be deduced from an abstract world of Platonic ideas and forms but something much easier to understand.[64]

First, there are some positive legal principles that stem from natural law like conclusions derived from principles (*sicut conclusiones ex principiis*). These are the principles whose validity may be considered unassailable by the legislator and which have been recognized even by prominent legal positivists. Consider, for example, what the great German jurist Georg Jellinek, in his *General Theory of the State*, deemed to be the inviolable foundations of criminal law, among which he included the prohibition of murder.[65] What characterizes these positive legal principles is that their deontic validity is prior to and independent of their own formulation. They are immediate rational conclusions that, expressly or tacitly, correspond to what the ancients called "the natural right," namely, what is just prior to and with complete independence of their positive formulation (*ius naturale, physikon dikaion*).[66]

The Roman jurists included these principles under the category of the *ius gentium*, as opposed to the *ius civile*. Nevertheless, though the *ius gentium* was made up of universally valid principles of justice, the Roman jurists distinguished it from the *ius naturale*. In his *Commentary on the Nicomachean Ethics*,[67] Thomas Aquinas explains that this is due to their partial idea of natural law, reflected in the famous passage of Ulpian: "natural right is what nature teaches all animals."[68] The Roman jurists reduced natural law to those teleological demands that the human species shares with the other species—for example, the self-preservation of the species or the union of the sexes—while the specific demands of rational beings would constitute the *ius gentium*. Aquinas, however, explains that natural law is, for rational beings, acting in accordance with reason, so the distinction made by Ulpian becomes problematic. Strictly speaking, the principles of the *ius gentium* are those principles of positive law that stem from natural law *sicut conclusiones ex principiis*.

Most norms, however, stem from natural law "as implementations of general directives" (*sicut determinationes quaedam aliquorum communium*), and their validity depends exclusively upon their authoritative positivation: *ex sola lege humana vigorem habent*. As John Finnis has explained, the Thomistic concept of *determinatio* should be translated as "concretization," "implementation," or "realization."[69] Just as the architect who constructs a building is simultaneously oriented and restrained by his purpose, while at the same time enjoying a great amount of freedom to execute his task, so the legislator has to promote the common good, which is simultaneously an end open to creative freedom and a constraint.[70] This is mainly the sense in which the classical tradition states that positive laws stem from natural law. As will be seen, this does not mean that the legislator can never behave otherwise or that arbitrary laws do not exist at all as positive laws.

3.3. The limit of government and law

Having described the ends of government and law, a reference to their limits in classical philosophy—namely, illegitimate government and unjust law—becomes necessary. Both the government that exceeds its powers or usurps those of others and the government that exercises them against their justificatory ends are considered illegitimate. The latter has been labeled tyrannical, since it behaves against the good that the ruler is bound to promote and preserve. With his behavior, the tyrant justifies disobedience,[71] for "justice being taken away, then, what are kingdoms but great robberies?"[72] In extreme cases, even tyrannicide can be justified.[73]

What we have generically said regarding illegitimate government is valid for *the law*. In a certain sense, unjust law is not law as it fails to achieve its final cause. Given that law's "final cause" is an integral part of the concept of law, the aphorism *lex iniusta non est lex* makes sense. This expression, which Aquinas borrows from Augustine,[74] dates back at least to Plato. Considered by modern legal positivists and several contemporary authors to be a naïve statement,[75] the truth is that, as occurs with so many practical aphorisms, it purports to express a commonsensical idea in a very simplified way. Thus, in order not to misunderstand it, further interpretation is required.

This aphorism does not attempt to deny the corruptions of law their legal nature in a purely positive sense but to define law by invoking its "focal meaning," the "central case" by reference to which all other uses of the term find their meaning. As occurs with other concepts (e.g., friendship, virtue, being, etc.), the equivocity in the uses of the term "law" is due to their proximity to a central meaning of the concept that justifies them by virtue of its similarity. Aristotle called this phenomenon homonymy or equivocity *pros hen* or "for reference to something."[76] Natural law tradition maintains that the concept of law should not be defined through a "factual" or "positive" common denominator that every possible use of the concept could meet but through its focal meaning. And in this focal sense, the concept of law must include a reference to its purpose. According to the classical natural law tradition, law is, in its focal meaning, an ordering of reason *for the common good*. When we renounce the meaning—the final cause—as a definitional element of human *praxis* and, for the sake of a "purer" theory, seek to define it in exclusively "factual" or "positive" terms—the project of a *wertfrei* social science[77]—the result is a nihilistic loss of reality itself, which ends up stripped of meaning.[78]

Obviously, not every just proposition is law: quite the reverse, it must be valid in a legal, positive sense. Following H. L. A. Hart's categories, we can say that every positive law must be backed by a valid "rule of recognition" and, in the case of the ultimate rule of recognition, that it must be "socially accepted."[79] Still, this is not an obstacle to saying that the law *is*, in its central case, just. The difference between legal positivism and classical natural law theory does not lie in a more "realistic" or "inclusive" approach by the former. Nor does it rest on an erroneous rejection of the "efficient cause" of the law (its positivity) by the natural law tradition, since the natural law tradition explicitly says that law emanates from an organ invested with authority.[80] The difference lies simply in the fact that legal positivism denies an objective, nonarbitrary "final cause" of the law, that is, the common good. Rejecting the idea of justice as an essential part of the concept of law, it tends to characterize law by its efficient cause: *auctoritas, non veritas, facit legem*.[81] The sophistication reached in the analysis of the genesis of law and of the logical relations between rules has been, undoubtedly, an advance in the understanding of the "mechanics of law" due to the efforts of legal positivism—let us consider, by way of example, the contributions of legal thinkers such as Georg Jellinek, Hans Kelsen, or H. L. A. Hart. Nevertheless, this progress in the study of the "mechanics" of law cannot compensate an abandonment of reflection upon the final cause, which would entail an inestimable loss. Within a teleological conception, law emanates "from the reason and will" (*a ratione et voluntate*) of the legislator.[82] As long as it ignores the common good, it departs from reason, ceases to be a "central case" of law, and becomes a "peripheral case," weakened or debilitated due to its disconformity with the central meaning of law.

Finally, though it may appear to be a truism, it is worth noting that unjust law is not only law that directly harms citizens but also law that leaves unpunished private conduct that is seriously harmful to the common good. Suppressing and avoiding evil is more pressing and compelling than positively promoting the common good. Thus, interpreting Isidore of Seville, Aquinas asserted that the law is "useful" in the promotion of the good but "necessary" in the suppression of evil.[83]

4. APPENDIX. THE REAPPEARANCE OF THE ANTITHESIS *PHYSIS/NOMOS* IN MODERNITY

In the preceding pages, I have attempted to give an accurate account of the classical political tradition, which is grounded in a teleological view of human nature. As we have seen, this tradition postulates a continuity between our rational and social nature and just human laws, which are precisely aimed at human fulfillment. I will finish this chapter with some observations on the modern return to the Sophists' antithesis—referred to at the beginning of the chapter—between *physis* and *nomos*.

I will draw on the work of Thomas Hobbes and Jean-Jacques Rousseau, due to their pioneering character and extraordinary influence on modern political thought. As a result of the rejection of a unifying natural human good or *telos*, their political theories reestablished the permanent tension between the *desire principle*, expressed in a pre-political nature, and the *reality principle*, expressed in the conventional political order. The methodological device through which they expressed this tension was the social contract.

Actually, the political contract as such has precedents that date back at least to Plato. Indeed, the idea of an implicit contract assumed by the citizen is an image deployed by Socrates to justify his duty to die for the sake of the laws,[84] and we can also find evidence of the idea of a political compact resting on popular consent among the Roman and medieval jurists.[85] In all these cases, however, contractualism does not presuppose a nonsocial or a nonteleological state of nature. It is merely an image aimed at expressing the due reciprocity between rulers and subjects in their respective duties but does not turn human society into a nonnatural artifact, a *superadditum* alien to a prior, nonpolitical nature. In contrast to these ancient and medieval compact-based explanations, the Hobbesian and Rousseauian contracts conceive of natural man as a being oriented toward the mere satisfaction of his desires.

4.1. A return to Glaucon: Thomas Hobbes

At the beginning of modernity, we find the most influential example of this understanding in Thomas Hobbes. Human nature has for Hobbes a non-teleological character, in the sense that "a common rule of good and evil" does not exist. Conversely, "whatsoever is the object of any man's appetite or desire; that is it, which he for his part calleth good; and the object of his hate and aversion, evil."[86]

Man is determined, thus, by the *desire principle*, and happiness is just "continual success in obtaining those things which a man from time to time desireth."[87] The potentially infinite character of desire is linked to the will to power, which leads man to ensure the means for satisfying any desire that could eventually appear in the future.[88] The emergence of a sovereign power is just a consequence of the selfish interest in self-preservation (*reality principle*), given that the unlimited expansion of desires in the state of nature leads to the "war of every man against every man."[89] As there is no common authority or natural law that goes beyond the passions of men, the state of nature is a state of "the right of all men to all things."[90] Under these circumstances, the transference of power to an absolute sovereign capable of imposing peace takes place.

The "law of nature" is the law of passions, among which fear and the instinct for self-preservation play a leading role.[91] Fear of self-destruction leads to a repression of one's own desires and to the submission of the will to an authority.[92] According to Hobbes, fear is what ultimately grounds a political contract whose essence is the surrender of rights by individuals "to confer all their power and strength upon one man, or upon one assembly of men."[93]

This grounding of political order by Hobbes has been extremely influential in modern political and legal theory. As has been said, it implies a rejection of classical natural law theory and a return to the antithesis *physis/nomos* of the Sophists. In fact, the basis of political obligation according to Hobbes entirely coincides with that expressed by Glaucon in his discussion with Socrates in *The Republic*. In effect, according to Glaucon, the good also lies in the satisfaction of one's desires (*desire principle*). Thus, committing injustice constitutes the highest good when the unjust man is able to avoid punishment. Nevertheless, "the excess of evil in being wronged is greater than the excess of good in doing wrong," and this is the reason why individuals "take the other determine that it is for their profit to make a compact with one another neither to commit nor to suffer injustice" (*reality principle*). This is, according to Glaucon, "the beginning of legislation and covenants between men" and "the genesis and essential nature of justice."[94] We can see in Glaucon the Hobbesian positivist *avant la lettre* or in Hobbes the modern Glauconian.

4.2. Antiteleological radicalism in Jean-Jacques Rousseau

The pre-Platonic antithesis between *physis* and *nomos* reappears in Rousseau even more strongly than in Hobbes.[95] In a more radical way, the natural man is for Rousseau neither a political animal (*zoon politikon*) nor a language animal (*zoon logon echon*). Both sociability and language constitute artificial additions to human nature, which is oriented to the satisfaction of one's instincts.

Once man has entered into society, the tension between nature (*desire principle*) and conventions (*reality principle*) arises within his soul in full force. Man is then obliged to repress his spontaneous instincts in favor of the social conventions and to disguise himself, pretending to be something other than what he is. An opposition between individual wishes and social restrictions emerges. What mostly distinguishes the Rousseauian from the Hobbesian point of view is that, unlike Hobbes, Rousseau does not approve of the resolution of the tension through acceptance of a heteronomy based on fear. He does not accept the alienating subjugation to an external power for the sake of a peace devoid of freedom. Yet, given that he has abandoned the classical teleological view of man as a political being whose individual flourishing *qua* human being is inextricably bound to social customs and laws, every social duty is to be deemed unnatural: "what causes human misery is the contradiction between our condition and our desires, between our duties and our inclination, between our nature and social institutions, between the man and the citizen."[96]

Throughout Rousseau's work, the *leitmotiv* is to solve the contradiction between human nature (*desire principle*) and social conventions (*reality principle*). Nevertheless, the solution to the conflict can only be achieved—in his view—through the complete embodiment of an autarchic and asocial *homme naturel* or the complete incarnation of a denaturalized *citoyen*. The only way out for the contradiction between natural instincts and social conventions lies in the abolition of one of the terms of the contradiction, be it the individual "structure" or the social "superstructure": "one must choose between making a man or a citizen, for one cannot make both at the same time";[97] "make man one and you make him as happy as he can be. Give him entirely to the state or give him entirely to himself. But if you divide his heart, you destroy it."[98] Since Rousseau did not believe in the possibility of returning to the state of nature, he found the only feasible way out in radical socialization, thus opening the path for all modern collectivist ideologies. He affirms that the best constitution is the one that best "denaturalizes" man.[99] In *The Social Contract*, the individual disappears in order to identify himself with the political community. The "superstructure" completely devours the "structure." The individual is annihilated and a collective subject with an unlimited will emerges instead: "the Sovereign, merely by virtue of what it is, is always what it should be."[100]

Rousseau ended up realizing that—leaving aside marginal exceptions—complete socialization is impossible in a modern individualistic society. Consequently, he proposed an interesting "third way" in *Émile*, a way which has become widespread in our societies: the education of a "savage made to inhabit cities," a *sauvage fait pour habiter les villes*,[101] a curious admixture between radical individualism and a resigned Stoic fulfillment of civic duties. Meanwhile, however, his essays have been a perennial source of inspiration for the radical ideologies that—antithetically—have attempted to overcome the contradictions that inevitably follow from this non-teleological nature: *totalitarian collectivism* in all its variants (nationalism, socialism, communism, etc.) and *revolutionary individualism* in all its variants (anarchism, libertarianism, etc.).

NOTES

1. See, mainly, the reply given by Callicles to Socrates in *Gorgias* 482e–384c. Similarly, see Hippias's intervention in *Protagoras* 337c–338b. See also Antiphon, *On Truth*, in M. Gagarin, *Antiphon the Athenian: Oratory, Law and Justice in the Age of the Sophists* (Austin: University of Texas Press, 2002), pp. 65 ff. For the genesis and historical evolution of the conflict of traditions in the interpretations of Greek *dike* and *areté*, see the fundamental research provided by A. MacIntyre, *Whose Justice? Which Rationality?* (Notre Dame, IN: University of Notre Dame Press, 1988), pp. 12–87.

2. *The Laws*, X, 889e–890a. The link between a teleological conception of the world in the classics and the political doctrine of natural law is rightly emphasized by Leo Strauss, *Natural Right and History* (Chicago, IL: University of Chicago Press, 1953), p. 7.

3. Isaiah Berlin, *The Crooked Timber of Humanity: Chapters in the History of Ideas*, 2nd ed. (Princeton, NJ: Princeton University Press, 2013), p. 25. See R. P. George, *Making Men Moral* (Oxford: Oxford University Press, 1993), p. 19.

4. See Aristotle, *De Anima* III, 10, 433a; Aquinas, *Summa Theologiae* I, q. 79, a. 10; and *Sententia Libri Ethicorum* (*Comment. Nic. Eth.*), VI, 2 (§ 1135).

5. *Comment. Nic. Eth.*, I, 12, § 144; see also *S. Th.*, I-II, q. 74, a. 1.

6. The tripartite division of the soul between rational part, aggressiveness (*thymos*), and libido (*epithymia*) comes from Plato (see, paradigmatically, the chariot myth in Socrates's speech in *Phaedrus*, 246a–257b, especially 253d–254d). See also *S. Th.*, I-II, q. 22, a. 3; q. 23, a. 1.

7. *S. Th.*, I-II, q. 59, a. 6; and q. 66, a. 4; and II-II, q. 58, a. 2.

8. *Cfr. S. Th.*, II-II, q. 58, a. 1; quoting Ulpian's definition in the *Digest*, Book I, Title I; and q. 57, a. 1.

9. *S. Th.*, I-II, q. 56, a. 3; and II-II, q. 47, a. 7, 8, and 16.

10. *S. Th.*, I-II, q. 32, a. 3; and q. 78, a. 2; and *Nic. Eth.*, VII, 10, 1152a, and II, 4, 1105b.

11. *Nic. Eth.*, I, 1098a; and *S. Th.*, I-II, q. 3, a. 2.

12. Regarding the coincidence between the "end" (*bonum*) and the "form" (*pulchrum*) in a particular individual, see *S. Th.*, I, q. 5, a. 4. On "the honest" as both "the virtuous" and "the beautiful," see *S. Th.*, II-II, q. 145, a. 1 and 2.

13. *Nic. Eth.*, I, 1097–1098a; 1102a; and T. Aquinas, *Comment. Nic. Eths.*, I, 10 and 19. In the words of Aristotle, the human good is "an activity of the soul in conformity with virtue" and "in a complete life" (*Nic. Eth.*, 1098a). Regarding the happiness of the virtuous person, see also, i. a., Plato, *Gorgias* 470d ff.; *The Republic* I, 354a, IX, 580b-c; and *The Laws*, 660e–662d, 716a–727d. For a careful examination of the concept of happiness in Aristotle, see Robert Spaemann, *Happiness and Benevolence* (Edinburgh: T & T Clark, 2005), pp. 8 ff., 82 ff.

14. *Cfr. S. Th.,* I-II, q. 18, a. 8–10.

15. Regarding the Aristotelian upright man or *spoudaios*, see *Nic. Eth.*, VI, 4, 1140a; and VI, 12, 1143b.

16. See *S. Th.*, I-II, q. 90, a. 3, ad 1 (on man as law for himself); and q. 91, a. 2, ad 3 (on freedom as the absence of subjection to the law). On freedom and autonomy as the rule of reason and the inner friendship between the powers of man, see the Platonic myth of the beast of several heads, the lion and the man, in *Republic* IX, 588b–590e.

17. Aristotle, *Metaphysics*, 1021b.

18. *Super Sententiis*, lib. 3, d. 25, q. 2, a. 1 qc. 2 ad 3: "Ad tertium dicendum, quod ad praecepta negativa tenemur semper et ad semper. . . . Sed ad praecepta affirmativa tenetur homo semper, sed non ad semper, sed loco et tempore determinato." See also, for example, *S. Th.*, II-II, q. 31, a. 2: "omnes enim actus virtutum sunt secundum debitas circumstantias limitandi"; and q. 33, a. 2: "et ideo praecepta negativa obligant semper et ad semper. Sed actus virtutum non quolibet modo fieri debent, sed observatis debitis circumstantiis quae requiruntur ad hoc quod sit actus virtuosus: ut scilicet fiat ubi debet, et quando debet, et secundum quod debet."

19. *Nic. Eth.*, 1107a. Regarding the connection between virtue ethics and intrinsically evil acts, see further Martin Rhonheimer, *The Perspective of Morality* (Washington, DC: Catholic University of America Press, 2011), pp. 201, 350–70.

20. "Terminus autem praefigitur homini, ut ultra non transeat, in moralibus per praeceptum negativum": *S. Th.*, II-II, q. 79, art. 2.

21. See *S. Th.*, I, q. 79, a. 12; *S. Th.*, I-II, art. 94, a. 6; and *Nic. Eth.*, VI, 1141a.

22. See *S. Th.*, I-II, q. 94, a. 2.

23. For an analysis of the argument and a reconstruction of the presuppositions on which conventionalism is based, see Strauss, *Natural Right and History*, pp. 97 ff.

24. See Aristotle, *Nic. Eth.*, VI, 1140b. Even more accurately, the same idea may be found in *S. Th.*, I-II, q. 57, a. 4; q. 58, a. 4; q. 85, a. 3; q. 93, a. 6; and q. 94, a. 2; II-II, q. 47, a. 16; as well as in Aquinas's *Comment. Nic. Eth.*, VII, 1 (§ 1294).

25. *S. Th.*, I, q. 79, a. 12.

26. See also Aristotle, *Nic. Eth.*, 1109a-b: "Hence also it is no easy task to be good. For in everything it is no easy task to find the middle . . . one can get angry—that is easy—or give or spend money; but to do this to the right person, to the right extent, at the right time, with the right aim, and in the right way, *that* is not for every one . . . up to what point and to what extent a man must deviate before he comes blameworthy it is not easy to determine by reasoning, any more than anything else that is perceived by the senses; such things depend on particular facts, and the decision rests with perception." I am indebted to Robert C. Koons for his wise remarks on this issue. In particular, I am grateful for his willingness to share with me his excellent paper, "Natural law, the moral imagination, and prudent exceptions."

27. Aristotle, *Topics*, A 1, 100b, 21–23.

28. On the difference between *populus* and *demos*, and between "the popular" and "the democratic," see the intelligent remarks of the great Spanish jurist and historian Álvaro d'Ors, *Nueva introducción al estudio del Derecho* (Madrid: Civitas, 1999), p. 59 (§ 37). It is a remarkable insight of Alasdair MacIntyre to have emphasized the importance that models of excellence and rules formed in the heart of traditions have for the development of virtues. See in this respect, for example, chapter 14 of *After Virtue. A Study in Moral Theory*, 3rd ed. (Indiana: University of Notre Dame Press, 2007).

29. Hans-Georg Gadamer, *Wahrheit und Methode. Grundzüge einer philosophische Hermeneutik*, in *Gesammelte Werke I* (Tubingen: Mohr Siebeck, 1990), p. 275: "Die grundgelegende Vorurteil der Aufklärung ist das Vorurteil gegen die Vorurteile überhaupt und damit die Entmachtung der Überlieferung." In the same vein, see also MacIntyre, *Whose Justice? Which Rationality?*, pp. 35 ff.

30. Gadamer, *Wahrheit und Methode*, p. 285: "Es kennzeichnet geradezu die Überlegenheit der antiken Ethik über die Moralphilosophie der Neuzeit, daß sie im Blick auf die Unentbehrlichkeit der Tradition den Übergang der Ethik in die 'Politik', die Kunst der rechten Gesetzgebung, begründet."

31. J. Annas, *The Morality of Happiness* (Oxford: Oxford University Press, 1994), p. 444.

32. See, in this vein, Gadamer's critique to historicism. In it, "the principled discredit of any prejudice" becomes "universal and radical" (*Wahrheit und Methode*, p. 280: "Die grundsätliche Diskreditierung aller Vorurteile, die das Erfahrungspathos der neuen Naturwissenschaft mit der Aufklärung verbindet, wird in der historischen Aufklärung universal und radikal").

33. On the dialectic method and the role of the *endoxa*, see E. Berti, "L'uso 'scientifico' della dialettica in Aristotele," in *Nuovi studi aristotelici* (Brescia: Morcelliana, 2014), pp. 265–82.

34. *Nic. Eth.*, XI, 1164b; see also, *v. gr.*, *S. Th.*, II-II, q. 31, a. 1: "omnes enim actus virtutum sunt secundum debitas circumstantias limitandi."

35. Gadamer, *Wahrheit und Methode*, p. 275. The same topic is widely and lucidly developed in, for example, Charles Taylor, *Sources of the Self: The Making of Modern Identity* (Cambridge, MA: Harvard University Press, 1989); see especially chapter 2 ("The Self in the Moral Space"), pp. 25–52.

36. *The Republic*, VII, 539b–d. Regarding a sound critical attitude, open to reality itself, see also Plato, *Euthyphro*, 9e.

37. *Politics*, I, 2, 1253a; Thomas Aquinas, *De Regno*, I, 1; *S. Th.*, I, q. 96, a. 4.

38. *Politics*, 1252a.

39. *Politics*, 1252b; and *De Regno*, I, 15.

40. *Nic. Eth.*, X, 1179b.

41. *De Regno*, I, 15: "Ad hoc enim homines congregantur ut simul bene vivant, quod consequi non posset unusquisque singulariter vivens."

42. Alasdair MacIntyre, *Dependent Rational Animals: Why Human Beings Need the Virtues* (Chicago, IL; La Salle, PA: Open Court, 1999), pp. 102–03, 107; see further chapters 9–11 (pp. 99–146); in a similar way, see also MacIntyre, *Whose Justice? Which Rationality?*, p. 35; as well as John Finnis, *Aquinas: Moral, Political, and Legal Theory* (Oxford: Oxford University Press, 1998), pp. 111–19.

43. See, paradigmatically, the dialogue between Thrasymachus and Socrates at the beginning of *The Republic* (I, 338c ff.). Similarly, Callicles says in Plato's *Gorgias* that what the so-called just laws enact does not correspond to a nonexistent common good but to the particular interests of the weak, who are *de facto* the ones who approve those laws (484b–d).

44. *Nic. Eth.*, I, 1094b.

45. *Summa contra Gentiles*, IV, 35; and II, 58, 5. See in this regard J. Budziszewski, *Commentary on Thomas Aquinas's Treatise on Law* (Cambridge: Cambridge University Press, 2014), pp. 33 ff. Several modern authors who—with good reason—have criticized the organicist idea of the state as a "big individual" unfortunately tend to overlook this important distinction (see, among others, Isaiah Berlin, "Two Concepts of Liberty," in *Liberty* [Oxford: Oxford University Press, 2002], p. 179).

46. *Nic. Eth.*, 1094a; and *Politics*, 1252a. See also Plato, *Statesman*, 305e.

47. "Nullus autem debet alicui nocere iniuste ut bonum commune promoveat" (*S. Th.*, II-II, q. 68, a. 3).

48. On the distinction between *legal or general justice* and *particular justice*, see more extensively, *Nic. Eths.*, V, 1129b–1130b; and *S. Th.*, II-II, q. 53, a. 5.

49. *S. Th.*, I-II, q. 61, a. 5.

50. *S. Th.*, II-II, q. 58, a. 6.

51. *S. Th.*, II-II, q. 47, a. 3 and 10; and I-II, q. 19, a. 10.

52. *S. Th.*, I-II, q. 90, a. 2.

53. *S. Th.*, I-II, q. 90. The intrinsic principles are the "powers" (see *S. Th.*, I, q. 77 ff.) and the "habits" (see *S. Th.*, I-II, q. 49 ff.).

54. *S. Th.*, I-II, q. 92, a. 1.

55. *Nic. Eth.*, 1179b.

56. *Politics*, 1326b.

57. See in this respect, MacIntyre, *Dependent Rational Animals*, pp. 132 ff.

58. *S. Th.*, I-II, q. 96, a. 1c. See also *Nic. Eth.*, VI, 8, 1142a; *S. Th.*, II-II, q. 47, a. 3. See also Plato, *The Republic*, III, 412b; and VII, 539b–d.

59. *S. Th.*, I-II, q. 91, a. 4.

60. *S. Th.*, II-II, q. 78, a. 1, ad 3; and *S. Th.*, II-II, q. 10, a. 11. Aquinas also quotes a famous passage of Augustine's from *De Ordine*, II, 4, 12, in *Corpus Christianorum Series Latina*, XXIX (Turnhout: Brepols, 1970), p. 114: "Aufer meretrices de rebus humanis, turbaveris omnia libidinibus."

61. *S. Th.*, I-II, q. 96, a. 2.

62. *S. Th.*, II-II, q. 77, a. 1, ad 1.

63. *S. Th.*, I-II, q. 95, a. 4; q. 96, a. 1.

64. *S. Th.*, I-II, q. 95, a. 2.

65. Georg Jellinek, *Allgemeine Staatslehre*, 3rd ed. (Berlin: Springer, 1921), p. 374: "The foundations of Criminal law, for example, are to a great extent fixed; the prohibition of heavy attacks to the most important juridical goods does not depend on the state's wishes. Declaring the decriminalization of murder lies outside of the real possibilities of the legislator." ("Die Grundlagen des Strafrechtes z. B. sind in großem Umfang feststehend, die Verpönung schwerer Angriffe auf die wichtigsten Rechtsgüter nicht von dem Belieben des Staates abhängig. Die Straflosigkeit des Mordes auszusprechen, liegt wohl außerhalb der realen gesetzgeberischen Möglichkeit.")

66. See the famous reply given by Antigone to Kreon regarding the prohibition of the burial of his nephew Polineikes, in *The Complete Sophocles I: The Theban Plays*, ed. P. Burian and A. Shapiro (Oxford: Oxford University Press, 2003), pp. 499–501. The passage is mentioned by Aristotle as an example of "the natural right" (*physikon dikaion; Rhetoric*, I, 13, 1373b). See also Thomas Aquinas, *S. Th.*, I-II, q. 95, a. 4; and II-II, q. 57, a. 2; and *Summa c. Gentiles*, III, 129.

67. *Comment. Nich. Eth.*, V, 12, § 1019; and *S. Th.*, II-II, q. 57, a. 3 (on the distinction between *ius naturale* and *ius gentium*).

68. "Ius naturale est, quod natura omnia animalia docuit": *Digestum Vetus Pandectarum Iuris Civilis*, Book I, Title I, Section 3, ed. Hugo a Porta (Lyon, 1558–60), p. 13.

69. See John Finnis, *Natural Law and Natural Rights*, 2nd ed. (Oxford: Oxford University Press, 2011), pp. 281–90.

70. *S. Th.*, I-II, q. 95, a. 2; cf. also *Comment. Nic. Eth.*, V, 12 (§ 1023).

71. S. *Th.*, I-II, q. 96, a. 4, ad 3.

72. Augustine, *De civitate Dei*, IV, 4; in *Aurelii Augustini Opera*, Pars XIV-1, in *Corpus Christianorum Series Latina*, XLVII (Turnhout: Brepols, 1955), p. 101: "Remota itaque iustitia quid sunt regna nisi magna latrocinia?" See also *S. Th.*, II-II, q. 104, a. 6.

73. *Super Sent.*, II, 44, Dist. 2, q. 2. In this early writing, Thomas Aquinas seems to justify Cicero's praise of those who conspired to kill Julius Caesar.

74. See Aquinas, *S. Th.*, q. 92, a. 1, ad 3; Augustine, *De Libero Arbitrio*, I, 5, in *Corpus Christianorum Series Latina*, XXIX (Turnhout: Brepols, 1970), p. 217: "Nam lex mihi esse non videtur, quae iusta non fuerit"; and Plato, *Hippias Major*, 284d.

75. See, for example, Hans Kelsen, *Allgemeine Staatslehre* (Berlin: Julius Springer, 1925), p. 336; H. L. A. Hart, *The Concept of Law*, 2nd ed. (Oxford: Oxford University Press, 1994), p. 8; and "Separation of Law and Morals," *Harvard Law Review* 71, 4 (1958): 615 ff. (with several references to Anglo-American utilitarian

authors, especially to Austin and Bentham); and Ronald Dworkin, *Law's Empire* (Cambridge, MA: Belknap Press of Harvard University Press, 1986), pp. 35–36.

76. On homonimy or equivocity "for reference to something" (*pros hen*), see Aristotle, *Metaphysics*, IV, 2, 1003a–b (with regard to the concept of "being" and the concept of "health"); *Nich. Eth.*, 1096b (with regard to the concept of "good") and 1159a (with regard to "friendship"); *Eudemian Eth.*, 1236a (also with regard to "friendship"); and *Politics*, 1275a–b (with regard to "citizenship"). The expression "focal meaning" is applied to the phenomenon of homonymy *pros hen* since G. L. E. Owen, "Logic and Metaphysics in Some Earlier Works of Aristotle," in *Aristotle and Plato in the Mid-Fourth Century. Papers of the Symposium Aristotelicum Held at Oxford in August 1957*, eds. I. Düring and G. E. L. Owen (Göteborg: Elanders, 1960), pp. 180–99. For the distinction between "central" and "peripheral cases" with regard to the concept of law, see the clear explanation offered by John Finnis in *Natural Law and Natural Rights*, pp. 9–18.

77. Max Weber, "Die 'Objektivität' sozialwissenschaftlicher und sozialpolitischer Erkenntnis," *Archiv für Sozialwissenschaft und Sozialpolitik* 19, 1 (1904): 22–87.

78. This loss of meaning lies at the core of the criticism that, at the end of World War II, Gustav Radbruch addressed to the prevailing German legal thinking during the end of the nineteenth century and the beginning of the twentieth century. See G. Radbruch, "Gesetzliches Unrecht und Übergesetzliches Recht," *Süddeutsche Juristen-Zeitung* 1, 5 (1946): 105–08; and "Die Erneuerung des Rechts," *Die Wandlung* vol. 2, 1 (1947): 8–16. See also Lon Fuller, "Positivism and Fidelity to Law: A Reply to Professor Hart," *Harvard Law Review* 71, 4 (1958): 657 ff. For an outspoken attack to the very possibility of a *wertfrei* social science, see more generally Strauss, *Natural Right and History*, pp. 35 ff.; and Isaiah Berlin, "Five Essays on Liberty: Introduction," in *Liberty*, pp. 22–23; and "Historical Inevitability," in *Liberty*, pp. 131 ff.

79. See, in this respect, Hart, *Concept of Law*, p. 109.

80. See *S. Th.*, I-II, q. 90, a. 4.

81. T. Hobbes, *Leviathan sive de materia, forma et potestate civitatis ecclesiasticae et civilis*, Pars II, Cap. XXVI, in *Thomae Hobbes Malmesburiensis Opera philosophica quae latine scripsit omnia*, vol. III, ed. John Bohm (London, 1841; repr. Aalen: Scientia Verlag, 1966), p. 202.

82. *S. Th.*, I-II, q. 97, a. 3.

83. *S. Th.*, I-II, q. 95, a. 3; see also, the mention to Isidore in q. 95, a. 1 (*sed contra*).

84. *Crito*, 51e–53a.

85. See in this vein, Brian Tierney, *Religion, Law and the Growth of Constitutional Thought 1150–1650* (New York: Cambridge University Press, 1982), pp. 39–42; Brian Tierney, *The Idea of Natural Rights. Studies on Natural Rights, Natural Law, and Church Law 1150–1625* (Grand Rapids, MI: Eerdmans, 1997), p. 249; and Larry Siedentop, *Inventing the Individual: The Origins of Western Liberalism* (Cambridge, MA: Harvard University Press 2014), p. 249.

86. Thomas Hobbes, *Leviathan, or the Matter, Form, and Power of a Commonwealth Ecclesiastical and Civil*, I, Ch. VI, § 7 (Oxford: Oxford University Press, 1998), p. 35.

87. *Leviathan*, I, Ch. VI, § 58, p. 41.
88. *Leviathan*, I, Ch. XI, p. 66.
89. *Leviathan*, I, Ch. XIII, § 13, p. 85.
90. *Leviathan*, I, Ch. XV, § 2, p. 95.
91. *Leviathan*, I, Ch. XIII, § 14, p. 86.
92. *Leviathan*, II, Ch. XVII, § 1, p. 111.
93. *Leviathan*, II, Ch. XVII, § 13, p. 114.
94. *Republic*, II, 358e–359a.
95. See further R. Spaemann, *Rousseau—Bürger ohne Vaterland* (München: Piper, 1980).
96. J.-J. Rousseau, "Sur le bonheur public," in *The Political Writings of Jean-Jacques Rousseau* (New York: Cambridge University Press, 1915), p. 326: "Ce qui fait la misère humaine est la contradiction qui se trouve entre notre état et nos désirs, entre nos devoirs et nos penchants, entre la nature et les institutions sociales, entre l'homme et le citoyen."
97. J.-J. Rousseau, *Émile*, in *Oeuvres complètes IV* (Paris: Gallimard, 1964), p. 248.
98. "Sur le bonheur public," p. 326.
99. *Émile*, p. 249.
100. J.-J. Rousseau, *Le Contrat social*, in *Oeuvres complètes III* (Paris: Gallimard, 1964), p. 363.
101. *Émile*, p. 111.

Chapter 2

Immanuel Kant

1. INTRODUCTION

In this second chapter, we will study the work of an eighteenth-century philosopher, Immanuel Kant, who attempted to rescue the rationality of the moral good from its subordination to the sensible inclinations, as the empiricists had postulated. Kant's constitutes one of the deepest and most valuable monuments to the theory of practical rationality, and as some academics have stressed, it bears important similarities with Aristotle's ethics.[1] Notwithstanding the obvious differences between Aristotelianism and Kantism, we also find in Kant's work a moral teleology—life according to the good determined by reason—that leads to a doctrine of virtue. Besides, though it is true that Kantian political theory cannot be called "perfectionist" in the same sense as the Aristotelian-Thomistic one, Kant's anti-relativism regarding the human good and its implications for the "coexistence of freedoms in accordance with a universal law" preclude placing him together with the "antiperfectionist liberals." A careful examination of the relationship between good and reason in Kantian practical philosophy will allow us to distinguish "what is Kantian" from other distinctive features of the work of contemporary philosophers inspired by him, such as John Rawls and Jürgen Habermas.

2. REASON AND GOOD IN KANT'S MORAL PHILOSOPHY

As with the Aristotelian-Thomistic tradition, we can only get an accurate idea of Kant's political thought by starting from his ethics. It is not possible to elucidate the role that "the good" plays in Kant's politics without previously understanding the role it plays more generally in his practical philosophy. In turn, it is also necessary to briefly consider the relationship between the human good and other concepts such as "happiness," "law," or "reason." I will therefore begin this chapter with some preliminary remarks on Kantian moral philosophy.

2.1. Matter and form in moral action

The so-called formalism of Kantian ethics easily leads to misunderstandings and confusions. This idea has even generated the wrong impression that there are no intrinsically evil acts. It has been suggested that, since the morality of an action does not lie in its material elements, it would be unsound to absolutely condemn any particular behavior. However, such a conclusion seems ungrounded. Neither Kantianism nor any sound moral philosophy examines raw material facts but the human *will*. And the will consists both of matter and form. As a *factum* of pure practical reason, the conscience of the categorical imperative does not exhaust morality, being only its formal criterion.[2] The fact that moral laws are valid *a priori* means that their validity is not grounded in experience, but not that they are pure in the sense of being deprived of any empirical element.

In Kantian thought, the subjective practical principle through which someone assumes a desire in the will is called a "maxim."[3] Thus, for instance, when someone borrows money knowing that he or she will not be able to repay it, the "object whose reality is desired"[4] is obviously the money, but the maxim followed is "to borrow money knowing that it will not be repaid." The subjective maxim includes a reference both to the sensible object—that is, to the desired end—and to the circumstances of the action.

The criterion for the rectitude of the will is given by the fulfillment of the categorical imperative: "So act that the maxim of your will could always hold at the same time as a principle in a giving of universal law."[5] The criterion of morality is thus the possibility of willing one's maxim to become a universal law. This possibility constitutes the source of morality of the action as opposed to the mere slavery of passions: "the lawgiving form, insofar as this is contained in the maxim, is therefore the only thing that can constitute a determining ground of the Will."[6]

Therefore, we find ourselves before a "hylomorphic" ethical theory in which the *form* of the will is what properly determines the morality of action:

> The matter of a practical principle is the object of the will. This is either the determining ground of the will or it is not. If it is the determining ground of the will, then the rule of the will is subject to an empirical condition (to the relation of the determining representation to the feeling of pleasure or displeasure), and

so is not a practical law. Now, all that remains of a law if one separates from it everything material . . . is the mere *form* of giving universal law. Therefore, either a rational being cannot think of *his* subjectively practical principles, that is, his maxims, as being at the same time universal laws or he must assume that their mere form, by which *they are fit for a giving of universal law*, of itself and alone makes them practical laws.[7]

Significantly, not every maxim referring to sensible objects is capable of being proposed as a universal law without contradiction. Insofar as they fall within maxims that cannot be "nomologized," there are behaviors that can never be morally good. Kant mentions several examples in this vein both in the *Groundwork* and in the *Metaphysics of Morals*. To repeat the example, borrowing money knowing it will never be repaid would be immoral. This maxim would not resist the categorical imperative, since it cannot take the form of a universal law without contradiction.

The fact that morality has its source in the form of the will obviously implies that "the moral worth of an action does not lie in the effect expected from it and so too does not lie in any principle of action that needs to borrow its motive from this expected effect"[8] but in the good will of the agent—that is, in his or her subordination to the categorical imperative. Having said this, it is crucial to notice that the form does not annul—but rather restricts—the matter of the action, referred to as the empirical desire. Correcting the misinterpretation of one of his critics, Kant endeavored to make it clear that being virtuous does not require renouncing the satisfaction of one's inclinations but subordinating them to the fulfillment of the moral law.[9] In the same sense, he affirms elsewhere that the subjective maxim of seeking one's own happiness cannot be adopted as an objective law if, at the same time, the happiness of the others is not included in that same maxim.[10]

"So act that the maxim of your will could always hold at the same time as a principle in a giving of universal law."[11] The first formulation of the categorical imperative conveys an extraordinary ethical insight and offers a criterion of morality in accordance with common sense. As a kind of refinement of the evangelical golden rule, it points toward the consideration of behavior in itself, disregarding any particular interest. It is an abstract reformulation of common moral experience, thus fulfilling one of the great tasks of moral philosophy: "Inexperienced in the course of the world, incapable of being prepared for whatever might come to pass in it, I ask myself only: can you also will that your maxim become a universal law?"[12]

The universalization of the maxim confers moral value on human action. For Kant, acting right is not enough for an action to be morally good: one also has to act for the sake of the law. Only to the extent that desires are submitted to the verdict of reason for the sake of reason is someone acting "morally."

The difference between Kantian legalism and classical eudemonism seems undeniable. Nevertheless, Kant's emphasis on taking the law as principle of moral action presents at least an analogy with the realization of virtue for its own sake—without seeking any egoistical return—in Aristotle's ethics.[13] Kant always contraposes the fulfillment of duty for the sake of duty to its fulfillment for egoistical motives. In contrast with the useful good, he identifies the *bonum honestum* with "the *will* insofar as it is determined by the *law of reason* to make something its object."[14]

2.2. Law, will, and good

As has been said, Kant represents the attempt to recover—with a different focus, certainly—the rationality of the *bonum* posed by classical political philosophy. What seems to differentiate him from classical ethics is not the existence of an objective rational good but the primacy of the law as a determining foundation of such good: "instead of the concept of the good as an object determining and making possible the moral law, it is on the contrary the moral law that first determines and makes possible the concept of good, insofar as it deserves this name absolutely."[15]

Consequently, the starting point of Kantian ethics is awareness of the law. Residing in the acting subject, this moral law could only be for Kant a legislation enacted by one's will. The moral law gives notice (*ratio cognoscendi*) of the existence of freedom, which is in turn conceived as the foundation of the existence (*ratio essendi*) of the moral law:[16] "*autonomy* of the will is the sole principle of all moral laws and of duties in keeping with them."[17]

Kant's will (*Wille*), however, should not be identified with arbitrariness (*Willkür*), since it is fully determined by reason, "from which alone can arise any rule that is to contain necessity."[18] According to Kant, an autonomous will is by definition a rational will. Conceived as a *factum* of reason, the categorical imperative constitutes "the formal and supreme determining ground of the will."[19] The will is, says Kant, "nothing other than practical reason,"[20] and its law determines the *bonum* in a binding and nonarbitrary way.

2.3. Happiness, good, and *summum bonum*

There is therefore, according to Kant, a good that, being formally determined by reason, man must pursue for its own sake. Notwithstanding this premise, Kant explicitly rejects any identification of this *bonum honestum* with human happiness. On this point, he distances himself from the Aristotelian-Thomistic tradition. Yet we must take into account that what we are dealing with here is not the classical understanding of "happiness" as human flourishing. "Happiness" for Kant means the mere satisfaction of all sensible inclinations. "The human being feels within himself a powerful counterweight to all the commands of duty, which reason represents to him as so deserving of the highest respect—the counterweight of his needs and inclinations, the entire satisfaction of which he sums up under the name happiness (*Glückseligkeit*)."[21] This opposition between happiness and duty is alien to the Aristotelian tradition, which understands the *eudaimonia* precisely as a virtuous life ruled by reason. It seems to me that Kant errs in giving no positive role to sensual desire, at least as indicative of the human good. It is true that we must distinguish right from wrong desire, but all desire is indicative of some apparent good, and the good life necessarily involves some satisfaction of sensual desires.

Notwithstanding the foregoing remarks, while it is unquestionable that a virtuous life accompanied by sensible discomfort does not do justice to our human aspiration for blessedness,[22] even less does a life of satisfied instincts against the dictates of reason fulfill such an aspiration. The satisfaction of our sensible inclinations at the expense of the rational good can never be a path of human fulfillment, according to the Aristotelian tradition. By contrast, the pursuit of our rational good at the expense of our sensible inclinations could be such a path if we assume the existence of a *summum bonum* after this life. This *summum bonum* constitutes—both for Kant and for the entire Christian tradition—a coincidence of goodness and well-being that we must rationally postulate and hope for.[23] Accordingly, "the constant though unattainable goal of our striving,"[24] the horizon of our conduct, is not mere sensible well-being but the complete identification of our will with the *bonum* determined by the law. When such an identification is attained, the will is holy and the moral law ceases to be experienced as a constriction.

2.4. Doctrine of virtue

Kantian moral teleology may be clearly appreciated in his doctrine of virtue, which deserves a brief consideration in these pages. Developed in the Second Part of the *Metaphysics of Morals*, the doctrine of virtue includes a classification of the moral duties of man with regard to (1) himself and (2) the others. As with the Aristotelian-Thomistic tradition, the double dimension of teleology as *end* and *limit* is patent:[25]

1. While referring to the *duties of man to himself*, Kant distinguishes between (a) "positive duties" and (b) "negative," "limiting," or "restricting" duties:

    (a) The former require man to strive for his own perfection, that is, to contribute to his own cultural improvement[26] and moral perfection,[27] cultivating all his faculties: *perfice te ut finem* (moral perfection); *perfice te ut medium* (culture).

(b) The latter also require man to preserve the integrity of his moral being, in accordance with his nature. This duty is stated as follows: "*preserve yourself in the perfection (Vollkommenheit) of your nature*," that is, respect the limits posed by your own nature: *naturae convenienter vive*.[28]

2. Regarding the *duties toward the others*, we can appreciate again the double teleological dimension of *end* and *limit*, of positive and negative or restricting duties.[29] Here, the classification is not as clear as in the case of the duties toward oneself and can be summarized as follows:

(a) On the one hand, Kant gives an account of the positive demands derived from the "duty of love" (*Liebespflicht*), the fulfillment of which has a "meritorious" (*verdienstlich*) character.
(b) On the other hand, he mentions the negative or restricting duties derived from the "duty of respect" (*Pflicht der Achtung*), the fulfillment of which has the character of debit (*schuldige Pflicht*).

3. REASON AND GOOD IN KANT'S POLITICAL PHILOSOPHY

Having completed our synthetic approach to Kantian moral philosophy, a similarly succinct approach to his political philosophy will be attempted. It is important to proceed carefully in order to avoid misunderstandings, given the subtlety of his distinctions and the dependence of several political concepts on the ideas developed in the *Groundwork* and in the *Critique of Practical Reason*.

3.1. The originary contract

If contractualism has its own distinctive features in every philosopher who has deployed such a device, in Kant it acquires a truly unique meaning, to the extent that there has even been discussion of a "Kantian turn of contractualism."[30] As occurs with other authors, Kant does not demand of his "originary contract" a historical reality: "It is instead *only an idea* of reason, which, however, has its undoubted practical reality."[31] What precisely differentiates Kant's position from that of his predecessors is, as will become immediately apparent, the practical meaning of the contract.

First of all, Kantian contractualism does not purport to distinguish a natural "pre-social" existence of man from a social existence. In fact, to speak of a "social contract" is misleading, and Kant prefers to use another term:

"originary contract." What the Kantian contract separates is a "natural state" from a "legal state" (*rechtliche Zustand*), the latter understood as a state of "public justice."[32] The originary contract is therefore a *pactum subjectionis* by which the citizens leave a situation where their rights are not properly protected—possessing a merely "provisional" character—in order to enter a new state in which their rights acquire a "peremptory" character. This second state is called "juridical" since only here are rights assured through the institutionalization of justice (*lex justitiae*), even though law and rights exist too in the previous state of nature (*lex iusti*). Moreover, it is precisely due to the fact that in the state of nature private rights already exist and may be transferred that we can speak of an obligation to advance toward a state of public justice that ensures them. "*Enter* a condition in which what belongs to each can be secured to him against everyone else"—says the Kantian postulate of public law.[33]

Second, the originary contract is not a mere factual consensus but a rational principle of justice. This is perhaps the most relevant feature that should be stressed here. Being a union of wills, the originary contract can be nothing but a "rational principle."[34] In a noteworthy passage of the *Critique of Practical Reason*, Kant asserts,

> But suppose that finite rational beings were thoroughly agreed with respect to what they had to take as objects of their feelings of pleasure and pain and even with respect to the means they must use to obtain the first and avoid the other; even then they could by no means pass off the *principle of self-love* as *a practical law*; for, this unanimity itself would still be only contingent (*KpV*, p. 26; *Cambridge Ed.*, pp. 159–60).

The will is the site or *locus* of practical reason, so it has to be neatly distinguished from sensible inclinations. To concur with someone in desire does not entail concurrence with them in the will. The union of wills that constitutes the originary contract ultimately emanates from the categorical imperative and consists in the necessary concurrence of all rational wills in leaving a precarious state of provisional justice (state of nature) to enter a state of public justice (civil union). For Kant, postulating the originary contract is the same as maintaining that public authority is legitimized as a requirement of the practical reason of citizens. Consequently, he goes so far as to prohibit the scrutiny of the origin of power with the intention of questioning its authority, and he connects the originary contract with Saint Paul's *non est enim potestas nisi a Deo*. As in the originary contract, the Pauline principle "is not an assertion about the *historical basis* of the civil constitution; it instead sets forth an idea as a practical principle of reason: the principle that the presently existing legislative authority ought to be obeyed, whatever its origin."[35] It is worth reemphasizing that the Kantian originary contract restates in legalistic terms the practical-rational duty to obey established civil authority, a duty that the Aristotelian-Thomistic tradition grounded in the common good.[36]

Kant seems to carry this duty to obey civil authority to an excessive point, since he strongly denies any right of resistance, which he sees as contradictory to the very nature of a political community. On this point, attentive Kantian commentators such as Byrd and Hruschka have introduced an important nuance: the right denied by Kant presupposes the existence of an originary contract—that is, the existence of a juridical state and of a general will unified in the existing legislator.[37] If a situation arose where public insecurity reached a point when we could no longer speak of distributive justice, a return to the natural state would have taken place. At that very moment, the postulate of public law would require moving again toward a juridical state, if necessary removing the false ruler: "when you cannot avoid living side by side with all others, you ought to leave the state of nature and proceed with them into a rightful condition, that is, a condition of distributive justice."[38]

3.2. Law and morals

(a) The external coercion of law

Now that the juridical state has been examined, the difference between legal and ethical duties should be analyzed. According to Kant, the former are characterized both by the external motive for their fulfillment—the coercion of public justice, as opposed to mere moral coercion—and by their content.[39] It should be noted that Kant does not deny a moral foundation to the duty to obey the law, as subsequently done by legal positivism. Yet, he does add to moral coercion—which belongs to the field of ethics and has an internal character—external coercion, which specifically belongs to the law. Nor does Kant deny that, within the conscience, legal obligations should be fulfilled for the sake of duty. What pertains to the legal sphere suffices, however, to fulfill them externally: "so act externally that the free use of your choice can coexist with the freedom of everyone in accordance with a universal law."[40]

(b) State and virtue

A point on which Kant seems to diverge from the classical Aristotelian-Thomistic tradition is his explicit denial that the state should seek to make men moral or virtuous. He unequivocally rejects any such political goal in his writing on religion:

> But woe to the legislator who would want to bring about through coercion a polity directed to ethical ends! For he would thereby not only achieve the very opposite of ethical ends, but also undermine his political ends and render them insecure.[41]

The identification of the legal community with an "ethical community" implies for Kant "a contradiction (*in adjecto*)": it is not possible to force someone to be virtuous because, in order to be virtuous, it is necessary to be free.[42] Actually, this is also conceded, at least in part, by the Thomistic tradition: being an "extrinsic" principle[43] of human acts, the law cannot produce virtues by itself. Notwithstanding this remark, it is clear that Kant traces a stricter distinction between the *legal aims* of the political community and its *ethical aims*. In order to accurately gauge the difference between both approaches, we cannot ignore the distance between the more homogenous medieval community or the narrow ancient Greek *polis* and the modern state, the circumstances of which impose evident boundaries in the pursuit of the human good of citizens, as has already been indicated.[44] Nor should we disregard, finally, Thomas Aquinas's contention that law is "unable to forbid all that is contrary to virtue; and it suffices for it to prohibit whatever is destructive of human intercourse, while it treats other matters as though they were lawful, not by approving of them, but by not punishing them."[45]

Kantian liberalism is neither relativistic nor skeptical about human moral good, and nor does it deny that the human good plays a relevant role in politics. It plays a role, for example, in public education and—as some authors have suggested—offers no exemption from the duty to protect favorable conditions for the development of virtue.[46] At the same time, however, it certainly acknowledges an important autonomy in the political as opposed to the moral sphere. Kant defines the law as "the sum of the conditions under which the choice of one can be united with the choice of another in accordance with a universal law of freedom." Therefore, "any action is *right* if it can coexist with everyone's freedom in accordance with a universal law, or if on its maxim the freedom of choice of each can coexist with everyone's freedom in accordance with a universal law."[47] The moral good acquires here at least a negative political role, because certain moral evils could hinder other citizens from pursuing a life in accordance with virtue. Indeed, Kant seems to confer a relevant place to the scope of obligations that may be imposed for their capability of influencing other citizens "indirectly."[48] In line with an age-old practice, he takes it for granted that the state should coercively preserve the "public decorum" (*sensum decori*) and even seems to take a strict view with regard to questions such as lotteries, "which produce more poor people and more danger to public property than there would otherwise be, and which should therefore not be permitted."[49]

(c) Legal duties to oneself?

Closely related to the previous point, another difference between law and morals relates to the question of the existence of legal duties to oneself. It is, in effect, a controversial issue, and even Kant seems to contradict himself with respect to this problem. Some of his writings discarding such legal duties have been deployed by contemporary antiperfectionist liberals to ground their proposals on Kant's authority.[50] However, the answer does not seem to be so easy. Before reaching any conclusion, it is worth making the following remarks:

(a) If we consider his early lessons on ethics (1775–1781), edited by Paul Menzer in 1924 on the basis of students' notes, it seems clear that Kant does not conceive the possibility of legal duties to oneself: "duties to ourselves . . . are not considered by the law, for the latter deals only with the relationship to other people. I cannot observe the law in regard to myself, for what I do to myself, I do with my own consent, and am committing no breach of public justice when I take action against myself."[51] *A fortiori*, it should be added that, at least in one paragraph of the *Metaphysics of Morals*—his most mature legal work (1797)—Kant describes the duties to oneself as specifically related to ethics.[52]

(b) Nevertheless, in a relevant part of the *Metaphysics of Morals*—his table of moral and legal duties—Kant includes within the category of "legal duties to oneself" all those that refer to "the right of humanity in our own person."[53] Besides, commenting on the beginning of Ulpian's formula, *honeste vive*, Kant mentions the duty to always be an end—and never become a mere means—for others.[54] These duties are violated, according to Kant, by particularly self-degrading actions such as the contract of slavery or bestiality. Being a violation of a genuine legal duty, the contract of slavery would be void, and an action like bestiality would result in one of the most serious punishments.[55]

The reading of both texts seems to suggest the conclusion that, on the one hand, Kant considers the duties to oneself as generally belonging to ethics, as follows from certain general statements. At the same time, however, in his more detailed analyses, Kant conceives of a core of legal duties, coercively enforceable, related to the "humanity in our own person." These legal duties are violated by especially self-degrading actions that could not be justified by the principle *volenti non fit iniuria*. Kant seems to consider that those actions do not simply remain in the agent's sphere but violate "the right of humanity in our own person."

If there is any basis for reproaching the Kantian approach explained above, it is certainly not an excess of liberalism. On the contrary, the debatable point is precisely the existence of coercively enforceable legal duties with respect to the right of humanity in someone's own person. The argument for an eventual limitation of self-degrading behavior ought to be found not so much in "oneself" or in "humanity" in general, as Kant seems to postulate, but in the negative social effects such behaviors might produce were they to gain public relevance or visibility. Inasmuch as they remain strictly hidden, however, there do not seem to be any legal reasons to prohibit them.

3.3. The ideal state

The "state in the idea" is, according to Kant, the state "as it ought to be in accordance with pure principles of right," an idea that "serves as a norm (*norma*) for every actual union into a commonwealth."[56] It is "that condition in which its constitution conforms most fully to principles of right; it is that condition which reason, *by a categorical imperative*, makes it obligatory for us to strive after."[57] In this ideal state, "the legislative authority can belong only to the united will of the people. For since all right is to proceed from it, it *cannot* do anyone wrong by its law."[58] We can discern in this way of speaking the unmistakable influence of Rousseau. However, we should not overlook the specific meaning that "the will" has for Kant: it is the site or *locus* of practical reason.[59] Thus, saying that the united will of the people can do no harm to anybody is tantamount to saying that the harmony of everybody in behaving in accordance with reason can do no harm to anybody.

Second, Kant defines the form of government (*forma regiminis*) as "the way a state, on the basis of its civil constitution (the act of the general will by which a multitude becomes a people), makes use of its plenary power." Kant distinguishes two ways of governing: (a) *republicanism*, which he defines as "the political principle of separation of the executive power (the government) from the legislative power," leading to the nonarbitrary execution of the laws and (b) *despotism*, characterized as the political principle of "high-handed management of the state by laws the regent has himself given, inasmuch as he handles the public will as his private will."[60]

The question of the ideal "form of state" (*forma imperii*)—democracy, aristocracy, monarchy—is treated by Kant in several works with apparently contradictory conclusions, due to the diversity of approaches he undertakes.[61] In any case, this issue is for Kant subordinated to the republican form of government, that is, to a form of government representative of the rational will of the people and not of the private interests of those who hold power. The best form of state is, in conclusion, that which adapts best to a republican form of government.[62]

It is important to emphasize that the republican form of government cannot be defined by the number of people governing but by how power is exercised, in a way that is representative of the general—and by definition rational—will of the people. The main constraint on this form of government lies in the fact that the ruler(s) cannot decide upon the subjective happiness of the individual, since they cannot make coercive decisions regarding the object of mere desires. Desires are subjective and contingent, so they fall outside the scope of the general will. Kantian liberalism is mainly opposed to any paternalistic guidance of the state with respect to individual desires:

> No one can coerce me to be happy in his way (as he thinks of the welfare of other human beings); instead, each may seek his happiness in the way that seems good to him, provided he does not infringe upon that freedom of others to strive for a like end which can coexist with the freedom of everyone in accordance with a possible universal law (i.e., does not infringe upon this right of another).[63]

To conclude, state coercion is designed to ensure the coexistence of liberties within a universal law; and individual liberty consists precisely in the ability to aspire, within this framework of rational coexistence, to the kind of happiness one wants. In a real and imperfect state, in which the rulers are not general, transcendent wills but flesh-and-blood legislators, the idea of a general will compels them to exercise their power in accordance with the dictates of practical reason:

> It is instead *only an idea* of reason, which, however, has its undoubted practical reality, namely to bind every legislator to give his laws in such a way that they *could* have arisen from the united will of a whole people and to regard each subject, insofar as he wants to be a citizen, as if he has joined in voting for such a will. For this is the touchstone of any public law's conformity with right. In other words, if a public law is so constituted that a whole people *could not possibly* give its consent to it . . . , it is unjust; but if it is *only possible* that a people could agree to it, it is a duty to consider the law just, even if the people is at present in such a situation or frame of mind that, if consulted about it, it would probably refuse its consent.[64]

It is difficult to express more clearly up to what point conformity to the general will—the criterion that every legislator must follow—constitutes a practical-rational principle and not a simple submission to factual consensus and agreements. Certainly, Kant does not place the language of the common good at the center of his discourse. However, he does place there the language of practical reason, to which all his considerations about the general will should be referred. Likewise, we find in his critique of despotism a firm condemnation of any attempt to replace the rational political *telos* with a dangerous state paternalism as well as a strong basis for supporting the principle of subsidiarity of the state.

We might still ask whether there is in Kant, as there appears to be in the Aristotelian-Thomistic tradition, a duty of prudence in the application of the rational principles of politics. As has been said, Thomas Aquinas insists that "law should take account of many things, as to persons, as to matters, and as to times,"[65] and that demanding excessively hard behaviors could lead—even when the behaviors demanded are good—to bad results.[66] In some passages, Kant seems to align himself with the principle *fiat iustitia et pereat mundus*. Nevertheless, the interpretation he makes of this principle is simply that of not subordinating the rational principles of politics to the utilitarian principle of welfare—a hardly objectionable thesis. Notwithstanding that the state should behave according to the rational principles of law, "it leads straight to the end, but with the reminder of prudence not to draw toward it precipitately by force but to approach it steadily as favorable circumstances arise."[67]

4. CONCLUSION: THE RIGHT TO FREEDOM IN KANT

> *Freedom* (independence from being constrained by another's choice), insofar as it can coexist with the freedom of every other in accordance with a universal law, is the only original right belonging to every man by virtue of his humanity.[68]

I would like to conclude this chapter on Kant with a brief comment on a central piece of his legal and political philosophy. In point of fact, the right to freedom constitutes for Kant the "originary right" (*Urrecht*) of each individual, and ensuring the coexistence of freedoms constitutes the primary end of law. It is, however, an end characterized by an important restriction, without which we can hardly understand Kant's work: the limitation of freedom for the sake of the harmonious coexistence of freedoms must be done "in accordance with a universal law." The mission of the legal order is precisely to carry out this limitation: "*Right* is the limitation (*Einschrankung*) of the freedom of each to the condition of its harmony (*Zusammenstimmung*) with the freedom of everyone insofar as this is possible in accordance with a universal law."[69]

The "universal law" constitutes the way by which further considerations on the human good analogous to those made by classical medieval thinkers can be introduced. Not in the sense of a state's mission to pursue the virtue of its citizens—something explicitly discarded by Kant—but at least of limiting those moral evils that prevent others living in accordance with virtue. In its task of limiting human freedom, the law has to take into account the "direct" and "indirect" influences of human conduct. It must not be indifferent to the moral ecology of a society, without which it is difficult to imagine (in my view) a true coexistence of freedoms "in accordance with a universal law." In defining the boundaries of the right to freedom, the legislator does not merely appeal to the factual consensus of the citizens—to their empirical desires—but to the general will as an idea of reason. The factual consensus concerns him to the extent that prudence requires it to be taken into account, since it is neither possible nor good to thoughtlessly hasten justice. In any case, the criterion for the legitimate limitation of freedom does not lie in the subjective desires of those who find their liberty curtailed but in what they should rationally be able to accept—that is, in the general will as an idea of reason.

After praising Kant's liberal attitude in affirming that no one person can compel others to be happy in his own way,[70] Isaiah Berlin criticized him "and the rationalists of his type" for departing from liberal orthodoxy by admitting the possibility of limiting liberty on the basis of this broad principle. For "in the name of reason anything that is non-rational may be condemned."[71] However, Kant does not say that *anything* nonrational may be coercively outlawed—as we have seen—but only those actions impeding the "coexistence of freedoms in accordance with a universal law." In my opinion, Berlin's misunderstanding lies—as happens with many contemporary authors—in his failure to neatly and clearly distinguish the right idea of society as a "unity of order" (*unitas ordinis*) from the wrong organicist idea of society as a "unity of nature" (*unitas naturae*).[72]

NOTES

1. With regard to this remark, I am indebted to several conversations with the prominent Kant scholar Alejandro G. Vigo. I am deeply grateful for his willingness to share his (as yet unpublished) article, "Aristóteles y Kant, en torno al origen de la cualidad moral de la acción." In the same line, see also the important article by Christine M. Korsgaard, "From Duty and for the Sake of the Noble: Kant and Aristotle on Morally Good Action" (1996), in *Kant on Emotion and Value* (Oxford: Oxford University Press, 2008), pp. 174–206.

2. See *Kritik der praktischen Vernunft* (Akademie-Ausgabe VI), p. 31; Eng. trans.: *The Cambridge Edition of the Works of Immanuel Kant—Practical Philosophy* (Cambridge: Cambridge University Press, 1999), pp. 164–65.

3. *KpV*, p. 27 (*Cambridge Ed.*, p. 160).

4. *KpV*, p. 21 (*Cambridge Ed.*, p. 155).

5. *KpV*, p. 30 (*Cambridge Ed.*, p. 164).

6. *KpV*, p. 29 (*Cambridge Ed.*, p. 162).

7. *KpV*, p. 27 (*Cambridge Ed.*, p. 160).

8. *Grundlegung zur Metaphysik der Sitten* (Akademie-Ausgabe IV), p. 401 (*Cambridge Ed.*, p. 56).

9. *Über den Gemeinspruch: Das mag in der Theorie richtig sein, taugt aber nicht für die Praxis* (Akademie-Ausgabe VIII), p. 281 (*Cambridge Ed.*, pp. 283–84).

10. *KpV*, p. 34 (*Cambridge Ed.*, p. 167).

11. *KpV*, p. 30 (*Cambridge Ed.*, p. 164).

12. *Grundlegung*, p. 403 (*Cambridge Ed.*, p. 58).

13. *Et. Nic.*, II, 1105a.

14. *KpV*, p. 60 (*Cambridge Ed.*, p. 188). On the distinction between *bonum honestum*, *utile*, and *delectabile*, see *S. Th.*, I, q. 5, art. 6.
15. *KpV*, p. 64 (*Cambridge Ed.*, p. 191).
16. *KpV*, p. 4 (n. 1) (*Cambridge Ed.*, p. 140).
17. *KpV*, p. 33 (*Cambridge Ed.*, p. 166).
18. *KpV*, p. 20 (*Cambridge Ed.*, p. 154).
19. *KpV*, p. 32 (*Cambridge Ed.*, p. 165).
20. *Grundlegung*, p. 412 (*Cambridge Ed.*, p. 66). For a further clarification of this passage, see L. Placencia, "Kant y la voluntad como 'razón práctica,'" *Tópicos* 41 (2011): 63–104.
21. *Grundlegung*, p. 405 (*Cambridge Ed.*, p. 59).
22. *S. Th.*, I-II, q. 4, a. 1: "non potest esse beatitudo sine delectatione concomitante"; and q. 4, a. 4: "rectitudo voluntatis requiritur ad beatitudinem et antecedenter et concomitanter."
23. *Cfr.* S. Augustine, *De Civitate Dei*, XIX, 4; in *Aurelii Augustini Opera*, Pars XIV-2, in *Corpus Christianorum Series Latina*, XLVIII (Turnhout: Brepols, 1955), p. 664; *S. Th.*, I, q. 6, a. 3; I-II, q. 2, a. 6; q. 3, a. 2, ad 4; q. 3, a. 4; q. 4, a. 1 and a. 2; and q. 5, a. 3.; and *KpV* 122–124 ("The Immortality of the Soul as a Postulate of Pure Practical Reason") (*Cambridge Ed.*, pp. 238–39).
24. *KpV*, p. 84 (*Cambridge Ed.*, p. 208).
25. *Die Metaphysik der Sitten* (Akademie-Ausgabe VI), especially pp. 419 ff. (*Cambridge Ed.*, pp. 544 ff.).
26. *MdS*, pp. 444 ff. (*Cambridge Ed.*, pp. 565–66).
27. *MdS*, pp. 446 ff. (*Cambridge Ed.*, pp. 566–67).
28. *MdS*, p. 419 (*Cambridge Ed.*, p. 545).
29. *MdS*, p. 448 (*Cambridge Ed.*, p. 568).
30. F. Schwember, *El giro kantiano del contractualismo* (Pamplona: Universidad de Navarra, 2007).
31. *Gemeinspruch*, p. 297 (*Cambridge Ed.*, p. 296).
32. *MdS*, pp. 306–07 (*Cambridge Ed.*, pp. 450–52). See an excellent explanation of the meaning of the different states in B. Sharon Byrd and Joachim Hruschka, *Kant's Doctrine of Right* (Cambridge: Cambridge University Press, 2010), pp. 44–76.
33. *MdS*, p. 237 (*Cambridge Ed.*, p. 393).
34. *Gemeinspruch*, p. 302 (*Cambridge Ed.*, p. 301).
35. *MdS*, p. 319 (*Cambridge Ed.*, p. 62).
36. *Cfr. S. Th.*, II-II, q. 104, a. 6. For the classical treatment of this question in the language of the common good and its evolution toward legalistic explanations, see Finnis, *Natural Law and Natural Rights*, pp. 245 ff.
37. *MdS*, pp. 318 ss (*Cambridge Ed.*, pp. 462 ff.). For a careful analysis of the Kantian theory in this point, see Byrd/Hruschka, pp. 90–93 and 181–84.
38. *MdS*, p. 307 (*Cambridge Ed.*, pp. 451–52).
39. *MdS*, pp. 218–21 (*Cambridge Ed.*, pp. 372 ff.).
40. *MdS*, p. 231 (*Cambridge Ed.*, p. 388).
41. *Die Religion innerhalb der Grenzen der bloßen Vernunft* (Akademie-Ausgabe VI), p. 96 (*Cambridge Edition of the Works of Immanuel Kant: Religion and Rational Theology* [Cambridge: Cambridge University Press, 1996], p. 131).

42. *RGV*, p. 95 (*Cambridge Ed.: Religion and Rational Theology*, p. 131).

43. *S. Th.*, I-II, q. 90. The "intrinsic" principles are, as has been said, the "powers" (see *S. Th.*, I, q. 77 ff.) and the "habits" (see *S. Th.*, I-II, q. 49 ff.).

44. See *supra*, chapter 1, 3.2.a.

45. *S. Th.*, II-II, q. 77, a. 1, ad 1.

46. *Gemeinspruch*, pp. 288–89 (*Cambridge Ed.*, pp. 289–90). See also J. T. Klein, "Kant and Public Education for Enhancing Moral Virtue: The Necessary Conditions for Ensuring Enlightened Patriotism," in *Kant and Social Policies* (London: Palgrave Macmillan, 2016), pp. 158–59. It is very interesting in this vein the work of Alejandro Vigo, "Kant: liberal y anti-relativista," *Estudios públicos* 93 (2004): 29 ff.

47. *MdS*, p. 230 (*Cambridge Ed.*, p. 387).

48. *MdS*, p. 230 (*Cambridge Ed.*, p. 387).

49. *MdS*, p. 326 (*Cambridge Ed.*, p. 468).

50. Outside the controversy, Byrd and Hruschka opt for asserting the nonexistence of such duties in Kant—by virtue of the principle *volenti non fit iniuria*—though they show through several examples that Kant "occasionally toyed with the idea that there were legal duties a person owed to himself" (Byrd/Hruschka, *Kant's Doctrine of the Right*, p. 63). On this particular problem, I consider Finnis's analysis to be more detailed: "Duties to oneself in Kant," in J. Finnis, *Collected Essays III* (Oxford: Oxford University Press, 2011), pp. 47 ff.

51. P. Menzer, ed., *Eine Vorlesung Kants über Ethik* (Berlin: Pan Verlag Rolf Heise, 1924), pp. 145–46 (*Cambridge Edition of the Works of Immanuel Kant: Lectures on Ethics* [Cambridge: Cambridge University Press, 1997], p. 122).

52. *MdS*, p. 220 (*Cambridge Ed.*, p. 385): "Ethics has its special duties as well (e.g., duties to oneself)."

53. *MdS*, p. 240 (*Cambridge Ed.*, p. 395).

54. *MdS*, p. 236 (*Cambridge Ed.*, p. 392).

55. *MdS*, p. 330 (*Cambridge Ed.*, pp. 471–72) (on the contract of slavery); and *MdS*, p. 363 (*Cambridge Ed.*, pp. 497–98) (on pederasty, rape, and bestiality). Bestiality deserves, according to Kant, the "permanent expulsion from civil society, since the criminal has made himself unworthy of human society" (*Cambridge Ed.*, p. 498).

56. *MdS*, p. 313 (*Cambridge Ed.*, p. 457).

57. *MdS*, p. 318 (*Cambridge Ed.*, p. 461).

58. *MdS*, p. 313 (*Cambridge Ed.*, p. 457).

59. As has been explained, out of the principle of self-love it would be impossible to build a practical law, and the mere coincidence in the object of sentiment—desire or pain—is just a casual coincidence (*KpV*, p. 26; *KpV*, p. 26; *Cambridge Ed.*, pp. 159–60).

60. *Zum ewigen Frieden* (Akademie-Ausgabe VIII), p. 352 (*Cambridge Ed.*, p. 324).

61. See a careful analysis in Byrd/Hruschka, *Kant's Doctrine of the Right*, pp. 175–81.

62. *Zum ewigen Frieden*, p. 353 (*Cambridge Ed.*, p. 325).

63. *Gemeinspruch*, p. 290 (*Cambridge Ed.*, p. 291). On the critique of the paternalistic "welfarism" in Kant, as well as on the justification and possible scope of public

redistribution, see the interesting essays published in Faggion, Pinzani, and Sánchez Madrid (eds.), *Kant and Social Policies* (London: Palgrave Macmillan, 2016), especially pp. 1–64, 93–124.

64. *Gemeinspruch*, p. 297 *(Cambridge Ed.*, pp. 296–97).
65. *S. Th.*, I-II, q. 96, a. 1c. See also *Nic. Eth.*, VI, 8, 1142a; *S. Th.*, II-II, q. 47, a. 3. See also Plato, *The Republic*, III, 412b; and VII, 539b–d.
66. *S. Th.*, I-II, q. 91, a. 4.
67. *Zum ewigen Frieden*, p. 378 *(Cambridge Ed.*, p. 344).
68. *MdS*, p. 237 *(Cambridge Ed.*, p. 393).
69. *Gemeinspruch*, pp. 289–90 *(Cambridge Ed.*, p. 290).
70. "Two concepts of Liberty," in Isaiah Berlin, *Liberty*, p. 183.
71. "Two concepts of Liberty," pp. 199–200.
72. See *supra* chapter 1, 3.1.

Part II

ANTIPERFECTIONIST LIBERALISM

Chapter 3

"Free and equals": John Rawls's political philosophy

1. INTRODUCTION

As we have seen, the two political traditions examined above give considerable importance to the moral good determined by reason. Notwithstanding the nuances already explained, necessary to avoid misinterpretations, the Aristotelian-Thomistic tradition understands the virtuous life as the final cause of law and government. In Kant's philosophy, political liberalism does not imply any skepticism regarding the human good and is also tempered with nuances. Considerations about what is morally good and evil must be taken into account in determining "the sum of the conditions under which the choice of one can be united with the choice of another in accordance with a universal law of freedom." In the Thomistic tradition, individual freedom imposes restrictions on the public pursuit of the good; and in Kantian philosophy, the good imposes restrictions on individual freedom. Thus, in neither case can human society be ordered without regard to the meaning of the moral good, that is, of a worthy or an unworthy life.

In clear contrast, contemporary "antiperfectionist" or "ateleological" liberalism—which will be studied in this part II—tends to leave aside considerations regarding the moral good in the exercise of political power. This is at least due to a denial that the meaning of the good life is relevant in defining the scope of political liberties. In my view, this position ultimately leads to an interpretation of liberties guided by what, following the framework deployed by Spaemann, I have described in the Preface as the "desire principle." Deprived of a rational *telos* to guide and limit them, liberties easily turn into licenses that legitimize any way of living that one desires. Supposedly, the only apparent limit would be the freedoms or licenses of others, a limit that leaves unresolved the fundamental problem of political coexistence: the conflict of freedoms.

* * *

Considered the most influential liberal political philosopher of the end of the twentieth and the beginning of the twenty-first century, John Rawls explicitly attempted to carry to a higher level of abstraction the classical liberal theory of the social contract. His two most important works, *A Theory of Justice* (1971, rev. ed. 1999) and *Political Liberalism* (1993, exp. ed. 2005, which includes a reply to the critique by Habermas and his most mature essay: *The Idea of Public Reason Revisited*, 1997) have given rise to an enormous amount of laudatory and critical studies. In *A Theory of Justice*, Rawls described what, in his opinion, would constitute a well-ordered society, that is, a political regime in which everyone cooperates rationally, in accordance with the demands of "justice as fairness."[1] Liberalism is presented here as a "comprehensive doctrine" that permeates the moral convictions of the people, something which he later considered as unrealistic in a plural society. In the essays and lectures published in *Political Liberalism*, he refused to present "justice as fairness" as a comprehensive doctrine. Instead, he came to conceive of it as a "political conception" of justice whose demands could and should be accepted by any reasonable citizen in the public forum, although he did not adhere to a liberal worldview in his private sphere.[2] In this chapter, I will expound and criticize central aspects of both *A Theory of Justice* and *Political Liberalism*.

I want to stress something that I have already explained in the Preface—namely, that *I do not claim* that Rawls defends a hedonistic ethical theory or a whimsical satisfaction of desires. Far from it, he has affirmed our capacity for noble virtues such as justice, benevolence or fidelity.[3] It would be quite unfair—and perhaps even ridiculous—to attribute to Rawls a hedonistic understanding of life. Yet, I think that central features of his political philosophy—especially the so-called priority of the right over the good—inevitably lead to an understanding of liberties that makes it politically difficult to discriminate between noble ethical claims and purely "desire-based" claims.

2. THE GOOD IN THE "ORIGINAL POSITION"

Rawls opposes his theory both to utilitarianism, which places the end of government in maximizing the welfare of society, and to perfectionism, which places the end of government in the moral good of the citizens and in their virtuous fulfillment. His theory of justice is presented as an attempt to carry out to a higher level of abstraction the classical theory of the social contract.[4]

As with other contractualist authors (e.g., Kant or Rousseau), the Rawlsian social contract does not claim to give an account of a historical fact. As in Rousseau's thought, it is a hypothesis used to derive political principles from a *natura pura* of man, one that enables us to discover the principles through which men "express their nature,"[5] leaving aside everything that is contingent in their lives. For Rawls, one of these contingencies is precisely the conception of the good that each has:

> It is not our aims that primarily reveal our nature but rather the principles that we would acknowledge to govern the background conditions under which these aims are to be formed and the manner in which they are to be pursued.[6]

What strictly speaking unveils our nature is the principles chosen in the "original position" from which the contract is agreed upon:

> A moral person is a subject with ends he has chosen, and his fundamental preference is for conditions that enable him to frame a mode of life that expresses his nature as a free and equal rational being as fully as circumstances permit.[7]

The ends, therefore, remain beyond consideration in the original position. In the act of defining the principles of justice, the conceptions of the good are covered by what Rawls calls the "veil of ignorance."[8]

Though the conceptions of the good are left behind the veil of ignorance, the desire of each individual to protect and advance his own interests—including the conceptions of the good that he will eventually have upon entering into society—is present in the original position: "each desires to protect his interests, his capacity to advance his conception of the good."[9] The interests taken into account in the original position, those that are not covered by the veil of ignorance, are labeled "primary goods" by Rawls. These are "things which it is supposed a rational man wants whatever else he wants." Together with self-respect or self-esteem, Rawls includes within the category of primary goods rights and liberties, opportunities, salary, and wealth. In particular, freedom to pursue and promote one's conception of the good—without considering its particular content—constitutes an essential primary good.[10]

In these situations, the parties agree upon the principles of justice that will shape, among other things, the constitutional bases of society and their authoritative interpretation. The theory of justice is part of a "theory of rational choice," that is, of a choice made by an individual in order to ensure a convenient situation, given the fact that he does not know what position he will finally occupy in society.[11] In the original position, the parties lack reciprocal interest with respect to the particular interests and conceptions of the good that they will have in society.[12] In this situation of "mutual disinterest," they adopt those principles of justice that would maximize their interests in the worst possible scenario (*maximin rule*).[13]

In the original position, the rational interest to ensure the best outcome in the worst possible scenario leads the parties to choose the "two principles of justice," which are known as (1) the "principle of equal basic liberty" and (2) the principle of "difference" and "fair equality of opportunity."[14] These principles constitute "the kernel of political morality"[15] and determine the whole social institutional system: the elaboration of the constitution and its interpretation as well as the legislation and execution of the laws.[16] The principle of equal liberty enjoys priority over the second principle and includes the capacity to pursue one's conception of the good, provided that it respects the basic liberties of other individuals.[17]

2.1. "Good" versus "contingent conceptions of the good"

Among the critiques that could be made of *A Theory of Justice*, I would like to focus mainly on the reduction of "the good" to mere subjective conceptions of the good—and, by implication, the reduction of "the evil" to mere subjective conceptions of the evil. It has been argued that *A Theory of Justice* does not take the good and the evil in the original position seriously. Rawls's reply runs in the following vein: by ensuring his liberty to pursue and promote his own convictions—whatever they may finally be—a party in the original position would "take one's religious or moral convictions seriously."[18] One's convictions would be taken so seriously that, behind the veil of ignorance, the parties in the original position would attempt to maximize the possibilities of asserting them in society, without any particular notion of their specific content. By trying to ensure what Rawls calls "primary goods"—property and liberty rights that will enable the individual to advance his own conception of the good—the parties in the original position prevent their respective conceptions of the good being damaged or set aside. By refusing to introduce a teleological understanding of their nature in the original position, the parties would be, according to Rawls, taking the good seriously.

But the fact is that it is not *the good* that the parties are taking seriously but *their conceptions* of the good. In the Rawlsian theory of justice, the good is not esteemed *qua* good, as Robert P. George has argued.[19] The value of the different conceptions of the good does not lie in the fact that they identify the good but in the fact that they represent their individual adherents. They say nothing about the good: they only speak about the "relative preferences" of the individuals defending them. This is the tacit premise of Rawls's thesis that conferring political relevance on the good in the original position "favors those of that persuasion"[20]—that is, those who hold fast to that view of the good. In the original position, we can never say anything objective and impersonal with respect to the good, which remains reduced to simple interest. Regarding our visions of the good, David Hume's antiteleological epigram holds absolutely valid: "we never really advance a step beyond ourselves."[21]

Thus, it is by no means clear that the parties take the content of their "moral convictions" seriously. At least, the statement should be completed by adding that it is not the good *qua* good that the parties take seriously but their convictions *qua* theirs. If the parties in the original position took the good *qua* good seriously, they would not agree upon a set of principles that would allow them to reaffirm themselves in their convictions before knowing the content of those convictions. Quite the contrary, they should be ready to sacrifice their eventual wrong convictions for the sake of the good. From the Rawlsian premises, however, it only remains possible to take one's convictions seriously, not as a sign that one is taking the good seriously but as a sign that one is taking oneself seriously. It is no coincidence that Rawls prizes self-respect as the most important primary good, nor that he frames the determination of the principles of justice in the context of so-called rational choice.

I think that, from a Kantian perspective, the transmutation of the good (the moral good or *bonum honestum*) into a simple contingent conception is also problematic. According to Kant, the moral good (*das Gute*) is determined by universal law: "it is . . . the moral law that first determines and makes possible the concept of the good, insofar as it deserves this name absolutely."[22] Rawls himself points out that, in any case, he is not seeking to make "an interpretation of Kant's actual doctrine." He just argues that "the original position may be viewed . . . as a procedural interpretation of Kant's conception of autonomy and the categorical imperative within the framework of an empirical theory."[23] Such an interpretation is made possible through an identification of the Kantian *homo noumenon* with the "original position"; the Kantian autonomy with the "mutual disinterest" of the parties in that position; and the categorical imperative with the Rawlsian principles of justice.[24] According to Rawls, this is not an abusive interpretation because it is possible to abandon the way Kant understood his own dualisms (necessary/contingent; form/matter; reason/desire) and maintain "what is distinctive in his theory,"[25] namely, "the constructivist method."[26] This method is characterized by not recognizing a moral order "prior and independent" of the subject and by deducing the moral order from a "procedure of construction."[27]

The "procedure of construction" proposed by Rawls strongly differs, as is obvious, from the "form" of morality as conceived by Kant. The great German philosopher conceives of the transcendental subject, the *homo noumenon*, as being beyond empirical experience, and of the criterion of morality, the categorical imperative, as the possibility of "nomologizing" one's subjective maxim. By contrast, the conditions of the "original position"—Rawls's "circumstances of justice" (conflictive plurality of conceptions of justice; interest in advancing one's project, even before knowing its content)—are highly empirical.[28] As Michael Sandel has pointedly said, Rawls's deontology is a "deontology with a Humean face."[29] In this sense, the unconditional priority claimed by Rawls for his own principles can hardly be compatible with the contingent, empirical circumstances from which he attempts to derive them.[30]

In my view, the distinctive feature of Rawlsian liberalism is the understanding of "the good life," generally speaking, as something that each one defines within the limits of the principles of justice chosen in the original position. We should note here that, for Kant, the priority of the moral law in the determination of "the good" (*das Gute*) does not mean that "the good"—distinguished by Kant from "well-being" (*das Wohl*)—is relative or contingent.[31] If that were the case, the doctrine of virtue set forth in the *Metaphysics of Morals* would be simply incomprehensible.

2.2. The partiality of primary goods

In the original position from which the principles of justice are defined, Rawls's theory requires the question of "the good" to be overlooked, except in the case of the so-called primary goods, namely those goods that everybody would want, whatever else they may additionally want. These are the goods that enable us to pursue and advance a life project, before considering its content. They are ultimately "useful goods" that enhance the individual's capacity to act. In his critique of *A Theory of Justice*, Thomas Nagel has noted that these goods promise an appealing neutrality but are in fact not neutral at all:

> The original position seems to presuppose not just a neutral theory of the good, but a liberal, individualistic conception according to which the best that can be wished for someone is the unimpeded pursuit of his own path, provided it does not interfere with the rights of others.

From this understanding of the human *natura pura*, the "primary goods"—those everybody wants to maximize independently of any additional want—are the rights to liberty and property. Yet, as Nagel rightly underlines, "the primary goods are not equally valuable in pursuit of all conceptions of the good," since "they are less useful in implementing views that hold a good life to be readily achievable only in certain well-defined types of social structure, or only in a society that works concertedly for the realization of certain higher human capacities and the suppression of baser ones, or only given certain types of economic relations among men." In sum, "the model contains a strong individualistic bias."[32] Given that they depend on cooperation, nonindividualistic conceptions of the good will either require an additional effort to convince other citizens or they will become a luxury that only those with enough money to pay for other people's consent and cooperation will be able to pursue. Consequently, and in the same line of thought exposed by Nagel, Joseph Raz has asserted that

> the very restrictions imposed on societies by the Rawlsian principles of justice make the implementation of some conceptions of the good more difficult and their pursuit by individuals less attractive than that of others. Furthermore, the implementation of some conceptions of the good is incompatible with the principles of justice and is ruled out altogether.[33]

3. POLITICAL LIBERALISM

3.1. Fundamental modifications

As has been pointed out, John Rawls introduced important modifications to his *Theory of Justice* in several subsequent lectures and writings edited together in his volume *Political Liberalism*. In *A Theory of Justice*, he proposed justice as fairness as an alternative to moral perfectionism and moral utilitarianism. In *Political Liberalism*, however, justice as fairness was presented as a strictly political, not metaphysical theory of justice,[34] and Rawls stressed its compatibility with any reasonable "comprehensive doctrine," be it utilitarian, perfectionist or any other type.

With strictly political aims, justice as fairness would be no more than the outcome of an "overlapping consensus" of all reasonable comprehensive doctrines. The possibility of a true human teleology defining our nature seems to be admitted, though it is considered unreasonable to argue from its principles in public discussions on the meaning and scope of the "constitutional essentials." In their identity as citizens, persons are above all free and equal, and that makes them independent from any particular conception of the good;[35] in their private sphere, though, they may consider themselves inseparable or indivisible from a certain conception of the good.[36] From the political-constitutional point of view, teleological considerations of human perfection are neither true nor false. They are simply inappropriate and are not taken into account.

The original position is now presented as a "device of representation." From this position, the parties defend the interests of those they represent, among which are to be found their future conceptions of the good.[37] This approach enables those who ideally enter in the original position to take a step back from their own conceptions of the good without being accused of not taking them seriously. For they are merely gaining the distance from themselves required to become representatives of a group of interests and ideas. By defending the possibilities of advancing the different conceptions of the good, even before knowing their content, one would not be (egoistically) affirming oneself against the truth but (altruistically) affirming the interests of those one represents.

In the public forum—especially in the discourse upon constitutional justice and above all in the interpretation of basic liberties—the parties can only make use of what Rawls calls "public reason," which is one of the central concepts—not to say *the* central concept—of his *Political Liberalism*. The main development of this concept appears in an article introduced at the end of the revised edition of that work: *The Idea of Public Reason Revisited* (1997).[38] The demands of public reason may be summarized as follows:

(a) Its nature and content is "given by the ideals and principles expressed by society's conception of political justice."[39] Notwithstanding the existence of several political conceptions of justice—one of them the conception developed by Rawls from the original position—every liberal political conception and, accordingly, every idea of public reason must have at least three features: first, it must endorse a list of basic rights, liberties, and opportunities; second, it must assert the priority of rights, liberties, and opportunities against perfectionistic values; and third, it has to confer on the individuals all-purpose primary goods to make effective use of their freedoms and to pursue their respective conceptions of the good.[40] Whenever the teleological considerations of human nature clash with the "basic liberties," they must be set aside.

(b) It is not possible to assess the meaning of the priority of basic liberties without providing a criterion specifying the importance of those liberties in the constitutional, legislative, and judicial sphere. "A liberty—Rawls says—is more or less significant depending on whether it is more or less essentially involved in, or is a more or less necessary institutional means to protect, the full and informed and effective exercise of the moral powers in one (or both) of the two fundamental cases [i.e. the capacity for a sense of justice (1) and the capacity for a conception of the good (2)]."[41] To put it more clearly, in the inevitable task of weighing the relative importance of basic liberties to resolve disputes, the direct appeal to the good must be replaced by the appeal to the importance of a certain liberty for the pursuit of one's conception of the good. This would be a requirement of public reason—characterized by Rawls as "the reasonable."[42]

(c) The constraints on public reason do not apply to public discussion within the civil society but only to the political sphere in a narrower sense[43]: to judges, public officers, and parliamentarians as well as candidates to occupy public positions. Citizens are only constrained by the requirements of public reason insofar as they act in a public capacity—namely, when they contribute to shaping the state's will through the exercise of their right to vote. In all these cases, the demands of public reason derive from a reciprocal civic duty of respect among the citizens. These demands become particularly important in public discussion of the constitutional essentials and most especially in the interpretation of constitutional rights and civil liberties by the highest courts. In sum, the aim of public reason is that public discussions regarding nuclear questions be based on arguments whose acceptance by each reasonable citizen could be reasonably expected.

To better understand the whole Rawlsian project, I would like to make a concluding reference to an important parallelism he establishes between his own political liberalism and the principle of religious tolerance that started to be recognized at the beginning of modernity.[44] According to Rawls, political pluralism is to philosophical pluralism what the principle of tolerance was to religious pluralism in the sixteenth century. Just as fairness then required the religious neutrality of the state, so fairness today requires its philosophical neutrality.[45]

3.2. Political not metaphysical?

The main criticism Rawl's *Political Liberalism* deserves is, in my view, that it does not deliver what it promises—namely, a purely political theory oriented to doing justice to the pluralism of comprehensive doctrines coexisting in a democratic society. In fact, it draws its conclusions from antiperfectionist premises that have metaphysical implications and are not, strictly speaking, circumscribed by the political sphere.

(a) Philosophical neutrality and religious neutrality

The Rawlsian attempt to apply the principle of neutrality to the philosophical realm is highly questionable, for example, given the different sources of philosophical and religious knowledge. The political principle of religious tolerance started to be recognized in the sixteenth century not solely on the basis of pluralism. It was also based on the premise that the religious question as such transcends the scope of natural reason. *Silete theologi in munere alieno!*—"*Let theologians* keep silence on matters outside their province!"—was the exhortation of Alberico Gentili, a jurist who was highly influenced by Bodin and the *politiques*,[46] to those who justified war on purely religious grounds.[47] Religious tolerance was only possible since, from a strict philosophical point of view, the assent of faith is given by reason of authority and not just by the authority of reason. Thus the principle of tolerance results from a double intent of "de-theologization" and "rationalization." In order for Rawls's analogy to be valid, we should assume that the discussion of the good is not a strictly rational discussion: we should carry through a "de-rationalization" of the good in the philosophical realm. In this sense, his *Political Liberalism* presents the same atelological features as *A Theory of Justice*.

(b) Rawlsian public reason

At first sight, however, Rawls's analogy seems to be justified through the differentiation between "the rational" and "the reasonable." In my view, the existence of certain boundaries imposed by public reason is not objectionable, and in general terms, those boundaries were also drawn by both Aquinas and Kant:

(i) First, the political community must not regulate all moral questions but only those that are relevant for the common life of men: for the common good, according to Thomas Aquinas,[48] and for the coexistence of freedoms in accordance with a universal law, according to Kant.[49] There exists a politically irrelevant sphere that remains removed from public coercive intervention.
(ii) Second, those who govern must never enforce morals ignoring the convictions and customs of those who are governed. Again, this principle is also recognized by both Aquinas[50] and Kant.[51] The *fiat Justitia et pereat mundus* is not compatible with the classical natural law tradition, since the possibility of justifying the exercise of power constitutes in itself a condition for realizing the common good. Thomas Aquinas would find no problem in maintaining with Rawls that the exercise of power has to be based on "publicly acceptable reasons."[52]

In spite of the suitability—and even necessity—of the concept of public reason, I think it is very problematic to understand this concept in the way Rawls does. As has been explained, his idea of public reason demands that all "reasonable" citizens admit the priority of liberties over the good. In this way, "public reason" is unfairly restrained, and civil liberties lose any appropriate reference for assessing their value beyond themselves. Such a restriction of public reason cannot be a fair solution to the reality of plural conceptions of the good, since it favors a "comprehensive doctrine" among the competing ones, namely, the conception that denies any intrinsic, rational superiority to any conception of the good. Again, we encounter ateological liberalism's lack of neutrality. Rawls justifies this requirement as not strictly rational but "reasonable." Yet if conceptions of the good exist that are effectively good and true, and conceptions of the good that are evil and false, "the reasonable" cannot consist in the irrelevance of this distinction in determining the scope of political freedom (in contrast to what Rawls's thesis suggests). Otherwise, fairness would require us to accept the existence of conceptions of the good that are simultaneously reasonable and evil (something I consider untenable). It should be noted that Rawls' liberalism does not just require us to accept the possibility that reasonable *persons* defend irrational conceptions of the good. In fact, this is perfectly possible and constitutes a reason to respect political adversaries and engage in a deliberative dialogue with them, no matter how mistaken we consider them to be. What Rawls suggests—if I have understood him correctly—is that the moral *ideas* a citizen deems irrational should be taken by him as reasonable, under the threat of becoming himself an unreasonable citizen.

(c) Philosophical neutrality and conflict of liberties

As I have already indicated, the reluctance to appeal to the discourse of the good in defining the scope of liberties leads to a situation in which liberties lack parameters of orientation to qualify them as worthy or unworthy of protection. Admittedly, the very effort to rank a catalogue of "basic liberties" above other freedoms seems to provide such an objective criterion. However, an abstract catalogue of basic liberties constitutes an insufficient parameter to solve particular, real-life conflicts.

How is it possible to decide a conflict of liberties with a "neutral" criterion of "the good"? This objection connects with the critique made by H. L. A. Hart of the (extraordinarily vague) Rawlsian principle that "each person is to have an equal right to the most extensive total system of equal basic liberties compatible with a similar system of liberty for all." In the conflict of liberties, Hart replies, we cannot avoid privileging "a liberty to do something which is more valuable for any rational person than the activities forbidden by the rules."[53]

In his *Political Liberalism*, Rawls attempted to reply to Hart's objection by identifying the importance of liberties with their relevance to ensuring the moral capacity of the subject—that is, to ensuring his capacity to develop a sense of justice and capacity to pursue his (subjective) conception of the good:

> A liberty is more or less significant depending on whether it is more or less essentially involved in, or is a more or less necessary institutional means to protect, the full and informed and effective exercise of the moral powers in one (or both) of the two fundamental cases [namely, the capacity for a conception of justice (1) and the capacity for a conception of the good (2)].[54]

I think that this criterion does not solve the problem. In reality, what should be deemed important to protect or advance a *subjective* conception of the good will depend on the content of that *subjective* conception of the good. Thus, the criterion deployed by a judge to define the relevance or significance of a liberty will lie in the *subjective* relevance or significance of that liberty for the party who invokes it. And the only *objective* indication for assessing that subjective importance will be the determination, emphasis, or strength with which it is claimed. In the absence of a prudential judgment regarding the good in each particular case, the Rawlsian public reason could end up privileging *lobbying*.

4. FULL THEORY OF THE GOOD AND RAWLSIAN LIBERTIES

4.1. Goodness as rationality

Before concluding the chapter, I would like to make some considerations regarding the Rawlsian theory of the good. Having settled the principles of the right in the original position—under circumstances that include, as has been explained, what Rawls deems a "thin theory" of the good—he proceeds to develop a "full theory" of the good in part III of *A Theory of Justice* (chapter VII). He labels his theory "goodness as rationality,"[55] and it contains, in my view, interesting ideas that should be considered more closely. In its broadest formulation, I think that his theory almost converges with the classical understanding of the good life. Nevertheless, the confluence turns out to be an illusion, swiftly vanishing when we become aware of the implications of the Rawlsian distinction between "the good" and "the just."

In a very broad sense, says Rawls, "something's being good is its having the properties that it is rational to want in things of its kind."[56] As we can see, this definition of the good is morally neutral, for it does not entail any judgment on "the point of view from which things are judged to be good or bad." However, "this moral neutrality of the definition of the good is exactly what we should expect"[57] from a descriptive theory of the good. Indeed, all other uses of the term to give advice, counsel, praise, extol, and so on, could be justified on the basis of this descriptive sense.

The question we should ask ourselves is what makes for a good plan of life. If we apply the descriptive definition of "goodness as rationality," we should conclude that a good plan of life is a plan that it is rational to want. In other words, "the rational plan for a person determines his good."[58] We arrive now at the decisive question: What ends, wishes, or desires is it rational for a person to have? In the "full theory of the good," a rational plan of life is a plan that fulfills the principles of *rational choice* and has been adopted with *deliberative rationality*.[59] The first of these features—rational choice—consists in choosing according to principles of quantitative rationality (most effective means, highest inclusiveness of the ends, and plausibility of carrying out the plan),[60] an issue that can be set aside here. Of more interest and complexity, in my opinion, is the second requirement, namely "deliberative rationality":

> The rational plan for a person is the one (among those consistent with the counting principles and other principles of rational choice once these are established) which he would choose with deliberative rationality. It is the plan that would be decided upon as the outcome of careful reflection in which the agent reviewed, in the light of all the relevant facts, what it would be like to carry out these plans and thereby ascertained the course of action that would best realize his more fundamental desires.[61]

Deliberative rationality presupposes knowledge of one's abilities, skills, possibilities, and desires.[62] It involves a rational introspection leading to the postponement of immediate desires in order to satisfy second-order desires,[63] and it demands embodying qualities such as the ability to see life as a whole, a certain continuity of purpose, and foresight: "without taking thought and seeing ourselves as one person with a life over time, we shall almost certainly regret our course of action."[64] We can say that, in such introspection, the decisive point is to assess the "intensity of our desires," given that deliberative rationality is ultimately oriented toward knowing what we really and ultimately want:

> I shall suppose that while rational principles can focus our judgments and set up guidelines for reflection, we must finally choose for ourselves in the sense that the choice often rests on our direct self-knowledge not only of what things we want but also of how much we want them. Sometimes there is no way to avoid having to assess the relative intensity of our desires. Rational principles can help us to do this, but they cannot always determine these estimates in a routine fashion.[65]

At this point, Rawlsian deliberative rationality seems to approximate the classical tradition, which also identifies the good life with *what we really and ultimately* want. However, this impression of coincidence disappears as soon as we realize that, contrary to what happens in the classical tradition, "what we ultimately want" is not connected by Rawls to objective parameters of the good life determining the moral goodness of a person and recognizable by reason. It is not possible "to construct the conception of moral goodness" until we introduce the principles of justice.[66] I think that Sandel has rightly noted that Rawls presents the good "as wholly mired in contingency" and, therefore, as "thoroughly heteronomous."[67]

4.2. An "ateleological teleology"

Finally, I consider that a political proposal that dismisses the relevance of the good in the definition of the scope of liberties ends up collapsing into contradiction. The teleology denied political relevance is surreptitiously replaced by an alternative teleology. In the words of Robert Spaemann, "The end of every teleology is the beginning of a new ateleological teleology."[68] In *A Theory of Justice*, the possession of primary goods—liberties and opportunities to advance one's conception of the good, without considering its future content—is presented as the true *naturale desiderium rationale*: the true natural, rational (and therefore "universalizable") desire of every human being, present even in the original position.[69] Rawls sees his theory of primary goods as the outcome of a "thin" concept of rationality.[70] However, when we analyze it carefully, we notice that his claim to offer a plain "thin theory of the good" is due to the "inarticulacy" of the strong value judgments it rests on, as Charles Taylor has rightly indicated.[71] It is, in sum, a "thicker" concept than it seems to be at first glance. A theory that aims at empowering individuals to protect and promote whatever conceptions of the good they wish is by no means a thin theory of the good. Among other consequences, it leads Rawls to suggest that, under certain "reasonable" criteria—he does not specify which—eugenic policies constitute a duty toward succeeding generations on the part of those that precede them, for such policies would be approved by the parties in the original position.[72]

This "ateleological teleology" appears again in the Rawlsian definition of a "good person." Applied to persons, the idea of "goodness as rationality" results in those properties that it is rational for them to want being seen in practically all their roles or functions. In Rawls's words, the "fundamental moral virtues," that is, "the strong and normally effective desires to act on the basic principles of right," are "undoubtedly" among the properties that define a good person.[73] Therefore, we can say that behaving in accordance with the liberal, antiperfectionist principles of justice defined by Rawls should be counted among the features that rationally characterize a good person. In my view, this is a highly illiberal excess.

Rawls's *Political Liberalism* does not include any substantial correction to this lack of neutrality. By promoting the maintenance of political institutions embodying a conception of justice that includes the principle of philosophical neutrality, Rawls places in the sphere of "the unreasonable" those who consider that it is neither prudent nor fair to rigidly juxtapose "freedom" and "good" or to give the former unconditional priority. Here too, the substantive reach of his principles only reveals their lack of neutrality when the author explains their practical applications. In a polemical footnote to *The Idea of Public Reason*, Rawls said that the right to abortion in the first three months of pregnancy is, in his view, a *sine qua non* condition for any reasonable balance of the values at stake:

> Suppose further that we consider the question in terms of these three important political values: the due respect for human life, the ordered reproduction of political society over time, including the family in some form, and finally the equality of women as equal citizens. (There are, of course, other important political values besides these.) Now I believe any reasonable balance of these three values will give a woman a duly qualified right to decide whether or not to end her pregnancy during the first trimester. The reason for this is that at this early stage of pregnancy the political value of the equality of women is overriding, and this right is required to give it substance and force. Other political values, if tallied in, would not, I think, affect this conclusion. A reasonable balance may allow her such a right beyond this, at least in certain circumstances. However, I do not discuss the question in general here, as I simply want to illustrate the point of the text by saying that any comprehensive doctrine that leads to a balance of political values excluding that duly qualified right in the first trimester is to that extent unreasonable; and depending on details of its formulation, it may also be cruel and oppressive; for example, if it denied the right altogether except in the case of rape and incest. Thus, assuming that this question is either a constitutional essential or a matter of basic justice, we would go against the ideal of public reason if we voted from a comprehensive doctrine that denied this right.[74]

This footnote aroused a considerable amount of criticism. In my view, it reveals a dangerous dialectic of intolerance in the very antiperfectionist tolerance defended by Rawls. It is fair to say here that, replying to his critics in *The Idea of Public Reason Revisited*, Rawls added an important nuance to this opinion. His clarification may be summarized in the following three points: First, he argued that the purpose of his footnote was just to illustrate the general thesis developed in the body of the text that "the only comprehensive doctrines that run afoul of public reason are those that cannot support a reasonable balance [or ordering] of political values [on the issue]"; second, he admitted that the controversial passage was not "an argument," though it expressed his "personal opinion"; and third, he left the possibility open that an opinion on abortion contradicting his own view satisfied the requirements of public reason.[75] Notwithstanding the fact that he softened the terms deployed in his previous essay, I have serious doubts that this reply in any way clears the shadow of intolerance cast by the footnote.

NOTES

1. J. Rawls, *A Theory of Justice*, rev. ed. (Cambridge, MA: Belknap Press of Harvard University Press, 1999), § 2, p. 8.

2. J. Rawls, *Political Liberalism*, exp. ed. (New York: Columbia University Press, 2005), I, § 1, p. 10; and § 6.3, p. 38; and pp. 440–41. A synthesis of Rawls's work may be found in his writing, edited by Erin Kelly, *Justice as Fairness— A Restatement* (Cambridge, MA: Belknap Press of Harvard University Press, 2001).

3. See, for example, his *Lessons on the History of Political Philosophy* (Cambridge, MA: Belknap Press of Harvard University Press, 2007), pp. 46 ff.

4. Rawls, *Theory of Justice*, § 3, p. 10.

5. Rawls, *Theory of Justice*, § 40, p. 222.

6. Rawls, *Theory of Justice*, § 84, p. 491.

7. Rawls, *Theory of Justice*, § 85, p. 491.

8. Rawls, *Theory of Justice*, § 3, p. 11. It is necessary to leave aside "those aspects of the social world that seem arbitrary from a moral point of view" (p. 14), among which Rawls includes the conceptions of the good (the same idea is reiterated in several passages: pp. 16, 27, 110, 118, 151, etc.).

9. Rawls, *Theory of Justice*, § 3, p. 13.

10. Rawls, *Theory of Justice*, § 15, p. 79.

11. Rawls, *Theory of Justice*, §§ 3–4, pp. 14 ff.

12. Rawls, *Theory of Justice*, § 25, p. 125.

13. Rawls, *Theory of Justice*, § 26, pp. 132 ff. The application of the *maximin rule* was refined by Rawls in later works (see, *v. gr.*, *Justice as Fairness*, §§ 28–34, pp. 97–120).

14. Rawls, *Theory of Justice*, § 11 ff., pp. 52 ff. The formulation of these principles presents variations in later writings (see *v. gr.*, *Justice as Fairness*, § 13, pp. 42 ff.) though substantially maintains its original meaning. In its development, Rawls divides the second principle of justice in two subprinciples: the *difference principle* ("economic inequalities are to be arranged so that they are reasonably expected to be to everyone's advantage") and *the principle of fair equality of opportunity* ("economic inequalities are to be arranged so that they are attached to positions and offices open to all") (see Rawls, *Theory of Justice*, pp. 52 ff.).

15. Rawls, *Theory of Justice*, § 35, p. 194.

16. Regarding the different stages at which the principles of justice work, see Rawls, *Theory of Justice*, § 31, pp. 171 ff.

17. Rawls, *Theory of Justice*, § 31, pp. 171 ff.

18. Rawls, *Theory of Justice*, § 33, p. 181.

19. George, *Making Men Moral*, pp. 134–36. For an explicit differentiation between "the good considered in itself" and the "conceptions of the good," see *S. Th.*, I-II, q. 34, a. 2.

20. Rawls, *Political Liberalism*, I, § 4.3, p. 24. The principles of justice are "principles that free and rational persons concerned to *further their own interests* would accept in an initial position of equality as defining the fundamental terms of their association" (Rawls, *A Theory of Justice*, § 3, p. 10; emphasis mine).

21. D. Hume, *A Treatise of Human Nature*, Book I, Part II, Section VI, ed. L. A. Selby-Bigge (Oxford: Clarendon Press, 1888), p. 67.

22. *KpV*, p. 64 (*Cambridge Ed.*, p. 191).

23. Rawls, *Theory of Justice*, § 40, p. 226.

24. Rawls, *Theory of Justice*, § 40, pp. 222–25.
25. Rawls, *Theory of Justice*, § 40, pp. 226–27.
26. On the distinctiveness of constructivism in Kant's philosophy, see J. Rawls, "Themes in Kant's Moral Philosophy," in *Kant's Transcendental Deductions*, ed. Eckart Förster (Stanford, CA: Stanford University Press, 1989), pp. 81 ff.
27. J. Rawls, "Kantian Constructivism in Moral Theory," *Journal of Philosophy* 77 (1980): 568. On the differences between both forms of "constructivism," see also O. O'Neill, "Constructivism in Rawls and Kant" in *The Cambridge Companion to Rawls*, ed. S. Freeman (Cambridge: Cambridge University Press, 2003), especially p. 352.
28. Rawls, *Theory of Justice*, § 22, pp. 109–12.
29. See Michael Sandel, *Liberalism and the Limits of Justice*, 2nd ed. (Cambridge: Cambridge University Press, 1998), pp. 13 ff.
30. Sandel, *Liberalism and the Limits of Justice*, p. 30.
31. *KpV*, pp. 62–63 (*Cambridge Ed.*, pp. 190–91); *Gemeinspruch*, pp. 282 ff. (*Cambridge Ed.*, pp. 282 ff.). On the priority of "the just" in Rawls, see *Theory of Justice*, § 6, p. 28.
32. T. Nagel, "Rawls on Justice" (1973), in *Reading Rawls*, ed. N. Daniels (Oxford: Blackwell, 1989), p. 9. See also, in the same vein, Joseph Raz, *The Morality of Freedom* (Oxford: Oxford University Press, 1986), pp. 118 ff.
33. Raz, *Morality of Freedom*, p. 120.
34. Rawls, *Political Liberalism*, I, § 1, p. 10.
35. Rawls, *Political Liberalism*, I, § 5, p. 30.
36. Rawls, *Political Liberalism*, I, § 5, p. 31.
37. Rawls, *Political Liberalism*, II, § 5, p. 74.
38. Rawls, *Political Liberalism*, pp. 440 ff.
39. Rawls, *Political Liberalism*, VI, p. 213.
40. Rawls, *Political Liberalism*, VI, § 4, pp. 223, 450.
41. Rawls, *Political Liberalism*, VIII, § 9, pp. 335–36.
42. Rawls, *Political Liberalism*, II, § 1, p. 53.
43. Rawls, *Political Liberalism*, pp. 442–45.
44. On the connection between modern state and secularization, see especially M. Kriele, *Einführung in die Staatslehre: Die geschichtlichen Legitimitätsgrundlagen des demokratischen Verfassungsstaates*, 5th ed. (Opladen: Westdeutscher Verlag, 1994), pp. 46 ff.; and Ernst-Wolfgang Böckenförde, "Die Entstehung des Staates als Vorgang der Säkularisation," in *Staat—Gesellschaft—Freiheit. Studien zur Staatstheorie und zum Verfassungsrecht* (Frankfurt am Main: Suhrkamp, 1976), pp. 42 ff.
45. Rawls, *Political Liberalism*, pp. 148–54.
46. Jean Bodin belonged to the group of the so-called *politiques*, a party deeply impressed by the bloody religious struggles taking place in France, which reached a critical point in the St. Bartholomew's Day massacre on August 24, 1572. The *politiques* advocated for the concentration of power in the hands of the sovereign as a means to effectively establish religious tolerance. On the role of Bodin and the party of the *politiques* during the religious wars in France, see Kriele, *Einführung in die Staatslehre*, pp. 46 ff.

47. Albericus Gentili, *De iure belli*, I, Cap. XI (Oxford: Clarendon Press, 1933, repr. ed. 1612), p. 92.

48. *S. Th.*, I-II, q. 100, a. 2. In the same sense, see also M. Rhonheimer, "The Liberal Image of Man and the Concept of Autonomy," in *The Common Good of Constitutional Democracy* (Washington, DC: CUA, 2013), p. 69; "Rawls's '*Political Liberalism*' Revisited," pp. 239–248; and J. Finnis, "Limited Government," in *Collected Essays: Vol. III* (Oxford: Oxford University Press), pp. 87 ff.

49. It should be remembered that, for Kant, the coexistence of freedoms embraces duties even regarding "the right of humanity in our own person" (*MdS*, p. 240).

50. *S. Th.*, I-II, q. 96, arts. 1–2.

51. *Zum ewigen Frieden*, p. 378.

52. Rawls, *Justice as Fairness*, p. 91.

53. H. L. A. Hart, "Rawls on Liberty and Its Priority" (1973), in Daniels, *Reading Rawls. Critical Studies on Rawls' "A Theory of Justice,"* p. 240.

54. Rawls, *Political Liberalism*, VIII, § 9, pp. 335–36.

55. Rawls, *Theory of Justice*, § 64, p. 366.

56. Rawls, *Theory of Justice*, § 62, p. 356.

57. Rawls, *Theory of Justice*, § 61, p. 354.

58. Rawls, *Theory of Justice*, § 63, p. 358.

59. Rawls, *Theory of Justice*, § 63, pp. 358–59.

60. Rawls, *Theory of Justice*, § 63, pp. 361–65.

61. Rawls, *Theory of Justice*, § 64, p. 366.

62. Rawls, *Theory of Justice*, § 64, p. 365.

63. On second order desires, see H. Frankfurt, "Freedom of the Will and the Concept of a Person," *Journal of Philosophy* LXVIII (1971): 5–20.

64. Rawls, *Theory of Justice*, § 64, p. 372.

65. Rawls, *Theory of Justice*, § 64, p. 365.

66. Rawls, *Theory of Justice*, § 61, p. 355.

67. Sandel, *Liberalism and the Limits of Justice*, pp. 165 ff.

68. R. Spaemann, *Natürliche Ziele. Geschichte und Wiederentdeckung des teleologischen Denkens* (Stuttgart: Klett-Cotta, 2005), p. 163.

69. Rawls, *Theory of Justice*, § 60, p. 348.

70. Rawls, *Theory of Justice*, § 3, p. 12.

71. Taylor, *Sources of the Self*, p. 89.

72. Rawls, *Theory of Justice*, § 17, pp. 92–93. On this question, see *infra*, chapter 8.

73. Rawls, *Theory of Justice*, § 66, p. 382.

74. Rawls, *Political Liberalism*, VI, § 7, pp. 243–44.

75. Rawls, *Political Liberalism*, p. 479.

Chapter 4

"Equal concern and respect": Ronald Dworkin's philosophy of rights

1. INTRODUCTION

If Rawls can be considered the most prominent liberal political philosopher of the past decades, Ronald Dworkin holds a similar position in the field of legal philosophy.[1] His name is mainly associated with the book *Taking Rights Seriously* (1977), a work that delivered the *coup de grâce* to the academic hegemony of legal positivism and contributed to consolidating rights as a central category in our legal systems. This book was, perhaps, the most influential legal-philosophical work of its age. However, Dworkin's intellectual dynamism has given rise to a vast bibliographic production, both academic and journalistic. Among his writings, a preeminent place should be given—together with *Taking Rights Seriously*—to his theory of political liberalism, initially sketched out in an essay published in *A Matter of Principle* (1985) and extensively revised in his *Tanner Lectures of Human Values* (1990); his "interpretive" theory of law, widely developed in *Law's Empire* (1986)—his most interesting book, in my opinion—and the great synthesis of his thought, completed shortly before his death: *Justice for Hedgehogs* (2011). In this last book, Dworkin elaborated an integrated theory of ethics and morals, politics, and law on the basis of the independence of value judgments from other dominions of thought.

2. CLARIFYING POLITICAL LIBERALISM

2.1. The principles behind the contract

As with my analysis of John Rawls, in the following pages I will introduce and criticize some of the presuppositions of Dworkin's philosophy. In order to link this chapter with the previous one, it is worth starting with a reference to Dworkin's reading and interpretation of Rawls's liberalism. In a critical essay written in the aftermath of the publication of *A Theory of Justice* and republished in chapter 6 of *Taking Rights Seriously* and in subsequent works, Dworkin pointedly identified the moral principle on which the Rawlsian theory rests, a principle that is tacitly assumed in the elaboration of the conditions of the original position: the right to "equal concern and respect." As Dworkin rightly said, the stipulation of the contract behind the veil of ignorance would just be an ideal construct to guarantee an underlying principle, namely, the principle of equality of all interests and preferences, including in this category the different conceptions of the good: "men who have no idea of their own conception of the good cannot act to favor those who hold one ideal over those who hold another."[2] Hence, the grounding principle of political and legal liberalism would not be a nonexistent absolute natural right to freedom but an absolute natural right to "equal concern and respect."

Rawls rejected Dworkin's attempt to characterize the original position as a mere device to verify the validity of moral principles previously assumed, again defending his theory as a development of certain moral intuitions, for example, the conception of persons as "free and equals."[3] It is not surprising, then, that Dworkin attributed to him a tacit acceptance of his main critical observation, namely, that "the original position is an expository device for testing the implications of certain basic moral and political principles we take to be true."[4] That the grounding principle of basic liberties is not a right to liberty, but to "equal concern and respect," is something that Dworkin has very convincingly argued. There cannot exist a strict general right to freedom, since such a right would call into question any limitation of freedom, and this would make political coexistence impossible.[5] For political liberalism, what qualifies certain liberties as basic is a strict general right to "equal concern and respect," a right that prevents any limitation on liberty that discriminates among the diverse preferences of the citizens.

In *Justice for Hedgehogs*, Dworkin clears up the liberal conception of "equal concern and respect" by deriving it from what he deems to be the most abstract of rights, namely, the "right to be treated as a human being whose dignity fundamentally matters."[6] The content of the principle of human dignity would in turn consist of two subprinciples:[7] on the one hand, the principle of "self-respect," which in itself includes a "duty to recognize the other" in which Dworkin grounds—rightly in my view—all moral obligations toward others;[8] and on the other hand, the principle of "authenticity," in which he grounds a "personal responsibility" of individuals "to define success in their own lives."[9] The distinctive feature of political liberalism is that such responsibility would preclude any political intervention. According to Dworkin, the right to equal concern and respect would prevent any intervention in this "ethical independence," that is, in this individual responsibility to define the meaning of one's good life.

We can hardly object to Dworkin's interpretation of Rawls. Actually, it is difficult to deny the close connection that exists between Rawls's "justice as fairness" and Dworkin's principles. Leaving aside the "constructivist" methodology of the contract, Dworkin clears up the liberal-ateleological position and plainly identifies the "constitutive morality" of antiperfectionist liberalism. By exposing the liberal understanding of the principle of human dignity and, subsequently, of the principle of equal concern and respect, he purifies the debate and places it in a clearer context.

2.2. POLITICAL LIBERALISM IN *A MATTER OF PRINCIPLE*

Initially developed in an essay included in *A Matter of Principle*, Dworkin's theory of liberalism insists on grounding this line of thought in the right to "equal concern and respect"—an idea that Dworkin links, as does Rawls with his entire theory, to the Kantian tradition.[10] Against the pure and simple assertion of one's freedom, the principle of equality always contains a moral act of recognition of the other as a neighbor and equal. Dworkin regards this principle—I think appropriately—as the very basis of human rights.[11]

1. Strictly speaking, however, the distinctive feature of antiperfectionist liberalism is not the fundamental character of equality, as Dworkin himself admits. The principle of equality is to be found at the very basis of innumerable moral and political traditions.[12] What is distinctive about antiperfectionist liberalism is an interpretation of the principle of "equal concern and respect" according to which "government must be neutral on what might be called the question of the good life."[13] In other words, "its constitutive morality is a theory of equality that requires official neutrality among theories of what is valuable in life."[14]

   Dworkin himself formulated four possible objections that could be made to antiperfectionist liberalism, and he attempted to give them a succinct reply:[15]

   (a) To the objection that liberalism "rests on skepticism about theories of the good," he replies that "its constitutive morality provides that human beings must be treated as equals by their government, not because there is no right and wrong in political morality, but because that is what is right."

   (b) To the objection that liberalism "is based on a mean view of human nature that assumes that human beings are atoms who can exist and find self-fulfillment apart from political community," Dworkin answers that "liberalism does not rest on any special theory of personality, nor does it deny that most human beings will think that what is good for them is that they be active in society."

(c) To the objection that "liberalism must itself be a theory of the good," Dworkin replies that "the liberal conception of equality is a principle of political organization that is required by justice, not a way of life for individuals."

(d) Finally, he rather more carefully confronts the objection that liberalism "denies to political society its highest function and ultimate justification, which is that society must help its members to achieve what is in fact good." In accordance with this thesis, liberalism "assumes that the opinions people have about the sort of lives they want are self-generated, whereas these opinions are actually the products of the economic system or other aspects of the society in which they live." Dworkin replies that, precisely because they are not self-generated, "it is all the more important that distribution be fair in itself, not as tested by the preferences it produces."

2. It is worth making some remarks on the way Dworkin confronts the objections to antiperfectionist liberalism in *A Matter of Principle*. Evading the complex reasoning on which each of them rests, he formulates his objections, in my view, in an oversimplified fashion—the first three in just one sentence—thus rendering them easy to criticize:

(a) It is true that liberalism does not explicitly pretend to be based on skepticism about the good but on a conception of political justice that demands neutrality with respect to the good. Yet, if we accept the existence of an objective, rational good—in Aristotelian terms, of a specifically human way of flourishing (*end*) that certainly includes a wide range of options but also excludes some of them (*limit*); or, in Kantian terms, of a life according to the good determined by the moral law—the liberal assertion of a right to completely decide one's conception of the good without any political interference becomes extremely problematic.

(b) The way Dworkin presents the second objection, asserting that liberalism treats men as "atoms who can exist and find self-fulfillment apart from political community," is also insufficient. It is difficult to glimpse what exactly the objection means when it is put in such laconic terms. As to Dworkin's response, that "liberalism does not rest on any special theory of personality," the fact is, as we have seen, that it rests on a right to ethical independence heavily charged with theoretical presuppositions about human nature.

(c) To the third objection, that liberalism contradicts itself since it is ultimately a "theory of the good," Dworkin replies by stressing the difference between the just and the good and underlining that liberalism is a theory of justice. Here too, the objection is introduced too briefly. Of course, liberalism does not introduce itself as a theory of the good but as a theory of justice based on a claim to ethical independence considered as a requirement of human dignity. In addition, liberalism sees this right to ethical independence as a right to fully define one's conception of the good, a claim that renders illegitimate any attempt to give intersubjective political validity to every consideration regarding the good life. And what is this but a relativistic theory of the good?

(d) Finally, Dworkin accepts that the conceptions of the good are not self-generated, and for that very reason he considers it a requirement of fairness that the exercise of public authority should not be guided by the preferences it produces. Analyzing this thesis, we can confirm the main objections formulated to liberalism (as set out in c and d). Dworkin denies the state any competence with regard to the conceptions of the good in order not to privilege some conceptions over others. Despite this starting point, he does not deny the communitarian premise that the ways of life, customs, and conceptions of the good are forged in moral traditions. What he says is that it is not just for the authority to have an impact on the birth and development of those ways of life. The basis for this assertion is the consideration of the different conceptions of good and evil as mere "preferences," as mere desires experienced by those who hold them. Neutrality among simple *preferences* would be, as Dworkin rightly points out, a requirement of fairness. However, if we reject the thesis that reduces the good to a preference, neutrality regarding the *good* is simply—as the objection holds, in the very terms deployed by Dworkin—to "deny to political society its highest function and ultimate justification, which is that society must help its member to achieve what is in fact good."

2.3. The *Tanner lectures*

(a) Ethical liberalism

Notwithstanding the relevance of the article just examined, the main exposition of Dworkin's theory of liberalism is contained in his *Tanner Lectures on Human Values,* first published in 1990 and included in chapter 6 of *Sovereign Virtue.*[16] In this essay, Dworkin thoroughly develops what he labels "ethical liberalism," a theory that purports to integrate the theory of justice with ethics. According to Dworkin, liberalism's "ethical neutrality" can only be maintained at a "relatively concrete" level of analysis. By contrast, at the more abstract levels, "liberalism cannot and should not be neutral."[17]

The idea of a "good" or "fulfilled life" is identified by Dworkin with what he calls "critical interests" or "critical well-being." In contrast to "volitional interests"—or "experiential interests," as he labels them in other writings—critical interests point toward the success of life as a whole.[18] But what, asks Dworkin, is the "metric" of the good life?[19] He distinguishes two models to measure the critical value of a life: an "impact model" and a "challenge model." The "impact model" resembles what has been called value-utilitarianism: a life is good inasmuch as it increases the amount of value in the universe. As for the "challenge model," the value of a life resides in responding appropriately to the circumstances and challenges posed by life. The good life is not so much defined by what someone produces externally but by their "skillful performance," which has an intrinsic value.[20]

Taking the "model of challenge" as a starting point, Dworkin tries to solve a series of dilemmas posed by the "ethical" question of the good life, one of which is, precisely, its relationship with the "moral" question of justice. From the perspective of value-utilitarianism, the circumstances faced by an individual—including the demands of justice—seem to draw limits to the content of value that anyone could produce. By contrast, if we conceive of ethics as appropriate coping with the world in which one lives, the external circumstances are no longer seen as limitations to a good life but, in some cases, even as constitutive "parameters" of that life.[21] According to Dworkin, this is exactly what happens with justice: the good life cannot be an unjust life, for justice constitutes a "normative parameter" of a good life.[22] Moreover, the injustice of a society undermines, at least to a certain extent, the very possibility of leading a good life, because a good life consists in "responding in the right way to the right challenge." Living immersed in an unjust environment or state of affairs makes it difficult to speak of "the right challenge," at least in its fullest sense. Consequently, we can say that society's injustice reduces—without completely eliminating—the possibility of living a good life.[23]

Now we come to the decisive dilemma that Dworkin contends will lead us to accept or reject the theoretical arguments in favor of ethical paternalism: must the "good life" be subjectively chosen in order to be objectively good? From a purely external conception of value—the utilitarian conception defended by the "model of impact"—the answer is evidently "no." From the model of challenge, however, the answer must be affirmative, since "intention is part of performance,"[24] and it is "skillful performance" that gives form to a good life. This conclusion leads Dworkin to reject any form of moral paternalism with regard to the critical interests of persons and to embrace the complete ethical neutrality of the state:

> The challenge view, on the other hand, rejects the root assumption of critical paternalism: that a person's life can be improved by forcing him into some act or abstinence he thinks valueless.... On the challenge model ... it is performance that counts, not mere external result, and the right motive or sense is necessary to the right performance.[25]

Dworkin's rejection of paternalism is not confined to the Millean *harm principle*,[26] that is, to the illegitimacy of prohibiting conduct that does not harm third parties. Dworkin's antiperfectionist liberalism also entails the rejection of what he labels "*cultural* paternalism," namely, "the suggestion that people should be protected from choosing wasteful or bad lives not by flat prohibitions of the criminal law but by educational constraints and devices that remove bad options from people's view and imagination."[27] From the "challenge model" he postulates, Dworkin argues that "a challenge cannot be more interesting, or in any other way a more valuable challenge to face, when it has been narrowed, simplified, and bowdlerized by others in advance, and that is as much true when we are ignorant of what they have done as when we are all too aware of it":

> Suppose someone replies that the challenge is more valuable when the chances of selecting a truly good life are improved, as they would be if the list of possibilities was filtered by wise collective rulers. That reply misunderstands the challenge model profoundly, because it confuses parameters and limitations. It assumes that we have some standard of what a good life is that transcends the question of what circumstances are appropriate for people deciding how to live, and so can be used in answering that latter question, by stipulating that the best circumstances are those most likely to produce the really correct answer.[28]

In short, the appropriate circumstances cannot be planned on the basis of a general criterion of the good, since there is no general criterion transcending the factual circumstances that may be used to improve them. For, according to the "model of challenge" developed by Dworkin, no criterion of the "good life" or "right performance" exists prior to and independent of the act of choosing: "the challenge model fuses value and choice" and rejects cultural paternalism insofar as this "assumes an independent, transcendent picture of ethical value, and the challenge model rejects any such picture." The only ideals whose endorsement by government is not ruled out by the challenge model are "ethical ideals not adequately supported by culture"—presumably to increase the range of choices. And finally, the challenge model also allows "compulsory education and other forms of regulation which experience shows are likely to be endorsed in a genuine rather than manipulated way, when these are sufficiently short-term and noninvasive and not subject to other, independent objection."[29]

To conclude, despite denying the coercive prohibition of a behavior for ethical reasons regarding the good life, liberal tolerance does not mean an ethical neutrality at an abstract level. Liberal tolerance, Dworkin admits, is not neutral in its *consequences*: "it must have the result that some kinds of lives are more difficult to lead than others." Nor is it neutral "toward ethical ideals that directly challenge its own," namely, "third-person ethics" that define value independently of choice.[30]

(b) Critical remarks

Having synthetically—and I hope faithfully and accurately—developed Dworkin's "ethical liberalism," I will now proceed to formulate some critical remarks on his theory. Nonetheless, I would like to start by pointing out that the "challenge model" he uses to characterize the good life is certainly closer to classical tradition than what he labels the "impact model." In Aristotelian terms, the model of impact conceives of morality as a purely technical production (*poiesis*), thus becoming a "third-person ethics," as Dworkin rightly affirms. It is clear enough that performing a right action motivated by external coercion does not necessarily make a life better, since ethics judges the human *will*. Furthermore, the effects of our actions sooner or later escape our control so that we do not really know what they will turn out to produce in the long term. Would it make any sense to assert that Hitler's mother did something wrong by giving birth to her son, merely for the fact that he ended up becoming a tyrant?

Embracing value-utilitarianism amounts to assuming the point of view of an all-knowing deity. Not even that, if we accept—as Thomas Aquinas and the entire Christian tradition does—that God does not work like a "value accountant" but like an artist.[31] Accordingly, I fully agree with Ronald Dworkin in dismissing out of hand what he calls the "impact model." Nevertheless, the alternative he proposes is not free from problems. As I will try to show, Dworkin associates his "challenge model" with an overtly relativistic conception of values:

> There is no settled canon of skill in living, and some people's lives, at least, make claims about ethical skill that if widely accepted would change prevailing views on the subject, and might even launch what would seem a new mode of living well, making, once again, ethical value from nothing.[32]

It is in this thesis—and not in the simple admission of a nonutilitarian model of ethical *praxis*—that the foundations of Dworkin's liberal ethical neutrality lie. It is true that the core of ethical life is *praxis* itself, even disregarding the outcomes; and that, in analogy with a work of art, the good life shows an extraordinary openness. It does not follow from these premises, however, that there are no transcendent parameters for ethical life or that those parameters are completely relative to the historical moment in which someone lives—as Dworkin suggests.[33] Practical reason identifies general parameters of a virtuous life and places limits, some of which appear to right reason—in my view—as moral absolutes incompatible with a good life, independently of the circumstances of the agent (the prohibition of lies, murder, adultery, etc.).

This rejection of ethical relativism does not yet include, however, a justification for legislation favorable to moral ecology—of a "culturally paternalistic" law, to use Dworkin's terms. Is it legitimate for legislation to advance and promote conditions favorable to the good life of citizens and to try to avoid situations that undermine those conditions? According to Dworkin, "a challenge cannot be more interesting, or in any other way a more valuable challenge to face, when it has been narrowed, simplified, and bowdlerized by others in advance." The problem with this argument—to which I will come back in chapter 6—is that, once we accept objective parameters of human excellence, a fulfilled life cannot be reduced to a life facing an "interesting" challenge. Once we admit the existence of an objective "honest good" (*bonum honestum*), the ethical perspective must be the perspective of *benevolence*, which demands us to cooperate so that our neighbor can attain it.[34]

3. "RIGHTS AS TRUMPS"

The liberal interpretation of the principle of equal concern and respect is legally institutionalized by Dworkin in his theory of *rights as trumps*. In accordance with this theory, "rights are best understood as trumps over some background justification for political decisions that states a goal for the community as a whole"[35]—be it the collective aggregated welfare (utilitarianism) or the "common good" in an Aristotelian sense (classical natural law).[36] The very object of democratic deliberation (positive freedom) consists in a decision upon the means, while everything which pertains to the ends of human life—the conceptions of the good—must be left to individual ethical responsibility (negative liberty).[37]

Particularly revealing is the fact that, in his defense of rights as "principles" that, like "trump cards," unconditionally prevail against "social policies," Dworkin tacitly assumes in several passages that teleological thought on the common good may be equated with interest utilitarianism. In his own words,

> The right to moral independence is part of the same collection of rights as the right of political independence, and it is to be justified as a trump over an

unrestricted utilitarian defense of prohibitory laws against pornography, . . . in much the same way as the latter right is justified as a trump over a utilitarian justification of giving Jews less or Sarah more in a society of Nazis or Sarah-lovers.[38]

It is evident that this way of speaking overlooks the distinction between a preference for Sarah or an aversion to Jews—a mere drive, in the first case, and a passion contrary to reason, in the second—and the rational will to pursue and advance the human good. Whether intended or not, the same inaccuracy is displayed in other passages of Dworkin's work—for example, when he affirms that rights prevail as trumps against "the desires and preferences of the majority, including their preferences about how others should lead their lives":[39]

> People have the right not to suffer disadvantage in the distribution of social goods and opportunities, including disadvantages in the liberties permitted to them by the criminal law, just on the ground that their officials or fellow-citizens think that their opinions about the right way for them to lead their own lives are ignoble or wrong.[40]

As Joseph Raz has indicated, this way of speaking is rather obscure, given that those who point to the unworthiness or moral evil of certain behaviors in order to favor limitations of freedom do not base those limitations on their convictions being this or that but on the behaviors in question being actually unworthy or evil.[41] It is not simply an appeal to preferences or desires, as Dworkin states, but to reason.

The paragraph transcribed above is especially revealing since, in it, Dworkin advocates for a fundamental right to publish and consume pornography. The prohibition of such behavior would illegitimately be grounded in the fact that "the *desires* and *preferences* of publishers and consumers are outweighed by the *desires* and *preferences* of the majority, including their *preferences* about how others should lead their lives."[42] However, in a case like this, it is plainly obvious that the argument appealing to public morality not only does not invoke mere irrational preferences or desires but is even formulated against people's irrational preferences and desires. For an irrational drive leads any human being toward the typical object of that drive, which has to be regulated and ordered by reason. The publication and consumption of pornography is not just a simple execution of subjective preferences equivalent to contradictory preferences but a departure from the "rule of reason" (*regula rationis*)[43]—and, consequently, an act of self-alienation. There is no need for a great hermeneutic effort to find the "desire principle" behind the Dworkinian right to ethical independence, for Dworkin himself uses that language. *In claris non fit interpretatio.*

4. CRITIQUE OF ETHICAL REALISM AND THEORY OF MORAL TRUTH

Even more clearly than in Rawls's work, Dworkin's liberalism rejects the possibility of giving political relevance to our propositions regarding the human good, that is, the good life. In contrast to Rawls, however, Dworkin did not limit himself to developing a political theory but also engaged in moral epistemology. In *Justice for Hedgehogs* (2011), he provided an account of what he called the "independence of value judgments," developing a whole theory of moral truth. In this last section of the chapter, I would like to make some critical remarks on his proposal.

4.1. Moral truth as responsibility

In a way that seems paradoxical, Ronald Dworkin attempts to rebut both moral realism and moral skepticism. Nevertheless, it has to be noted that his conception of "moral realism" is somewhat narrow. He understands this concept in a manner that is very distinct from how the classical tradition might understand itself as "realist." The *moral realism* criticized by Dworkin—so-called naturalistic realism or Cornell realism—is wrongly based, in his opinion, on what he labels the myth of "the causal impact hypothesis," that is, the "hypothesis" that moral truth makes an impact or has an influence on moral opinions. According to Dworkin, the assertion of an impact of moral truth on moral opinion is plainly ungrounded. Yet, *skepticism* is also based on an ill-founded premise, namely the myth of what he calls "the causal dependence hypothesis." This "hypothesis" states that the existence of truth in morals depends upon "causal impact," that is, upon an effective influence of moral truth on moral opinions.

The problem with moral skepticism is, Dworkin argues, that it relies on the same theory of moral truth as moral realism. Both skepticism and realism claim that, in order to believe in moral truth, it is necessary to assert the existence of an impact of the objective moral truth on subjective moral opinions (*causal dependence*). Since moral realism affirms this impact, it believes in moral truth; since moral skepticism denies the very same impact, it does not believe in moral truth. In Dworkin's opinion, both are mistaken, for the major premise—the "causal dependence hypothesis"—is groundless: the existence of a moral truth does not depend upon the influence or impact of reality on our opinions. Dworkin constructs a theory of moral truth that is not understood in the classical way (*adaequatio rei intellectus*) but, as we will see, in a distinctly modern sense, namely, truth as responsibility or coherence (*res sponsio*).

As has just been explained, Dworkin begins by denying what he calls the "causal impact hypothesis," because "there is no causal interaction between moral truth and moral opinion."[44] The very impossibility of this thesis lies, in his opinion, in the fact that moral or value judgments can only be defended by invoking other moral and value judgments. There is simply no way of testing, through the "counterfactual question" of whether I would think the same were the reality different, if moral truth produces moral opinion.[45] Over and over again, we appeal to *our own* moral judgments in order to defend the judgments that *we ourselves* endorse. We should thus conclude, Dworkin argues, that there is no sufficient basis for saying that moral truth *causes* moral belief; and that, being built upon such a baseless hypothesis, moral realism is a myth. "We never advance a step beyond ourselves," we must say again with David Hume.

In any case, this kind of "solipsistic internalism" of values does not lead Dworkin to embrace moral skepticism but to reformulate the very meaning of moral truth. By dismissing the "causal dependence hypothesis," what he ultimately denies is the hypothesis which holds that "if moral truth does not cause moral opinion [that is, if there is no causal impact], then people can have no reliable or responsible grounds for those opinions."[46] Moral skepticism denies "causal impact" but shares with moral realism the endorsement of "causal dependence." As a consequence, it dramatically concludes that there are no reliable or responsible grounds for our moral opinions. Dworkin, by contrast, denies the need for any interaction between moral truth and moral opinion in order to hold ourselves responsible for our moral opinions.

Dworkin's central claim is that moral responsibility is independent of moral realism and, strictly speaking, constitutes moral truth itself. In effect, he builds a theory of moral truth independent from any *adaequatio rei*: moral truth as "responsibility."[47] After dismissing the interaction between moral truth and moral opinion, and any further claim about the correspondence between moral judgment and moral reality, he reformulates the meaning of moral truth in subjective terms. Truth ceases to point toward "adaptation" to reality (*adaequatio rei*) and becomes "commitment" to reality (*res sponsio*). Within the independent world of values, Dworkin demands of us consistency and effort to harmoniously integrate our own values;[48] he demands of us responsibility, without claiming that some judgments fit better with reality than others. For "we cannot say that when sincere people are in the right they are guided by moral truth, while insincere people can be right only by accident."[49] It is necessary to "seek the truth," but we can never affirm that truth is guiding us.[50] Strictly speaking, moral truth lies in being responsible and consistent—even though, expressly for the sake of responsibility, we must still speak of moral truth.[51]

4.2. Critical remarks

In what follows, I want to raise some objections to the moral epistemology developed by Dworkin. With regard to his criticism of moral realism—embodied in what he labels "causal impact hypothesis"—it is worth stressing, above all, that his criticism by no means affects the classical tradition, for that is not how the classical tradition conceives of itself as "realist." As has been indicated, Dworkin seems to exclusively address his criticism to so-called naturalistic realism. The classical tradition does not say that moral judgment is generally determined by moral truth but only that the moral opinion of the prudent or upright person (*phronimos, spoudaios*) is determined by moral truth. Even almost universal moral truths—for example, that sexual abuse of a child is abhorrent or that the life of a handicapped person has the same dignity as the life of a strong young man—are denied by some people. Experience teaches that the denial of such truths is usually the result of a deep personal or even social depravity. The experience, in ourselves and in others, of corruption and conversion, of vice and virtue, leads us to conclude that moral integrity and lucid moral judgment are closely connected. In the Platonic dialogue on knowledge, the first opinion to be rebutted by Socrates is Protagoras's thesis that "man is the measure of all things." Instead, Socrates affirms that the true measure is the wise man.[52] As for the link between knowledge and virtue, that is asserted with the utmost firmness by Socrates in several statements, only he who acts well may be said to know the good.[53] To understand this thesis, it is important to note that his idea of "knowledge" (*episteme*) does not correspond to mere "right opinion" (*orthos doxa*) but involves a true identification with the known object that determines the very conduct of the person who knows.[54]

Following Aristotle's view, Thomas Aquinas recommends distinguishing—against Plato's Socrates—between the knowledge of the good and its effective realization, though he declares himself aware of the deep truth conveyed by Socrates's thesis in several passages. "There is some truth in the saying of Socrates that so long as a man is in possession of knowledge he does not sin: provided, however, that this knowledge (*scientia*) is made to include the use of reason in this individual act of choice,"[55] says Aquinas in a passage from the *Summa Theologiae*. And he insists in another passage that Socrates "was somewhat right, because, since the object of the will is a good or an apparent good, it is never moved to an evil, unless that which is not good appear good in some respect to the reason; so that the will would never tend to evil, unless there were ignorance or error in the reason."[56]

In any case, what Aristotle maintains and Aquinas reaffirms is that, in order to rightly judge—*kata ton orthon logon*, "in accordance with right reason," to use Aristotle's expression—it is necessary to be well disposed.[57] The fulfillment of the moral law is a source of wisdom, and the violation of the moral law is a source of ignorance. This is why certain forms of moral ignorance deserve our reproach more than our arguments.[58] It is not that evaluative or value judgments—judgments whose object is "the good"—are not true, or that they are the outcome of a purely arbitrary decision. It is just that their truth cannot be guaranteed by "empirical experience" but requires a connaturality of the subject with his or her object of knowledge. In the field of practical reason—whose object is the human good—that connaturality amounts to an inner harmony with one's good that is indispensable to achieving it: "in moral matters a man has a right estimate about the end through a habit of virtue."[59] Addressing Simmias in a passage from the *Phaedo*, Socrates expresses this idea with an incomparable sentence: "for one who is not pure himself to attain to the realm of purity would no doubt be a breach of universal justice."[60] This statement should not be taken as an expression of "moral elitism" but rather as the result of an insight into one's own experience of vice and virtue, corruption and conversion, blindness and clarity of moral judgment. Knowledge of one's *telos* is not purely "objective" but requires a purification of one's feelings.[61]

What has been said certainly implies that there is no criterion of moral truth *de facto* acceptable to everybody, which the classical tradition has admitted since Socrates. In one of the most beautiful and tragic dialogues, the Greek philosopher expresses himself in this way:

> So one ought not to return a wrong or an injury to any person, whatever the provocation is. Now be careful, Crito, that in making these single admissions you do not end by admitting something contrary to your real beliefs. I know that there are and always will be few people who think like this, and consequently between those who do think so and those who do not there can be *no agreement on principle;* they must always feel contempt when they observe one another's decisions.[62]

Dworkin's demand for a counterfactual test acceptable to all presupposes, on the one hand, that moral truth is nothing but "an idealization of the concept of warranted assertibility,"[63] as MacIntyre has pointedly characterized the concept of moral truth underlying this kind of "internalism." But this "warranted assertibility" would only be possible if the moral realm could be mastered like the causal regularities of physical phenomena. In that case, morality would not be conditioned by the judging and acting subject's identification with the good. Yet we consistently experience that knowledge of the human good resists such mastery. As happens with every fundamental philosophical question, the decisive issue is who has the burden of proving what. Against the requirement for an impossible *probatio diabolica*—the "counterfactual question" demanded by Dworkin—the classical tradition does not deny a certain circularity in the moral arguments, and it reasonably recalls an experience that almost everybody is able to verify through introspective inquiry: the experience, in ourselves and others, of the simple fact that moral corruption and improvement are, respectively, followed by moral ignorance and wisdom.

As to the theory of moral truth as "responsibility," it represents a consistent solution given Dworkin's presuppositions. Once we have discarded any possibility of affirming the correspondence between reality and value judgments, ideas such as authenticity, responsibility, or coherence come to fill that vacuum. If there is no criterion of truth outside of myself, then moral truth can only exist within me.[64]

We could still ask Dworkin, however, why we have a duty of coherence or consistency in our moral behavior. Consistency and responsibility are indeed values and, according to Dworkin's epistemology, they cannot claim any moral truth. In other words, if we cannot claim any correspondence between value judgments and reality, we cannot claim any correspondence between the judgment "*x* should be responsible" and reality, either. Dworkin's proposed "responsibility" could only claim to represent the deepest value within Dworkin's internal and independent world of values—which is to say, the backbone of his particular version of the *Ecce homo*. Using Max Weber's words, Ronald Dworkin's ideal of responsibility can have no other claim than to obey "the daemon that holds the threads of *his* life."[65] But he lacks any objective reason to demand that others observe his own parameters.

NOTES

1. At the time of his death, the renowned liberal constitutional law professor Laurence Tribe said that Dworkin had been "the preeminent legal philosopher of the past half century" (*Harvard Law Review* 127, 2 [2013]: 507). In fact, his ideas have widely transcended the boundaries of the academic field, making him, in the words of Thomas M. Scanlon, the "leading public philosopher" ("Partisan for Life," *New York Review of Books* [July 15, 1993]: 45) of the leading Western nation.

2. Dworkin, "The Original Position," in Daniels, *Reading Rawls*, p. 50.

3. J. Rawls, "Justice as Fairness: Political Not Metaphysical," *Philosophy and Public Affairs* 4, 3 (1985): 236.

4. R. Dworkin, *Justice for Hedgehogs* (Cambridge, MA: Belknap Press of Harvard University Press, 2011), p. 64.

5. R. Dworkin, *Taking Rights Seriously* (Cambridge, MA: Harvard University Press, 1977), pp. 269 ff. The idea of an absolute right to freedom seems to be the

basis of the political philosophy of authors such as Robert Nozick. Starting from a conception of rights as "libertarian side constraints" (*Anarchy, State and Utopia* [New York: Basic Books, 1974, repr. 2013], pp. 30 ff.), Nozick exclusively admits a minimal state holding the monopoly of security and general protection. By the logic of the free market, this minimal state would spontaneously emerge from the state of nature through an invisible hand.

6. Dworkin, *Justice for Hedgehogs*, p. 335.
7. Dworkin, *Justice for Hedgehogs*, pp. 191 ff.
8. Dworkin, *Justice for Hedgehogs*, pp. 255 ff. On the "duty of recognition" as the foundation of all duties toward the others, see R. Spaemann, *Persons: The Difference between "Someone" and "Something"* (Oxford: Oxford University Press, 2012), pp. 183–84.
9. Dworkin, *Justice for Hedgehogs*, p. 336.
10. See Ronald Dworkin, *A Matter of Principle* (Oxford: Oxford University Press, 1985), especially pp. 181–204 ("Liberalism"); the appeal to Kant may be found in p. 191; in a similar sense, see Dworkin, *Taking Rights Seriously*, p. 198.
11. See Dworkin, *Justice for Hedgehogs*, pp. 255–70, with references to the works of Kant, Rawls, and Scanlon.
12. For an account of the ambivalence of the concept and the plurality of historical conceptions, see, for example, F. Simón-Yarza, "De la igualdad como *límite* a la igualdad como *tarea* del Estado: Evolución histórica de un principio," *Revista Española de Derecho Constitucional* 97 (2013): 76–113.
13. Dworkin, *Matter of Principle*, p. 191.
14. Dworkin, *Matter of Principle*, p. 203.
15. Dworkin, *Matter of Principle*, pp. 203–04.
16. R. Dworkin, *Foundations of Liberal Equality* (Salt Lake City: University of Utah Press, 1990); "Equality and the Good Life," in *Sovereign Virtue. The Theory and Practice of Equality* (Cambridge, MA: Harvard University Press, 2000): pp. 237–84.
17. Dworkin, "Equality and the Good Life," p. 239.
18. Dworkin, "Equality and the Good Life," p. 242. We will come back to this distinction below.
19. Dworkin, "Equality and the Good Life," p. 238.
20. Dworkin, "Equality and the Good Life," p. 253.
21. Dworkin, "Equality and the Good Life," pp. 260–63.
22. Dworkin, "Equality and the Good Life," p. 264.
23. Dworkin, "Equality and the Good Life," p. 265.
24. Dworkin, "Equality and the Good Life," p. 268.
25. Dworkin, "Equality and the Good Life," p. 269.
26. See *infra* chapter 9, 3.4.b.
27. Dworkin, "Equality and the Good Life," p. 272.
28. Dworkin, "Equality and the Good Life," p. 273.
29. Dworkin, "Equality and the Good Life," p. 274.
30. Dworkin, "Equality and the Good Life," p. 283.
31. "Deus est causa rerum per suum intellectum et voluntatem, sicut artifex rerum artificiatarum. Artifex autem per verbum in intellectu conceptum, et per amorem suae

voluntatis ad aliquid relatum, operator" (*S. Th.*, I, q. 45, a. 6). "Deus autem per suam sapientiam conditor est universarum rerum, ad quas comparatur sicut artifex ad artificiata" (*S. Th.*, I-II, q. 93, a. 1). See also Spaemann's critique to value-utilitarianism in *Happiness and Benevolence*, pp. 124–25.

32. Dworkin, "Equality and the Good Life," p. 258.
33. Dworkin, "Equality and the Good Life," p. 259.
34. For a deep exposition of the ethical viewpoint of "life as a whole," understood as a perspective of benevolence, see Robert Spaemann's book *Happiness and Benevolence*, several times quoted.
35. R. Dworkin "Rights as Trumps," in *Theories of Rights*, ed. Jeremy Waldron (New York: Oxford University Press, 1984), p. 152.
36. Dworkin's thesis on the absolute primacy of rights against social ends was first expounded in chapter 7 of *Taking Rights Seriously*, pp. 184–205; for a more synthetic explanation of his theory, see "Rights as Trumps," pp. 153–67; its last development may be found in *Justice for Hedgehogs*, pp. 327–50.
37. Dworkin, *Justice for Hedgehogs*, p. 365.
38. Dworkin, "Rights as Trumps," pp. 158–59.
39. Dworkin, "Rights as Trumps," p. 154.
40. Dworkin, "Do We Have a Right to Pornography?" in *A Matter of Principle*, p. 353.
41. Raz, *Morality of Freedom*, pp. 157–58.
42. Dworkin, *A Matter of Principle*, p. 360 (emphasis mine).
43. *S. Th.*, I-II, q. 75, a. 1.
44. Dworkin, *Justice for Hedgehogs*, p. 70.
45. Dworkin, *Justice for Hedgehogs*, p. 73.
46. Dworkin, *Justice for Hedgehogs*, p. 76.
47. Dworkin, *Justice for Hedgehogs*, pp. 109 ff.
48. Dworkin, *Justice for Hedgehogs*, p. 108.
49. Dworkin, *Justice for Hedgehogs*, p. 112.
50. Dworkin, *Justice for Hedgehogs*, p. 113.
51. Dworkin, *Justice for Hedgehogs*, pp. 121–22.
52. *Theaetetus*, 179a–b.
53. See, for example, *Protagoras*, 352b–358d; and Plato, *Gorgias*, 466d–e.
54. *Cfr. v. gr. Meno*, 97b–98a; *Theaetetus*, 201a–c; and *Symposium*, 202a.
55. *S. Th.*, I-II, q. 58, a. 2.
56. *S. Th.*, I-II, q. 77, a. 2.
57. *Nic. Eth.*, VI, 1138b and 1144b.
58. Aristotle, *Topics*, I, 11, 105a.
59. *S. Th.*, II-II, q. 8, a. 5: "in moralibus rectam aestimationem habet homo de fine per habitum virtutis." See also Aristotle, *Nic. Eth.*, IX, 8, 1168b, regarding the good man as he who loves himself most (*malista philautos*). See also II, 6, 1106a–1107b; *S. Th.*, I-II, q. 1, a. 7; and II-II, q. 25, a. 7: "boni autem, vere cognoscentes seipsos, vere seipsos diligent."
60. *Phaedo*, 67a.
61. *S. Th.*, I-II, q. 1, a. 7: "Et similiter illud bonum oportet esse completissimum, quod tanquam ultimum finem appetit habens affectum bene dispositum"; and *S. Th.*,

I-II, q. 9, a. 2: "qualis unusquisque est, talis finis videtur ei" (quoting Aristotle, *Nich. Eth.*, III, 1114a).

62. *Crito*, 49d–e; emphasis mine.

63. MacIntyre, *Whose Justice? Which Rationality?*, p. 169.

64. This line of thought was consistently followed, for example, by Jean-Jacques Rousseau. A confessed radical in his views—"there never was for me the least thing intermediate between everything and nothing" (*OEuvres complètes*, vol. I [Paris: Gallimard, Bibliothèque de la Pléiade, 1959], p. 332)—Rousseau attempted to resolve the contradictions of men, as has already been explained (see chapter I, 4.2). Man's truth still requires, as in Plato and Aristotle, integrity or consistency, but this integrity is no longer subject to any natural teleological measure. The only source of evil consists in being an *homme double*. It is necessary to choose "between the most austere democracy and the most perfect Hobbism" ("Lettre à Mirabeau," in *The Political Writings of Jean-Jacques Rousseau*, vol. II, ed. Vaughan [Cambridge: Cambridge University Press, 1915], p. 161), between the wild *homme naturel* and the Spartan *citoyen*. For "*all the institutions that* put man in *contradiction* with himself are worthless" (*Contrat social*, en *Oeuvres complètes*, vol. III [Paris: Gallimard, Bibliothèque de la Pléiade, 1964], p. 464). Self-consistency does not need to be justified through an *adaequatio rei*, since self-consistency has already become the ultimate measure of moral truth: "Make man one and you will make him as happy as he can be" ("Du Bonheur Public," in *The Political Writings of Jean-Jacques Rousseau*, vol. I, p. 326). Regarding the problem of teleology in Rousseau's work, see R. Spaemann, *Rousseau—Mensch oder Bürger* (Stuttgart: Klett-Cotta, 2008). See also Jean Starobinski, *Jean-Jacques Rousseau: la transparence et l'obstacle* (Paris: Gallimard, 1971).

65. Max Weber, "Science as Vocation," in *The Vocation Lectures: Politics as a Vocation—Science as Vocation* (Indianapolis: Hackett, 2004) p. 31 (emphasis in the original).

Chapter 5

Goods and processes: Jürgen Habermas's ethical-political project

1. INTRODUCTION

The previous chapters have been dedicated to critically examining so-called antiperfectionist liberalism in the work of two of its most prominent exponents in Anglo-American legal and political theory. It would seem remiss to close part II of the book without a reference to the political philosophy of Jürgen Habermas, a thinker who holds a comparably preeminent position in the Old Continent. Strictly speaking, Habermas's work is more nuanced and open to teleological considerations than Rawls's and Dworkin's liberalism. However, he firmly maintains some of the premises of ateleological or antiperfectionist liberalism and seems to confer on his own proceduralist moral theory a substantive moral potential that is in my view excessive.

Habermas's proposal is linked to an issue that runs parallel to the problem of the meaning of freedoms, namely, the problem of who decides that meaning. *Quis iudicabit?* is the question that, since Hobbes, modern political philosophy has posed again and again. Answering this question in a manner suited to the conditions of a plural society constitutes one of the basic demands of the same practical reason that, on a different level, leads to the defense of certain contents in the adoption of decisions. Thus, we should not try to find incompatibilities between the *substantive* discourse about the human good and the *procedural* discourse about the legitimate decision-making body or authority. Both discourses have their source in practical reason, while responding to different questions. In facing the *Quis iudicabit?* question central to a pluralistic modern society, the quest for fairness in the deliberative processes within a context of ideological fragmentation assumes, as has just been said, a crucial importance and to a great extent explains the success of Habermas's discourse theory.

2. "DISCOURSE ETHICS"

Developed from 1960s on the basis of his theory of communicative action, discourse ethics was introduced by Habermas in two essay compilations published in the early 1990s as *Moral Consciousness and Communicative Action*[1] and *Remarks on Discourse Ethics*.[2] In 1992, the Habermasian project experienced a fruitful development in a theory of the democratic constitutional state, *Between Facts and Norms*,[3] which was extraordinarily well received in academic legal circles. Earlier, though, his discourse theory had already borne significant fruit in the legal field due to—among other things—the notable work of Robert Alexy.[4]

Discourse ethics does not offer any substantive guidance but fixes a procedure to test the claims of validity of hypothetically proposed norms. In Habermas's opinion, the "postmetaphysical age" no longer allows the philosopher to offer generalizable substantive contents. This would not be in line with the pluralism of our society.[5] Leaving aside the *ethical* question of the good life, *moral* philosophy should focus on "the categorially different question of the norms according to which we want to live together and of how practical conflicts can be settled in the common interest of all."[6] In sum, it should limit itself to exploring a procedure of rational verification of the normative contents regulating social relations, which would for their part originate in the "real life" of communities. Responding to the label of "formalism," Habermas stresses that discourse ethics does not deny valid moral norms their content, but "the content that is tested by a moral principle is generated not by the philosopher but by real life."[7] Habermas's project purports to establish such a procedure for testing public normative rationality.

Discourse ethics does not explicitly embrace moral skepticism. It claims to be "cognitivist" in that it recognizes in moral discourse a genuine claim of normative validity, of the "correctness" of the moral propositions. Nevertheless, the substantive, nonprocedural theses should be left outside the scope of political philosophy. What the philosopher may offer is simply a verification procedure for testing the rationality of the substantive contents provided by real life. Habermas builds his procedure by replacing the Kantian categorical principle with another "principle of universalization" (U). In accordance with the universalization principle of discourse ethics, every valid norm must satisfy one condition:

> (U) *All* the affected can accept the consequences and the side effects its *general* observance can be anticipated to have for the satisfaction of *everyone's* interests (and the consequences are preferred to those of known alternative possibilities for regulation).[8]

This principle is introduced as a reformulation of the Kantian categorical imperative in two senses.

On the one hand, it has a discursive as opposed to a monological nature. The application of the principle is not a competence of a single subject but of a plurality of participants engaging in a real discourse.[9] For Kant, the moral point of view would be the first-person singular; for Habermas, the first-person plural: "controversial questions of normative validity can be thematized only from the first-person plural perspective, that is, in each instance 'by us.'"[10] This intersubjectivity in the application of the universalization principle is just a corollary of the very nature of discourse, which constitutes "an exacting form of argumentative decision making."[11] As a principle for testing hypothetical norms that claim to regulate social life, Habermas's universalization criterion must be intersubjectively applied.

On the other hand, the universalization principle also differs from the Kantian categorical imperative in not being a *factum* of pure reason. Habermas justifies it in what he calls, following Karl-Otto Apel, a "transcendental-pragmatic" way. It is an inherent principle of the rules of discourse, rules that every participant in an argumentative discourse must accept in order not to fall into a performative contradiction. Indeed, in order to enter a process of argumentation with the purpose of arriving at a rational and noncoercive understanding, it is necessary to take for granted certain incontestable presuppositions, for example, the right of others to take part in the discourse and all of the conversation partners' purpose of reaching a rational understanding—what Habermas calls a "communicative attitude," as opposed to a purely "strategic attitude."[12] Anyone who opposes these preconditions falls into a performative contradiction, for they cannot achieve a rational understanding while excluding them. These communicative rules implicitly carry, in their turn, Habermas's principle of universalization (U): "every person who accepts the universal and necessary communicative presuppositions of argumentative speech and who knows what it means to justify a norm of action implicitly presupposes as valid the principle of universalization." Thus, the principle of universalization is to normative justificatory discourses what the principle of induction is to scientific discourses.[13]

After having carried out the "transcendental-pragmatic" justification of the principle of universalization, Habermas proceeds to formulate the "principle of discourse ethics":

(D) Only those norms can claim to be valid that meet (or could meet) with the approval of all affected in their capacity as participants in a practical discourse.[14]

As transcendental-pragmatic presuppositions, "free speech" and "equal recognition" embody, in Habermas's view, two fundamental moral intuitions:

justice and solidarity or sympathy. Though having a procedural character, discourse ethics says something about substance: on the one hand, it demands the overcoming of egocentrism and recognizing the other in his communicative attitude (solidarity); and on the other hand, it demands a basis of equal liberties in line with the inviolability of each individual (justice).[15]

Finally, Habermas rejects the accusation of formalism that Hegel makes against Kantian morality, one that could be transposed to discourse ethics. As with the Kantian categorical imperative, the principle of universalization is only the "criterion of morality." It is a formal principle to test hypothetical norms, which are in turn fraught with substantial contents regarding the good. Habermas limits himself to leaving the question of the good life outside of philosophical enquiry and to place it in the domain of the real lives of communities. "In moral argumentation" this question "must be left to the participants themselves" so that they "find concrete answers in particular cases; it cannot be known in advance."[16] Therefore, in the context of real discourses, the various conceptions of the good life serve as a basis for hypothetical normative proposals whose validity has to be tested through the rules of discourse, including the principle of universalization.[17]

Over time, Habermas has expanded the scope of legitimate discussion to the point of admitting that religious traditions may contribute to the public discourse with normative proposals regarding the good life—adequately translated, though, into a secular language that makes them universalizable.[18]

3. CRITICAL REMARKS ON DISCOURSE ETHICS

Before commenting on the indubitable value of discourse ethics in the realm of politics, I would like to make some critical remarks. My aim is not so much to oppose his procedural proposals as to show the limits that, in my view, the Habermasian ethical project has. Some of the following remarks have been in one way or another advanced by several authors, and in some cases Habermas himself has attempted to reply to them. Nevertheless, as far as I have been able to investigate, Habermas's replies seem to me insufficient.

3.1. The "postmetaphysical age" and the problem of the good

The first criticism directly points to the premise from which Habermas starts his argument, namely that in the "postmetaphysical age" philosophy can no longer offer valid answers to the problem of the good life. The pluralism of opinions would require moral philosophy to be confined to the question of "the just"—as opposed to the good—in the way suggested by Rawls and reaffirmed by Habermas. Habermas's proceduralism thus begins with a philosophical self-imposition of teleological agnosticism. Against this premise, I would want to raise several objections.

First, I think that such a strong claim should not depend on so vague and obscure a thesis as "We live in a postmetaphysical age." Philosophical reflection on the human goods the state is called upon to protect must certainly be based on the demands and lessons provided by real life. It is a genuine task of moral and political philosophy and one that does not depend on any metaphysical theory. A vague appeal to the "postmetaphysical age" is not a sufficient argument to dismiss philosophical claims regarding the good life. Denying the very possibility of a moral and political philosophy transcending pure procedural questions would lead to an irreparable loss for philosophy itself.

Such a serious premise as the one proposed by Habermas cannot be supported, as I have just indicated, by a vague appeal to the "postmetaphysical age." Together with numerous thousand-year-old traditions from all over the planet, I think we can state "in advance" that contempt for truth, egocentrism, fanaticism, adultery, sexual debauchery, infidelity, or dishonor to parents are behaviors that no authority should foster or encourage. We can say this even before entering into a discourse. Moreover, if the discourse resulted in opposite conclusions, it would not be a rational discourse, and we could appeal against it—as indeed Tocqueville does in a famous passage in his *Democracy in America*—to "the sovereignty of mankind,"[19] which is to say, to reason. Or we could say, with Socrates, that it is preferable to contradict the majority of mankind than to lose inner harmony with oneself.[20] Obviously, if the majority is against the above-mentioned statements, they will not achieve an intersubjective positive validity. However, this does not mean that their rational evidence needs any discursive verification. On the contrary, it is the rationality of discourse that has to be verified through its compatibility with certain substantive ethical truths upon whose political implications the philosopher is bound to reflect. Of course, it is correct to say that the proposals regarding the good life acquire their positive legal validity not by virtue of philosophers' propositions but by virtue of authoritative decisions made by society. I do not think, however, that Habermas's thesis removing the question of the good life from moral and political philosophy is limited to this soft claim, because in that case it would be trivial: *Quod omnes tangit ab omnibus approbari debet*.

I roughly agree with Habermas, however, in what he calls the "contingency" that "pervades ethical knowledge."[21] We have already examined this question with reference to the historicity of understanding duly emphasized by the hermeneutic tradition,[22] though it is also acknowledged by the classical tradition. Only the first principles of understanding, whose genesis rests—as with all knowledge—on the senses,[23] are so bound to the apprehension of being and of the good that they cannot be erased. Beyond these first principles, moral knowledge becomes contingent, and the historical experience of prejudice enables us to speculate that many of our convictions are perhaps wrong. Concerning the contingency of moral knowledge, Thomas Aquinas recalls the ancient custom of the Germans, narrated by Julius Caesar in *De Bello Gallico*, according to which plunder or banditry (*latrocinium*) was not considered morally wrong when it was practiced in the land of foreign tribes.[24] Yet the fact that the ancient Germans denied the moral evil of plundering in *terra aliena* should not occasion in us the slightest doubt regarding the wickedness of such practice. Being aware of the historicity of understanding faces us with our own finitude and compels us to question ourselves about the right attitude to understanding. Against mistrust in the power of reason, a straight or right intention (*intentio recta*) always calls us to open ourselves to reality. Knowing is nothing but "awakening to reality," as Heraclitus[25] saw, and in order to remain awake it is necessary to be attentive. "Reasonable pluralism" constitutes, of course, part of that reality toward which we have to direct our attention, and it requires us to be reflective, prudent, and critical regarding our own ideas, always knowing that certainty in error is an age-old experience to which no one is immune. Nevertheless, all this does not require us to give up philosophical enquiry into the good. Such a resignation, incidentally, would be as philosophical, metaphysical, and fallible as its opposite. As we will immediately see, dismissing the question of the good life also involves a judgment upon the good and a rather historically conditioned one.

3.2. "Ateleological teleology" in Habermas's proceduralism

Finally, the "priority of the just over the good," as John Rawls and Jürgen Habermas understand it, implies an unparalleled hierarchy of goods. By reducing morality to the principles of discourse, Habermas protects the goods implicit in his discursive idea of justice against any possible interference. Once again, we are before an "ateleological teleology," to use Spaemann's words as quoted above. The goods underlying proceduralism—tolerance, freedom, participation, and so forth—receive a radical priority over all other goods. Charles Taylor has expressed this idea with special clarity:

> The more one examines the motives—what Nietzsche would call the "genealogy" —of these theories of obligatory action, the stranger they appear. It seems that they are motivated by the strongest moral ideals, such as freedom, altruism, and universalism. These are among the central moral aspirations of modern culture, the hypergoods which are distinctive to it. And yet what these ideals drive the theorists towards is a denial of all such goods. . . . Impelled by the strongest metaphysical, epistemological, and moral ideas of the modern age, these theories narrow our focus to the determinants of action, and then restrict our understanding of these determinants still further by defining practical reason

as exclusively procedural. They utterly mystify the priority of the moral by identifying it not with substance but with a form of reasoning, around which they draw a firm boundary. They then are led to defend this boundary all the more fiercely in that it is their only way of doing justice to the hypergoods which move them although they cannot acknowledge them.[26]

In its endeavor to exclude the problem of the good from the scope of moral philosophy, Habermas's proceduralist theory hides—according to Taylor—the goods that could provide his theory with any motivational power. These are true goods, and they are genuinely modern: tolerance, participation, dialogue, and so forth. In fact, we may catch a glimpse of the connecting point between Habermas's moral theory and the goods tacitly supporting that theory when he says that, in order to be feasible, discourse ethics must take root in communities whose understanding of the good life converges with the approach of discourse ethics:

> Universalist moralities are dependent on forms of life that are rationalized in that they make possible and prudent application of universal moral insights and support motivations for translating insights into moral action. Only those forms of life that meet universalist moralities halfway in this sense fulfill the conditions necessary to reverse the abstractive achievements of decontextualization and demotivation.[27]

Habermas seems to admit that, for his theory's "abstract" and "decontextualized" proceduralism to be effective, the community must identify itself with values embracing proceduralism. Only then, a "reversion" (*Rückgangigmachung*, in the German original version) of the "abstractive achievements of decontextualization and demotivation" (*die Abstraktionsleistungen der Dekontextualisierung und der Demotivierung*) takes place. In other words, discourse ethics ceases to be a value-neutral theory. The "forms of life" mentioned by Habermas are, strictly speaking, those that could turn discourse ethics into a true ethics, the forms of life that tend to identify with the goods discourse ethics avoids making explicit for the sake of a broader universalism. The problem is that, by taking them out of the rejected "particularism of the good" and elevating them into the superior category of "procedural universalism," the unarticulated goods underlying this proceduralism gain an inflexible supremacy over any other competing goods or values. Paradoxically, the postponement of the discourse upon the good finally leads into an unconditional prevalence of a couple of goods, into a "tyranny" of some values, to use Carl Schmitt's famous expression.[28] Those values underlying proceduralism—tolerance, altruism, respect—escape from the right balance of practical reason and are asserted as absolutes from behind the mask of proceduralism. In classical terms, they become "vices by excess."[29]

3.3. The reformulation of the "categorical imperative"

Habermas's reformulation of the categorical imperative also deserves some criticism. In place of the Kantian categorical imperative, he proposes a principle to be applied in dialogue, in real discourses. As we have seen, this suggestion rests on the assumption that the *moral point of view* is the first-person of an empirical plural: the "we" of real discourses. The reason for this assumption is that Habermas reduces the object of moral philosophy to "controversial questions of normative validity."[30] Nevertheless, the question is precisely whether morality can be reduced to the solution of intersubjective conflicts. It seems that Habermas does not envisage an ethical theory, nor even a morality, but a constructive theory to solve normative conflicts within society. It is not by chance that his project resulted in a theory of constitutional democracy. Martin Rhonheimer has quite rightly said that Habermas reduces ethics to "political ethics."[31] Even more incisive is Spaemann's criticism that Habermas mistakes ethics for law.[32] As a jurist, Martin Kriele seems to be more sympathetic to Habermas's discourse theory and recognizes its positive features for law, though he also points out its insufficiency as a moral theory.[33] Habermas's principle of universalization cannot be a true alternative to the Kantian categorical imperative, for the intersubjective point of view of factual discourses *is not* the moral point of view. By saying that the discursive and non-monologic nature of the principle of universalization provides with "advantages" against the Kantian imperative, Habermas seems to place them in competition with one another, which entails an implicit distortion of the moral point of view.

3.4. Real discourses

Another problem we can observe with so-called discourse ethics is that it appeals to discursive conditions that never exist in the real world.[34] Real discourses are ingrained with preunderstandings and particular affections. The parties never enter into the discourse in symmetric conditions, as they differ in authority, rhetorical power, empathy, character, knowledge, and so forth. Reason itself tells us that the persuasive power of real discourses is dependent on thousands of contingencies besides the intrinsic power of rational arguments. Habermas shows himself to be aware of this objection, responding that the lack of transparency in real discourses should not prevent us from adopting the necessary institutional measures to take them closer to the ideal conditions of discourse. In my view, Habermas's response is correct, though insufficient for several reasons.

First, it is obvious that fostering transparent discourses cannot be detrimental but on the condition that we do not lose sight of the fact that *every* political discourse takes place in conditions of real asymmetry. This is an inevitable fact, regardless of whether we give an equal voice and vote to all concerned, something that is in itself impossible, for there are relevant groups whose participation is excluded *per definitionem*. Thus, for instance, future generations, the unborn, infants, and severely ill or mentally handicapped people do not have their own voice, and their rational consent has to be anticipated or represented by others. Under the presupposition of the inevitable asymmetry of all real discourses, a fair decision can only emanate from the moral virtue of the ruler. Politics cannot be reduced to discourse. It always bears within itself the *power* and *discretion* of some people over others. And when someone has power to discretionarily enforce their decision, only moral virtue guarantees the fairness of that decision: "every power which may be variously directed to act, needs a habit whereby it is well disposed to its act."[35]

Second, it is also worth commenting on Habermas's idea that he who engages in a discourse with the purpose of reaching a rational understanding must assume the same communicative attitude in others. Strictly speaking, I think this thesis is true: I cannot believe in the possibility of a rational understanding with a counterpart who adopts a strategic attitude. Having said this, it is no less true that, if I observe in my counterpart a strategic attitude, I may consider myself morally compelled by the virtue of prudence to give up discursive transparency and adopt the same strategic attitude. A "communicative attitude" is not always recommendable, since practical reason itself demands at times the adoption of a strategic silence for the sake of preserving a good. Classical ethics is in this sense both positive and realistic. On the one hand, it encourages the adoption of a communicative attitude, so as to enter the public forum with a truthful attitude that is open to dialogue. However, if one perceives that the "rules of the game" are different, one must keep seeking the common good through prudent and strategic behavior in a strategic context. In the political realm, the viability of a communicative attitude depends on the context and cannot be forced. In short, the classical theory of prudence or the Kantian anticipation of a universal rational consensus is indispensable.

Third, it should be noted that every discourse inevitably concludes at the moment of making the concrete decision, that is, with the application of norms.[36] Political theory inexorably requires then an ethical reflection upon the good, an "anticipation of a rational consensus" regardless of its effective occurrence. We could seemingly solve the uncertainty of the application of norms by setting interpretive rules to reduce discretion, but this way of proceeding would just shift the problem. The selection of the interpretive rule applicable to a particular case would still require further meta-rules to keep reducing the discretion, and this problem could be carried back *ad infinitum*. Anyone acquainted with constitutional jurisprudence knows this problem.

In politics, then, only the ruler's prudence (*phronesis*) as understood by the classical tradition ensures fair decisions. Spaemann criticized Habermas for envisaging a "utopia of the dialogue free from domination." Habermas, for his part, defended himself by attributing to Spaemann the "utopia of the good ruler"[37] and recalling the *Quis iudicabit?*: "Who will elect the good ruler?" I think, however, that this reply is hardly convincing, since it points to an imaginary objection. Affirming the ineluctable need for a doctrine of virtue does not mean denying the need for checks and balances to protect society from a bad ruler. Discourse ethics constitutes a valuable contribution to designing fair political decision-making procedures. The problem is that it cannot and should not promise the emergence of truth from real discourses. Such a promise encourages a dangerous attitude and has often served to exonerate those who freely execute—despite having the power not to—intersubjectively approved but unjust decisions. We find a paradigmatic example of this risk in a well-known passage from Kelsen's *The Essence and Value of Democracy*. According to the celebrated Austrian jurist, relativism regarding the truth—which in his view is an intrinsic feature of democracy—finds a "tragic symbol" in Pontius Pilate's behavior as described in chapter 18 of St. John's Gospel. Yet the fact is that Pilate's decision was not "tragic" in the sense suggested by Kelsen.[38] It was not a decision immediately imputable to an anonymous, abstract, and transcendent subject—"democracy"—but to he who "handed him over to be crucified" (John 19,16).

4. THE VALUE OF HABERMAS'S PROJECT: A CRITERION OF PUBLIC REASON

4.1. An impartial criterion

After the critique made in the previous section, I consider it appropriate to conclude this chapter by highlighting the value that discourse theory has. Discourse theory is not a complete political theory, but it does offer important ethical-political principles, which are particularly valuable for a pluralistic society. Habermas's principle of universalization is in my view a formal criterion to elucidate which hypothetical norms meet "public reason." Precisely due to its formal and abstract nature, it is a much more impartial criterion than the Rawlsian account of public reason. Habermas himself has underlined this contrast between "discourse ethics" and the *Theory of Justice*, stressing that the procedure offered by discourse ethics excludes any substantive content:

> *Any* content, no matter how fundamental the action norms in question may be, must be made subject to real discourse. . . . Once a normative theory like

Rawls's theory of justice strays into substantive issues, it becomes just one contribution to practical discourse among many.[39]

If the Kantian moral imperative serves as a criterion of morality, the Habermasian principle of universalization seems to serve as basis for a (notably, impartial) criterion of public reason. It is no coincidence that it has been praised by authors who can hardly be included within "ateleological" liberalism. This is the case, for example, with Martin Kriele. Though indicating its insufficiency as an ethical theory, Kriele has defended the theory of discourse as a "renewal of the classical theory of democracy."[40] For we cannot deny, in effect, that the validity of legal norms should depend, as far as possible, on the agreement of those affected.[41]

Notwithstanding this, it should be noted that discourse cannot legitimize what is irrational before engaging with it, as Kriele points out. The purpose of discourse is to publicly and reciprocally undertake the communicative verification of the rationality of norms whose validity is hypothetically proposed, not to create that rationality. Hence, the "fruitfulness" of discourse rests on "making us aware of something which is already presupposed in every discourse, namely, the possibility of reason." Discourse theory identifies, in the end, with a state that is open to discussion, namely the "democratic constitutional state."[42]

This should not make us lose sight of the fact that the theory of discourse does not provide the ultimate grounds for defending democratic procedure. Procedural fairness does not receive its justification—at least, its ultimate justification—from discourse theory but from the requirement of "equal recognition" of all those affected by political decisions. This remark is far from being superfluous, as Habermas himself has explicitly maintained, in a critique to Ernst Tugendhat, that the justification of the right to engage in a political discourse does not rest on the idea of participation or balance of power but on a communicative understanding of moral reasoning.[43] Habermas wants to avoid falling prey to pure decisionism, and he therefore situates his theory in a cognitive sphere: discourse is not a mere decision-making formula but an appropriate procedure for arriving at fair norms. Conceived of as a cognitive procedure for verifying the rationality of norms, it takes into account the conditions for rational argumentation more than the conditions for a balance of power or fair decision making.

However, considering the intrinsic asymmetry of real discourses and the impossibility of fulfilling the ideal conditions of discourse, I think we should disagree with Jürgen Habermas on this point. More than a method for arriving at the truth, constitutional democracy constitutes a fair and balanced decision-making procedure. We do not need to assume a Schmittian standpoint—to mention a thinker whose views are the polar opposite of Habermas's—to notice that politics has to do with authoritative decisions, with decisions that are not simply proposed but coercively imposed. *Prima facie*, it seems right to aspire to discursive deliberation before making a decision, though maintaining a "communicative attitude" is not always a prudent option. One cannot and should not aspire to adopt the standpoint of one's counterpart on realizing that, as happens with Calicles in the Platonic *Gorgias*,[44] the counterpart holds a manifest contempt for the truth. Once we notice the strategic attitude of the interlocutor, we should not expect the truth to arise from the interlocution. It is not surprising, in this sense, that in the *Gorgias* the truth does not arise from the dialogue—which is abruptly interrupted by Callicles[45]—but from a monologic deliberation carried out by Socrates with himself.

In addition to the previous considerations, we should underline that, as has been indicated, political discourses end up with coercive decisions. Once we notice the strategic attitude of our counterpart, practical reason itself—virtue—may recommend or even demand the adoption of an equally strategic attitude, which by definition precludes discourse in Habermasian terms. The reason why democratic principles still hold valid in these situations is that, rather than being a discursive method for arriving at the truth, democracy constitutes a fair decision-making procedure for a plural society. *Quod omnes tangit ab omnibus approbari debet*.

4.2. An eminently procedural criterion

A second important remark with regard to the value of discourse theory is that its application must be concretized through the articulation of adequate decision-making procedures. Here, it may be worth recalling the terms in which Habermas formulates the principle of discourse:

> (D) Only those norms can claim to be valid that meet (or could meet) with the approval of all affected in their capacity as participants in a practical discourse.[46]

To avoid misguided interpretations of the principle, I deem it necessary to make some comments on its application:

(a) It would be plainly nonsensical to understand the principle as a requirement of unanimity in the adoption of any type of norms. The idea of public reason embodied in this principle points toward the *possibility of meeting with the approval* ("could meet") rather than to a factual unanimity ("meet"). How should we interpret, then, the "possibility of meeting with the approval of all affected"? A nonempirical, purely ideal interpretation of the Habermasian principle of discourse must be ruled out, for it would be clearly alien to Habermas's conception of discourse.

Furthermore, it would make the principle superfluous as a political concept, since it would add nothing to the statements of several great exponents of political thought. Tocqueville's appeal to the "sovereignty of mankind"[47] is also an appeal to the *ideal* consensus of natural reason, though it does not require a factual consensus. And the same happens with Kant's "general will": "it is instead *only an idea* of reason," which does not exclude the justice of the law "even if the people are at present in such a situation or frame of mind that, if consulted about it, they would probably refuse its consent."[48]

(b) In Habermas's work, the "possibility of meeting with the approval of all affected" bears within itself empirical demands, for it requires matching one's reasons with the logic of politics. Having said this, in an *open democracy*, in which any exercise of power should always be open to rational discussion and justification, the rebuttal of an argument with a mere appeal to its *public* unacceptability should be viewed with caution. Such an argument is a purely conservative one that, as such, should not exempt the advocate of the *status quo* from the need to provide further rational justification. Otherwise, the argument of *public* reason would turn into a device for expelling dissidents from the political forum through an easy appeal to the "reality principle," through a mere referral to established *praxis*. The argument that defends a social practice by invoking its *public acceptability* must be given no more than the presumption of rationality, namely the presumption of legitimacy that such practices deserve for the very fact of their being publicly sanctioned. From a strictly rational viewpoint, however, it is always a *iuris tantum* presumption that could be rebutted with arguments demonstrating their irrationality.

(c) In order to avoid abusing the concept of public reason, it should be understood as a principle inspiring a procedural political *ethos*. Discourse ethics must be mainly embodied in an adequate scale of political majorities for the adoption of different political decisions. Those majorities should depend on the constitutional significance of the issues at stake. Hence, the "constitutional essentials" must always be subjected to qualified majorities, since they result in legal *topoi* expressing the basic convictions of society as a whole. Those who question the intersubjective validity of such agreements should carry the burden of proving the intersubjective validity of their own reasons, and this can only be ensured through an appropriate regulation of the constitutional processes and majorities and in a context of freedom of speech. Of course, all this does not prevent the citizens from appealing—as a substantive argument—to the public non-acceptance of their adversaries' opinions. Notwithstanding the legitimacy and even the intrinsic rationality of such appeals, they should never be deemed as a definitive argument against dissidents.

NOTES

1. J. Habermas, *Moralbewußtsein und kommunikatives Handeln* (Frankfurt am Main: Suhrkamp, 1983). I hereinafter quote the translation by Thomas McCarthy, *Moral Consciousness and Communicative Action* (Cambridge: MIT Press, 1990). This edition was supervised by Habermas and adjusted to the English linguistic usage.

2. J. Habermas, *Erläuterungen zur Diskursethik* (Frankfurt am Main: Suhrkamp, 1991). I hereinafter quote the partial translation—adapted to English usage—by Ciaran P. Cronin, *Justification and Application: Remarks on Discourse Ethics* (Cambridge: MIT Press, 1993).

3. J. Habermas, *Faktizität und Geltung. Beiträge zur Diskurstheorie des Rechts und des demokratischen Rechtsstaats* (Frankfurt am Main: Suhrkamp, 1992). I use the careful translation, closely followed by Habermas, of William Rehg: *Between Facts and Norms: Contributions to a Discourse Theory of Democracy* (Cambridge: MIT Press, 1996).

4. See mainly R. Alexy, *Der Theorie des rationalen Diskurses als Theorie der juristische Begründung* (Frankfurt am Main: Suhrkamp, 1983); and, also in the line of the discourse theory, his *Theorie der Grundrechte* (Frankfurt am Main: Suhrkamp, 1986).

5. "Moral Consciousness and Communicative Action," in McCarthy, *Moral Consciousness and Communicative Action*, p. 121.

6. "Remarks on Discourse Ethics," in Cronin, *Justification and Application*, p. 24.

7. "Morality and Ethical Life: Does Hegel's Critique of Kant Apply to Discourse Ethics?" in McCarthy, *Moral Consciousness and Communicative Action*, p. 204.

8. "Discourse Ethics: Notes on a Program of Philosophical Justification," in McCarthy, *Moral Consciousness and Communicative Action*, p. 65.

9. "Discourse Ethics," pp. 66–67; and "Morality and Ethical Life," p. 203.

10. "Remarks on Discourse Ethics," in Cronin, *Justification and Application*, p. 49.

11. "Morality and Ethical Life," p. 198.

12. "Moral Consciousness and Communicative Action," in McCarthy, *Moral Consciousness and Communicative Action*, pp. 133 ff.

13. "Discourse Ethics," p. 86.

14. "Discourse Ethics," p. 93.

15. "Morality and Ethical Life," pp. 199 ff.

16. "Remarks on Discourse Ethics," p. 24.

17. "Discourse Ethics," p. 102; and "Morality and Ethical Life," pp. 204–05.

18. J. Habermas, "Religion in der Öffentlichkeit: Kognitive Voraussetzungen für den 'öffentlichen Vernunftgebrauch' religiöser und säkularer Bürger,'" in *Zwischen Naturalismus und Religion: Philosophische Aufsätze* (Frankfurt am Main: Suhrkamp, 2005), pp. 119–54. In this context, the conversation between Jürgen Habermas and Joseph Ratzinger, *Dialektik der Säkularisierung. Über Vernunft und Religion* (Freiburg-Basel-Vienna: Herder, 2005), attracted very special attention; see mainly paragraphs 4 and 5 of Habermas's presentation for the discussion, which was held in the Catholic Academy of Bavaria on January 19, 2004.

19. *De la démocratie en Amérique I, II*, 7, in *Oeuvres*, vol. II (Paris: Gallimard, Bibliothèque de la Pléiade, 1992), pp. 287–88.
20. Plato, *Gorgias*, 482b–c.
21. "Remarks on Discourse Ethics," p. 22
22. See *supra*, chapter 1, 2.4.
23. *S. Th.*, I-II, q. 51, a. 1.
24. *S. Th.*, I-II, q. 94, a. 4; cf. *De Bellico Gallico*, VI, 16. For an accurate interpretation of this text of the *Summa*, see Budziszewski, *Commentary on Thomas Aquinas's Treatise on Law*, pp. 274–75.
25. "For those who are awake there is one common world, while those who sleep each turn away into their own" (H. A. Diels, *Die Fragmente der Vorsokratiker* [Berlin: August Raabe, 1897], Heraclitus, § 89).
26. Taylor, *Sources of the Self*, pp. 88–89.
27. "Discourse Ethics," p. 109.
28. See C. Schmitt, "Die Tyrannei der Werte," in Ernst Forsthoff et al., *Säkularisation und Utopie. Ebracher Studien. Ernst Forsthoff zum 65. Geburtstag* (Stuttgart-Berlin-Cologne-Mainz: W. Kohlhammer, 1967), pp. 37–62.
29. Incidentally, I want to note that, in his important essay *The Abolition of Man*, Clive Staples Lewis decried this way of proceeding—reducing practical reason to arbitrarily selected "fragments of truth"—as a distinctive feature of what we call "ideologies." "What purport to be new systems or (as they now call them) 'ideologies', all consist of fragments from the *Tao* itself, arbitrarily wrenched from their context in the whole and then swollen to madness in their isolation, yet still owing to the *Tao* and to it alone such validity as they possess" [C. S. Lewis, *The Abolition of Man* (New York: HarperCollins, 2001), pp. 43–44].
30. "Remarks on Discourse Ethics," p. 49.
31. Rhonheimer, *Perspective of Morality*, pp. 7–13, 248–50.
32. R. Spaemann, "Sittliche Normen und Rechtsordnung," in H. Marré, D. Schümmelfeder, and B. Kämper (eds.), *Das christliche Freiheitsverständnis in seiner Bedeutung für die staatliche Rechtsordnung* (Münster: Aschendorff, 1996), pp. 5 ff.
33. M. Kriele, *Recht und praktische Vernunft* (Götingen: Vandenhoek & Ruprecht, 1979), pp. 30–34.
34. See in this vein R. Spaemann, "Die Utopie der Herrschaftsfreiheit," *Merkur* 26 (1972): 735–52.
35. *S. Th.*, I-II, q. 50, a. 5.
36. Habermas himself faces this problem in "Discourse Ethics," pp. 104 ff. His answer appeals to impartiality and coherence and—as has been said—emphasizes that discourse ethics is only compatible with particular forms of life capable of assuming moral judgments "dissociated from the local conventions."
37. See J. Habermas, "Die Utopie des guten Herrschers," *Merkur* 26 (1972): 1266 ff.; followed by Spaemann's retort.
38. H. Kelsen, *Vom Wesen und Wert der Demokratie*, 2nd ed. (Tubingen: J. C. B. Mohr, 1929), pp. 103–04.
39. "Moral Consciousness and Communicative Action," in McCarthy, *Moral Consciousness and Communicative Action*, p. 122.

40. Kriele, *Recht und praktische Vernunft*, p. 30.
41. See Habermas, *Between Facts and Norms*, p. 158.
42. Kriele, *Recht und praktische Vernunft*, p. 31.
43. "Discourse Ethics," pp. 68–76.
44. Plato, *Gorgias*, 484b ff. See, in this vein, Finnis's critique of Habermas in "Discourse, Truth, and Friendship," in *Collected Essays*, I, pp. 43–44. Relying on the Platonic *Gorgias*, Finnis conducts in this essay a brilliant exposition of the ideal conditions of discourse and issues a judgment regarding its viability and appropriate context.
45. Plato, *Gorgias*, 505c.
46. "Discourse Ethics," p. 93.
47. *De la démocratie en Amérique I, II, 7*, in *Oeuvres*, vol. II (Paris: Gallimard, Bibliothèque de la Pléiade, 1992), pp. 287–88.
48. *Gemeinspruch*, p. 297.

Part III

THE DEHUMANIZATION OF HUMAN RIGHTS

Chapter 6

Mutual disinterest and civil liberties

1. INTRODUCTION

In part II of this book, I have attempted to critically explain some of the main features of contemporary antiperfectionist liberalism, well represented in the works of John Rawls, Ronald Dworkin, and—in a more nuanced way and not without proposals I consider valuable—Jürgen Habermas. In my view, antiperfectionist liberalism has attained a disturbing hegemony in the intellectual sphere. Nevertheless, it has always had sharp and illustrious critics, many of whom have been quoted in these pages. Likewise, authoritative witnesses of our age have called the attention of Western society to the "dehumanization" that such an understanding of freedoms involves.

I think that the loss of relevance of the human good in the political and legal interpretation of rights constitutes the *proton pseudos*, the mistake at the root in our public understanding of rights. Teleological agnosticism with regard to human life has an immediate effect on human rights understanding and enforcement, which is manifested both in jurisprudential theory and in judicial and political decisions. In part III, I will touch on both aspects, taking some of the most important ethical-political contemporary issues as examples. In this chapter, I will begin by developing the general implications arising from political indifference toward the integral moral good of citizens.

* * *

According to a very well-known formula, coined in the nineteenth century by the great German jurist Rudolf von Ihering and widely accepted by legal authors and treatises, an individual right is a "legally protected interest" (*rechtlich geschütztes Interesse*).[1] The substrate of a right is thus provided by an "interest," a concept that may receive different meanings depending on the idea of human being we are basing ourselves on. If we assume the teleological nature of man, we can affirm that, beyond the subjective desires and inclinations *de facto* experienced by a human being, there are some objective interests provided by nature and not subject to human arbitrariness. Reducing those interests to subjective inclinations would make the liberation of desire a key hermeneutic principle in understanding the meaning of rights. Then, the fulfillment of a human person's life may exclusively be defined from the subjective perspective of the person whose fulfillment we are talking about. Even so-called noble goods are relativized, as we clearly observe in Ronald Dworkin's work.

As we have seen, Dworkin distinguishes between what he labels "experiential interests"—enjoying a delicious meal, reading an entertaining novel, and so forth—and "critical interests"—forming a family, carving out a brilliant professional career, and so forth. In contrast to the former, critical interests are not attached to "experience" but to a deeper personal fulfillment.[2] They are, so to speak, what ultimately determine the "rational plan of life" described by John Rawls.[3] Dworkin's "critical interests" seem to identify what constitutes a good life in the classical sense, though the truth is that—as happens with the Rawlsian plan of life—they are completely subordinated to the subjective impression of those who hold them. There are no rational and objective parameters to define and limit them beyond the subjective interests—either critical or experiential—of others. If we identify experience with bodily pleasure and pain, Dworkin's critical interests are certainly not experiential; but if we consider experience as the satisfaction of our subjective preferences, critical interests are completely experiential. As we shall see, this is the only way to explain why for Dworkin the *nasciturus* lacks critical interests. Plainly, it lacks them because it cannot consciously experience them—because it is not aware of them. If critical interests were defined in a more "objective"[4] way, that is, as a teleological tension of the subject toward its personal, vital fulfillment, we should then say that any human being has interests, including the *nasciturus*. By contrast, if there is no human interest pointing toward the protection of unassailable parameters of human fulfillment—either because there are no such parameters or because they have no public import—society cannot but remain indifferent in this respect.

2. LIBERAL TOLERANCE AS INDIFFERENCE

2.1. Precarious recognition

As has been stated above, the "recognition" of the reality of the other constitutes the foundation of any moral obligation toward him.[5] Even the demand of impartiality "is grounded in the evidence of a perception, in the evidence of the reality of the other and of one's own reality as that of a subject and not primarily that of an object of instincts." This evidence demands recognition, and in the recognition of this evidence we discover the true basis of all practical-rational obligation.[6]

Consequently, the extent of our recognition of the other determines the extent of our awareness of the duty toward him. Both in morals and in politics, the content of this act of recognition yields crucial consequences. If we admit the existence of objective parameters of the good life, our very natural sociability—the natural openness of every human being toward others—prevents us from defining "the just" independently from "the good." The good of the agent's neighbor *is* part of the agent's own good, for the agent's social nature points beyond the agent himself: "everything which, as such, naturally belongs to another, is principally and more strongly inclined to that other to which it belongs, than toward itself."[7] This does not imply that we may egoistically justify our pursuit of the good of others in pure terms of our own good, for that would mean ceasing to consider it as the good of others—it would be self-stultifying.[8] More simply, reason orients the person toward the good of the other for the sake of the other. Accordingly, justice toward the political community as a whole—what Aquinas calls "general" or "legal justice"—demands concern about the integral human fulfillment of all citizens, and disregarding this obligation implies denying the rest of the citizens their due, their *ius suum*.[9]

By denying the teleological nature of the other, we exclude from the realm of benevolence—at least in the political field—any duty toward our neighbor's objective human fulfillment. Yet it seems impossible to speak of a true *bene*-volence if there is no objective criterion of the good. In which case, "willing" the other's "good" seems to mean respecting his subjective desires or even helping him to satisfy them, no matter their content. An extreme example of this attitude is Justice Holmes's famous statement: "if my fellow citizens want to go to Hell I will help them."[10]

But that is just an extreme attitude, verging on cynicism. Though far from Holmes's effrontery, Rawls's appeal to "mutual disinterest" in the determination of the principles of justice seems to compel us to divide our personality in a very problematic way. Politically, we must identify the good of our neighbors with their subjective preferences, no matter how harmful the satisfaction of those preferences is considered for the neighbor in question or even for society as a whole.[11] In addition, Rawls's theory entails a further indifference with regard to the effects that the expansion of ways of life perceived as harmful may have on persons under the age of reason or on future generations.

2.2. Indifference calls to indifference

I want to highlight a further problem that Michael Sandel has insightfully noted: the indifference postulated by antiperfectionist liberalism hastens the empirical conditions that eventually justify such indifference.[12] In order to support his thesis, Sandel alludes to David Hume's distinction between the *circumstances of justice* and the *circumstances of benevolence*. It is worth mentioning, though, that this distinction is much older, and that we can also find it in the work of Thomas Aquinas. As the medieval philosopher explains, "Justice properly speaking demands a diversity of persons (*diversitatem suppositorum*)."[13] In a certain sense, the differences between persons fade through loving benevolence. By creating a communion between persons, benevolence dissipates the "diversity of persons" through a reciprocal interest and mutual belonging that transcend any sense of impartiality—something that paradigmatically happens among parents and their children.[14]

Rawls awards justice—which, as we have seen, includes impartiality toward the question of the good—the rank of supreme social virtue and, at the same time, makes it dependent on a contingent empirical reality, namely, the conflicting views upon the good which in fact split society. It is the circumstance of radical pluralism about the good that demands we define justice independently of the good. Already present in *A Theory of Justice*, this Rawlsian premise is clearly formulated in *Political Liberalism*.

What happens, though, when there is still a shared ethical "substrate"? What happens when there exists an (at least partial) idea of the good around which society is able to cooperate? In this case, the pluralism of opinions that leads Rawls to give an inflexible supremacy to the virtue of justice—understood as impartiality regarding the good—has not taken place, at least not so radically. Hence, hastening a situation of "mutual disinterest" toward the good could even be a perverse action, the "original fall" introducing a new, less desirable state of affairs. Let us imagine a family whose members share a common understanding of the good life and are committed to its pursuit. At the moment when one of the family members begins to behave with indifference, the other members are compelled to distance themselves, to apply new criteria of "indifference toward his fate" instead of cooperative criteria of "collective friendship." For the sake of the common good of the family, justice as impartiality may gain a prudential—not unconditional, as in Rawls's model—priority over more intense considerations of benevolence.

Mutatis mutandis, the same could be applied to political society, where the common sharing of ideals regarding "the good" is usually a matter of degree. *My* indifference with regard to the common good currently binding us gives rise to a new state of "ethical discord" that compels *you* to treat me with the same indifference regarding the good and to redefine our relationship under contractual, self-interested terms. Postulating as a principle of justice general indifference toward the question of the good life leads to a progressive destruction of all the bonds between us regarding the good life, to an increasing dissolution of all those common domains in which we still hold a community of affection. Far from constituting virtue, elevating the Rawlsian principles of justice to the category of supreme political principles gives rise to a state of affairs in which those principles become prudently necessary, not because they are better but because the circumstances of benevolence have deteriorated.

Wherever there is a shared collective ethical substrate, indifferent behavior toward it contributes to hastening the circumstances that will trigger the need for such indifference in order to avoid conflict. By fostering this behavior as a principle, instead of accepting it as a mere prudential criterion that reason discerns while presenting itself as public reason, antiperfectionist liberalism opts for a society in which indifference toward the integral good of the citizens spreads progressively.

2.3. Ethical indifference and deterioration of justice

Finally, there is a sharp observation made by Rawls in his critique of Robert Nozick's libertarianism that, by analogy, could also be applied to his own antiperfectionist political liberalism. In his defense of an institutional framework correcting market dysfunctions and creating a "background justice," Rawls notes that "an initially just social process will eventually cease to be just, however free and fair particular transactions may look when viewed by themselves." Moreover, "fair background conditions may exist at one time and be gradually undermined even though no one acts unfairly," at least when their conduct is judged "by the rules that apply to transactions within the appropriately circumscribed local situation." In sum, Rawls concludes that "the tendency is rather for background justice to be eroded even when individuals act fairly."[15]

I honestly see no reason not to extend this social application of the principle of entropy to the relationship between the promotion of the human good and the "background justice" of a political system. Even more clearly than economic *laissez-faire*, systematic agnosticism on the part of the public authority with respect to the human good has a negative impact on background justice: the rulers and courts ignore what is good or evil for the people, rights are deprived of their reference to the human good in their interpretation, individuals believe themselves legitimized by their own rights to corrode social ecology, and once social customs are perverted, justice itself decreases.

This problem may be more clearly appreciated if we consider that moral ecology is a "non-excludable" public good, that is, a good whose possession by one individual does not decrease—but rather increases—its possession by others. In a recent book advocating for a political perfectionism quite different to the one defended in this book, Matthew Kramer has rightly noted that non-excludable goods "tend to be underproduced in the absence of measures by public or private organizations to overcome problems of collective action":

> Given that every person P stands to benefit from the availability of a public good G irrespective of whether P has contributed to covering the costs of bringing about G, and given that contributions to covering those costs can be quite onerous, and given that P's abstention from pitching in with such a contribution is very unlikely in itself to make the difference between the provision and non-provision of G, there will be strong incentives for free-riding in the absence of actions to counter those incentives.[16]

Given the "non-excludable" character of social ecology, we can emphatically conclude that the coercive role of the state in creating conditions favorable to the human good is indispensable. Moving back to an already cited Kantian formula, the restrictions of citizens' freedoms should be regarded as legitimate whenever they can be rationally accepted. From a strictly rational-practical point of view, this is true "even if the people are at present in such a situation or frame of mind that, if consulted about it [the restrictive measure at stake], they would probably refuse their consent."[17] A restriction of freedom in such a situation would perhaps be imprudent if we proceeded without a certain amount of public opinion favorable to the restriction,[18] yet it would not contradict personal moral autonomy. Quite the opposite, Kant rightly demands that the public authority ensures the "coexistence of freedoms in accordance with a universal law." Paving the way for those who propagate subjective behavior that destroys the moral good determined by reason, the state would cease to represent the united will of the people. It would be allowing the private interests of some people to prevail against the general will—understood as an idea of practical reason.[19]

2.4. Indifference and cultural paternalism in Ronald Dworkin

In the case of Ronald Dworkin, political indifference toward the good appears, for instance, in the arguments he deploys in his *Tanner lectures* to criticize what he labels "cultural paternalism." Dworkin affirms that "a challenge cannot be more interesting, or in any other way a more valuable challenge to face, when it has been narrowed, simplified, and bowdlerized by others in advance, and that is as much true when we are ignorant of what they have done as when we are all too aware of it."[20]

Reducing our responsibility toward the good life of our fellow citizens to the preservation of an "interesting" or "valuable challenge" represents, in my view, an extremely impoverished idea of our duties of benevolence. For a young person, for example, living immersed in a depraved social environment may constitute a more "interesting" challenge to his human stability than living without such threats. That does not mean, however, that in order for the challenge to be more "exciting" or "interesting," we should not attempt to politically discourage or avoid such environments, all the more so if we take into account that the failure to properly face the challenge could result in harmful consequences for third parties (family, friends, colleagues, etc.). As has been said, once we admit the existence of an objective *bonum honestum*, the ethical perspective is always the perspective of *benevolence*, which requires us to cooperate so that people can attain that good.

Certainly, we have to be aware that the human good can only be attained freely. From this premise, though, we cannot derive the ethical neutrality of the state. Tending the social ecology—what Dworkin labels, not without any negative connotation, "cultural paternalism"—constitutes an ethical duty of benevolence toward the whole political community. Of course, this thesis "assumes that we have some standard of what a good life is"—and of how a good life is frustrated—that "transcends" the particular circumstances in which someone lives and may therefore be used to stipulate which circumstances are adequate or inadequate for a good life. Inasmuch as Dworkin's "model of challenge" rejects this premise outright,[21] I think it is plainly wrong. For I am convinced that growing up in an unstructured family, with an alcoholic mother and a porn-addicted father, does not give rise to a mere "different challenge" but is rather *objectively worse* than growing up in a solid family with temperate, hard-working, and virtuous parents; that the virtues of fortitude and temperance constitute appropriate standards to judge which familiar circumstances are desirable or undesirable to lead a flourishing human life; and that, notwithstanding the obvious restrictions posed by a healthy pluralism and by public reason itself, the ethical perspective requires everybody—the ruler included—to foster circumstances leading to human integral fulfillment.

2.5. Indifference and rights talk

As has been stated, the Dworkinian eschewal of public protection of a "moral ecology" has taken the form of an influential theory of rights. In a suggestive essay, Mary Ann Glendon insightfully described the moral indifference conveyed by such a discourse. The Harvard professor illuminated with many examples from case law and legal doctrine some of the features and risks of the prevailing "rights talk": the lack of a language of responsibility or dimension of sociality; the absolute and assertive nature of rights claims; individualism and insularity.[22] Such risks are encapsulated, in my opinion, in the Dworkinian conception of "rights as trumps": "if someone has a right to something, then it is wrong for government to deny it to him even though it would be in the general interest to do so."[23]

Such an individualistic discourse is overtly indifferent toward what is really good for the citizens. Though cloaked in freedom and rights, it is ultimately detrimental to those individuals lacking robust communities to support them in cultivating their character. It is of course less detrimental for those who belong to the intellectual establishment. An enlightened egoism can lead by itself to cultivating the virtues and talents necessary to achieve some vital stability and reach positions of social reputation.[24] The person with opportunities to develop by himself seems to need only autonomy. In their character formation, an enlightened egoism can make it the rest of the way. Those persons whose egoism is not so enlightened through an initial lack of the necessary means of formation are much more in need of an institutional framework that fosters moral ecology. A rights discourse oriented to satisfying the preferences of individuals regardless of their content does no favors at all to such people.

In this line, Glendon has called attention to the fact that it was a utilitarian theorist of elite domination—John Stuart Mill—who provided one of the most incisive modern apologias of liberal autonomy. Mill's autonomy is not—at least immediately—at the service of the most vulnerable subjects. It rather caters to the fulfillment of singular and exceptional characters—as was indeed the case with Mill himself, a genius of the Enlightened establishment, son of the philosopher James Mill, and mentored by Jeremy Bentham. Paradoxically, these are the characters who end up determining for the whole of society what a good life and a bad life is, and their autonomy would ultimately be at the service of their leadership.[25]

3. HUMAN RIGHTS AND LIBERATION OF THE LIBIDO IN JURISPRUDENCE

3.1. The expansion of the right to privacy

Infused with the connotations outlined above, current rights discourse ends up becoming, in Glendon's words, a vindication of "infinite and impossible desires,"[26] where "if rights are good, more rights must be even better, and the more emphatically they are stated, the less likely it is that they will be watered down or taken away."[27] Especially in this context, to speak of the pleasure principle or desire (*Lustprinzip*) demands a reference to sexual libido. The abandonment of teleology, together with technical mastery of the reproductive mechanisms—permitting both blocking its natural purpose and simulating it experimentally—has produced an unprecedented emancipation in this area in the last half century. It is hard to deny that the institution of marriage benefits from certain social restrictions with regard to sex. Wherever there is public morality, there will inevitably be some degree of hypocritical or exaggerated prudery, because in any society with moral standards, those who want to transgress them have at least to feign morality: "hypocrisy is the homage that vice pays to virtue"—said La Rochefoucauld.[28] Hypocrisy is deplorable, and historical experience has taught us to be alert to and to oppose puritan excesses. Having said this, endorsing social cynicism or public moral indifference as a valid alternative dehumanizes society. The unscrupulous find an open door to poison the soil needed for the formation of ethical traditions and, as has been said, moral convictions can only survive and develop amid those traditions. As always happens, a radical *laissez-faire* works to the benefit of the unscrupulous.

It is not necessary to give many examples of the liberation of libido through rights discourse, for it is a well-known subject of constitutional controversies and debates. Nevertheless, it may be worth mentioning a couple of cases evidencing the worrying extent to which rights have been used as a vehicle for the expansion of desire. In this vein, the *right to privacy* has been the most common instrument.

This fundamental right—which lacks an explicit mention in the American Constitution—was created by the Supreme Court of the United States in its famous decision *Griswold v. Connecticut*.[29] Some years later, it would be the right invoked in *Roe v. Wade*,[30] the decision creating a constitutional right to abortion. In the early 1980s, in the controversial decision *City of Akron Center for Reproductive Health Inc.*,[31] followed by *Thornburgh v. American College of Obstetricians & Gynecologists*,[32] and subsequently repealed by *Planned Parenthood v. Casey*,[33] the U.S. Supreme Court said that the requirement to inform a woman about issues that could deter her from taking the decision to have an abortion—the state of the fetus, adoption alternatives available, and so forth—infringed upon her right to privacy.

In the case law of the European Court of Human Rights, we also find judgments that are striking not so much for their final ruling as for the legal reasoning on which they are based.[34] Thus, for instance, in *Akdaş v. Turkey*,[35] the court did not consider the prohibition by the Turkish authorities of an extremely pornographic novel by Guillaume Apollinaire (*Les Onze Mille Verges*) to fall within the states' margin of appreciation to protect public morality. Most striking about this case is the basis supporting the court's ruling, namely, that the controverted book constitutes a part of "European literary heritage"[36]—and we must suppose that the court means a *relevant* part, because otherwise the argument would be trivial.

In *Dickson and another v. United Kingdom*,[37] the Grand Chamber of the European Court of Human Rights condemned the United Kingdom for violating the right to privacy by denying prisoners access to artificial insemination. It must be noted that the applicant was serving life imprisonment, that both he and his partner were of an advanced age, and that they had met in prison. At the time of the prohibition, she had been released and it was difficult to ensure the stability of the couple in the future. Having rationally assessed the circumstances and with due legal support, the authorities' refusal to permit the insemination ultimately responded to the best interest of a prospective child. Nevertheless, the Grand Chamber held by twelve votes to five that, in view of such an intimate decision as having a child, the state's margin of appreciation should be curtailed. The desire to have a child prevailed over the good of the child.

One of the most staggering decisions was, in my view, the one issued by the European Court of Human Rights in the case *Stübing v. Germany*. On this occasion, the court had to decide whether the sentence imposed on a man who had fathered four children—three of them severely handicapped—with his sister violated the right to privacy. What is more astonishing about this case is not so much the final ruling of the court, which confirmed the sentence, but the *ratio decidendi*. In the court's opinion, "the applicant's criminal conviction had an impact on his family life and, possibly, attracted protection under Article 8 of the Convention, as he was forbidden to have sexual intercourse with the mother of his four children."[38] Under such premise, a restrictive measure could only be justified by proving its "necessity" in a "democratic society," a test that—according to the court's judgment—is particularly strict when applied to issues affecting something as intimate as sexuality.[39] In the end, the European Court of Human Rights did not justify the restriction directly, that is, by issuing an opinion on the punishability of incest as such. It certainly confirmed the sentence and dismissed the application but cautiously avoided a strong ruling against incest. Surprisingly enough, the court grounded its judgment on a bare reference to the lack of consensus among the member states regarding the criminalization of incest, thus leaving the door open to a future social acceptance of incest that would render its judgment obsolete.[40]

In *Stübing*, the European Court of Human Rights has imposed as a limit on the forty-seven states of the Council of Europe the *prima facie* protection, through Article 8 of the European Convention of Human Rights, of *any* form of exercise of sexuality, including incest. Hence the court confirms the assertive and insular character of rights referred to at the beginning of this section. Their content is taken in isolation from any teleological consideration regarding the human good. Considerations of public order are only taken into account *a posteriori*. But once a conduct has been covered under the abstract protection of rights, public order reasons are regarded with mistrust and subjected to a strong presumption against them, for they oppose a freedom that is *prima facie* regarded as legitimate. In the realm of sexuality, any kind of practice is *prima facie* considered legitimate through its inclusion within the right to privacy.

In cases like *Dickson* or *Stübing*, we can clearly perceive the moral indifference that such decisions entail with respect to the potential interests of the persons affected by the sexual behaviors covered under the cloak of rights rhetoric. The result is, in my view, deeply dehumanizing: actions such as incest, the outcomes of which are anything but "private," receive the protection of our legal order's *pars selecta:* human rights. The cases analyzed are far from constituting an exhaustive account of the judicial "privatization" of sexuality and the liberation of libido through rights discourse. In any case, the line of reasoning followed by those decisions shows that a false premise is more resistant to arguments on the abstract level than when confronted with reality. To say that sexuality is a completely private issue may perhaps sound reasonable in theory. But once we assume this premise, we feel perplexed before cases like *Stübing*. Instead of giving up the premise, the Strasbourg Court maintains it with references to abundant precedents but without taking into account the serious consequences of its conclusions. I honestly do not think that criticizing such jurisprudence can be labeled as exaggerated moralism or prudery.

A final recent decision I would like to mention is *Paradiso Campanelli v. Italy*, a judgment regarding the controversial question of 'rent-a-womb' surrogacy. The applicants in the case were an aged Italian couple who, after several attempts at procreating through *in vitro* fertilization, contracted a Russian womb rental services company to make their desire a reality for 50,000 euros. Specialized in assisted reproduction techniques, the company carried out *in vitro* fertilization and implanted an embryo—which had supposedly been fertilized with an anonymous mother's ovum and the applicant's semen—in the "surrogate mother." The baby was born in February 2011; in March, the Italian couple was registered in Russia as parents of the child, without any mention of the 'rent-a-womb' gestational surrogacy; and in April, the mother obtained from the Italian Consulate the documents that allowed her to go back to Italy with the baby. In May, however, the Italian Consulate in Moscow told the Italian administrative and judicial authorities that the official documents regarding the child's birth contained false data. The applicants were then accused of "altering civil status" and "forgery," as they had taken a child who was not theirs. They had additionally violated the adoption laws, which prohibited adopting such a young baby. In the course of the procedure, a DNA test was done and revealed that the applicant was not the child's father.

In October 2011, the Youth Court decided to remove the child from its parents, for several reasons. Among other causes, the court said that several adoption provisions of international law had been violated, and that the agreement signed by the applicants with the Russian company was contrary to the Italian Medically Assisted Reproduction Act, which bans heterologous assisted fertilization. The situation created was entirely unlawful, and the court deemed it appropriate to remove the child from the parents and declare him eligible for adoption. The court remarked that "given that the applicants had preferred to circumvent the adoption legislation, notwithstanding the authorization they had received, it could be thought that the child resulted from a narcissistic desire on the part of the couple or indeed that he was intended to resolve problems in their relationship." This reflection led the court to "cast doubt on whether they were genuinely capable of providing emotional and educational support." Consequently, according with the Italian legislation, the child was entrusted to the social services and placed in a foster family in January 2013.[41]

After unsuccessfully opposing these measures through all the available means in Italy, the applicants appealed to the European Court of Human Rights. In its judgment of January 27, 2015, Strasbourg condemned Italy for breaching the right to family life of Article 8 of the Convention. The decision gathered several elements of the case and, in an overall balance of those elements, concluded that reasons based on public order should cede to the applicants' interest in maintaining their affective ties with the child—even though they had only lived a couple of months together. What seems most striking in this decision is, in my view, the small weight given by the court to the common good protected by public order. It actually refers to public order in a very restrictive way, just to limit its scope,[42] and ignores the profound link that exists between the preservation of public order in a community—in this case, the Italian state—and the welfare of children in that community. By contrast, it gives a strong weight to the individual "emotional aspects" of the case, including the difficulties of the couple to procreate[43]—which by themselves constitute a circumstance incapable of justifying a breach of the civil status and still less of justifying that breach in terms of human rights. In short, the desire principle prevails against reason.

Decided by five votes to two, the judgment raised various objections and was appealed to the Grand Chamber, which overturned the Chamber's decision on January 24, 2017, by eleven votes to six. Among the arguments held by the Grand Chamber, it is worth praising, in my opinion, the fact that it expressly declared that "the legitimate aim of preventing disorder" is linked to "that of protecting children—not merely the child in the present case but also children more generally."⁴⁴ Fortunately, reason finally prevailed against desire.

3.2. Dialectic of liberal tolerance: The restriction of conscientious objection

An additional negative consequence of the wrong understanding of tolerance that influences rights jurisprudence needs to be highlighted here. As has been indicated, the understanding of tolerance held by antiperfectionist liberalism ends up involving a dangerous dialectic of intolerance. Depriving authorities of the power to interpret the content of rights with reference to the human good, the only criterion for solving conflicts of liberties is the subjective significance that liberties have for those who exercise them. In turn, the only "objective" criterion for weighing such subjective significance is the strength with which they are asserted. The assertive and absolute character of contemporary rights talk denounced by Glendon—the Dworkinian conception of *rights as trumps*—is precisely associated with the absence of objective teleological parameters to determine the importance of rights. In the absence of rational criteria regarding how relevant the good to be realized through this or that exercise of freedom is, and of how relevant this or that exercise of freedom is to achieving such a good, the balance between freedoms becomes a mere wrestling match.

The outcome is a dangerous dialectic within the very discourse of tolerance. In the name of freedom, the more intensely defended ways of exercising freedom end up turning into "forms of good life" that not only claim respect but also acquiescence and public recognition. Legal casuistry on freedom of conscience reveals some well-known examples. In the Decision *Pichon and Sajous v. France*,⁴⁵ for example, the majority of the European Court of Human Rights denied pharmacists the protection of their freedom of conscience against the obligation, coercively imposed by the authorities, to dispense abortion pills. Thus, the consumption of abortifacient drugs functions not just as a freedom but also as a conduct that demands to be acknowledged or recognized by pharmacists who are compelled to aid in their distribution. Now, can it really be maintained that the freedom to access abortifacient pills in each and every pharmacy represents a more important or significant element for fulfillment than the freedom not to be involved in their sale? On strictly rational criteria—that is, leaving aside ideological interests of pressure groups—I think it is very difficult to answer affirmatively.

In contrast to what the Strasbourg Court concluded in *Pichon and Sajous*, the conservative majority of the Spanish Constitutional Court has safeguarded the freedom of conscience of pharmacists who refuse to sell the pill.⁴⁶ Nevertheless, the Constitutional Court's judgment is followed by three dissenting opinions and has been strongly criticized by liberal intellectuals. Their criticism basically points toward a dangerous—and in my view wrongly construed—*reductio ad absurdum*: we should not admit a general right to conscientious objection, for it would lead to the dissolution of the whole legal system. This *reductio ad absurdum* was suggested in 1980s by the Spanish Constitutional Court itself: "conscientious objection in general, that is, a right to be exempted from the fulfillment of constitutional or legal duties for being that fulfillment contrary to one's convictions, is neither recognized nor imaginable to be recognized in our legal system nor in any legal system, since that would mean the denial of the very idea of state. What could happen is that it may be exceptionally admitted, with respect to one particular duty."[47]

In my opinion, the Constitutional Court mistakes here an "absolute" right with a "general" right, that is, with a right *simpliciter*, without any further specification in its abstract *prima facie* formulation. All legal mandates are subordinated to multiple constitutional "general" rights that, absolutely affirmed, would lead to "the denial of the very idea of state." If, by declaring that a *general* right to conscientious objection does not exist, the court wants to express the view that an *absolute* right to conscientious objection does not exist, we could simply reply that this must be applied to any abstract constitutional right. An absolute right to conscientious objection—the same as an absolute right to freedom of speech, or to privacy, or to freedom and security, or to equality, and so forth—"is neither recognized nor imaginable to be recognized." By contrast, a general right to conscientious objection is perfectly imaginable and does not necessarily lead to the disappearance of the idea of state. Partly following Robert Alexy, we can confidently say that the just measure of such a right shall depend on the structure and content of the reasoning leading from the "*prima facie* legal positions"—the abstractly expressed right—to the "definitive legal positions"—the concretely recognized legal power.[48] If we accepted the thesis denying the existence of an abstract or general right to conscientious objection, the collision between subjective conviction and legal mandate would inexorably be solved in favor of the legislator, regardless of the seriousness of the objection and the social importance of a uniform compliance with the legal obligation.[49]

4. IMPOSSIBLE NEUTRALITY AND SOCIAL POLICIES

I have just made reference to the dialectic of intolerance into which liberal tolerance easily falls while pretending to be neutral. The neutrality that liberalism preconizes ends up being a chimera, a conceptual impossibility that is systematically disproved by the facts. As we shall immediately see, social policies are perhaps the most evident proof of this lack of neutrality in liberalism, given that the taxes used to fund such policies are inevitably coercive.[50]

In a well-known article published some decades ago, Robert Nozick dealt with the idea of "coercion" through a careful distinction between the concepts of "threats" and "offers." In his essay, Nozick explained that the difference between them is precisely the coercion of the first versus the noncoercion of the later. In the case of "threats," there is always a subordination to the other's will, whereas "offers" do not entail such subordination:

> If P intentionally changes the consequences of two actions A_1 and A_2 available to Q so as to lessen the desirability of the consequences of A_1, and so as to increase the desirability of the consequences of A_2, and part of P's reason for acting as he does is to so lessen and increase the desirability of the respective consequences, then
>
> (a) This resultant change predominantly involves a *threat* to Q if he does A_1 if Q prefers doing the old A_1 (without the worsened consequences) to doing the new A_2 (with the improved consequences).
> (b) This resultant change predominantly involves an *offer* to Q to do A_2 if Q prefers doing the new A_2 (with the improved consequences) to the old A_1 (without the worsened consequences).[51]

To refine his analysis, Nozick asks himself what *baseline* or factual reference we should confront our proposals with to ascertain whether they are *offers* or *threats*. This baseline could be either the *morally legitimate* course of events or the *normal* course of events. To use his own example, if someone beats his slave every day and promises him that, if he (the slave) performs certain fastidious acts, he (the master) will stop beating him, the promise will be considered either an *offer* or a *threat* depending on the course of events we take as *baseline*. If the promise is superposed on the normal course of events—a situation in which the slave is daily beaten—we will certainly conclude that the promise is an *offer*. If it is superposed on the morally legitimate course of events—a situation in which the slave is not beaten at all—the proposal will be considered a *threat*. Nozick rightly concludes that the relevant reference or baseline will depend on the case though will usually be the morally legitimate course of events.

Now, if we take the morally legitimate course of events as baseline and accept value-neutrality as a basic principle of political morality, we should give up political liberalism with its defense of the welfare state and embrace the principles of political *libertarianism*. As soon as a behavior entails a controversial judgment regarding the good—for example, abortion, euthanasia, or the use of contraceptive drugs—subsidizing that behavior through public funds constitutes a violation of liberal neutrality. Wouldn't those citizens who ethically oppose the subsidized conduct prefer to do A_1 (not contribute to this social policy) in the first situation (i.e., without the legal consequences of not paying taxes) rather than A_2 (contribute to this social policy) in the second situation (i.e., avoid with their contribution the legal consequences of not paying)? Were they not better off in the first situation, in which the state was "socially neutral" and they were not forced to pay taxes under the threat of administrative penalties or even criminal punishments? It is obvious that, to the extent that social policies are publicly funded, they are not mere offers but "offers conjoined with threats"[52] addressed to taxpayers. If we really embrace liberal neutrality, we cannot consistently support social policies affecting—even superficially or incidentally—controversial questions regarding the good life.

Nevertheless, the fact is that we should unequivocally reject both liberal and libertarian antiperfectionist neutrality. With sound judgment, Joseph Raz has highlighted the core problem that may serve to rebut each one:

(a) With regard to *libertarianism*, the mistake lies in the fact that the morally legitimate course of events—the "baseline" with which social policies should be confronted—is not a situation in which private property absolutely belongs to the taxpayer. To use a felicitous expression coined by Catholic social teaching, private property is burdened by a "social mortgage." Or in the terms of Article 14.2 of the German Basic Law, "property entails obligations" (*Eigentum verpflichtet*). Strictly speaking, the morally legitimate course of events does not justify libertarianism, for there is a natural moral obligation to contribute to the integral good of all citizens with one's property.

(b) The above observation, however, not only discredits the libertarian claim against subsidized social policies but—if consistently understood—also opposes the claims of neutrality wielded by all forms of antiperfectionist *liberalism*. If we assume that every citizen has an original duty to contribute to the common good with their *property*, should we not say the same, *in genere*, with regard to an original duty to contribute to the common good with their *freedom?* Though libertarians are more consistently "antiperfectionist" than liberal "welfarists," both of their neutralities are ill-founded.

NOTES

1. R. von Ihering, *Geist des römischen Rechts auf verschiedenen Stufen seiner Entwicklung*, III-1 (Leipzig: Breitkopf und Härtel, 1865), p. 339.

2. R. Dworkin, *Life's Dominion. An Argument about Abortion, Euthanasia and Individual Freedom* (New York: Random House, 1993), pp. 201 ff.

3. See *supra*, chapter 3, 4.1.

4. I use the term "objective" not as belonging to a "view from nowhere" but as intersubjectively "true" or "valid" (see, e.g., J. Finnis, *Fundamentals of Ethics* [Washington, DC: Georgetown University Press, 1983], pp. 60–66).

5. See *supra*, chapter 4, 2.1.

6. Spaemann, *Happiness and Benevolence*, p. 99.

7. "Unumquodque autem in rebus naturalibus, quod secundum naturam hoc ipsum quod est, alterius est, principalius et magis inclinatur in id cuius est, quam in seipsum" (*S. Th.*, I, q. 60, art. 5).

8. Annas, *Morality of Happiness*, p. 9.

9. *Cfr. S. Th.*, II-II, q. 59, a. 1.

10. Oliver Wendell Holmes, *Letter to Harold J. Laski (March 4, 1920)*, in *Holmes-Laski Letters I*, ed. Mark DeWolfe Howe (Cambridge, MA: Harvard University Press, 1953), p. 249.

11. As John Finnis said, "The benevolent spectator cares, not for the conflicting self-loves that the objects of his benevolence happen to have and the conflicting claims they happen to raise, but rather for the intrinsic value of the goods they could be educated to enjoy and of the various perfections and excellences they thus could variously realize" ("Rawls's A Theory of Justice," in *Collected Essays*, III, pp. 72–73).

12. Sandel, *Liberalism and the Limits of Justice*, pp. 31 ff.

13. "Iustitia ergo proprie dicta requirit diversitatem suppositorum" (*S. Th.*, II-II, q. 58, a. 2).

14. "Et ideo patris ad filium non est comparatio sicut ad simpliciter alterum, et propter hoc non est ibi simpliciter iustum, sed quoddam iustum, scilicet paternum" (*S. Th.*, II-II, q. 57, a. 4).

15. Rawls, *Political Liberalism*, VII, pp. 266–67. The idea of justice as a process of fair transfers of legitimately acquired holdings is developed by R. Nozick in *Anarchy, State and Utopia*, especially pp. 150 ff.

16. M. H. Kramer, *Liberalism with Excellence* (Oxford: Oxford University Press, 2017), p. 65.

17. *Gemeinspruch*, p. 297.

18. See *Zum ewigen Frieden*, p. 378.

19. See *Zum ewigen Frieden*, p. 352.

20. Dworkin, "Equality and the Good Life," p. 273.

21. Dworkin, "Equality and the Good Life," p. 273.

22. M. A. Glendon, *Rights Talk. The Impoverishment of Political Discourse* (New York: Free Press, 1991), p. 14.

23. Dworkin, *Taking Rights Seriously*, p. 269.

24. For a careful account of the possibility of grounding several virtues on the "effectiveness" of self-interest, see *v. gr.* MacIntyre, *Whose Justice? Which Rationality?*, pp. 40 ff.

25. Glendon, *Rights Talk*, p. 75 (in a chapter suggestively entitled: *The Lone-Rights Bearer*).

26. Glendon, *Rights Talk*, p. 45.

27. Glendon, *Rights Talk*, p. 16.

28. La Rochefoucauld, *Collected Maxims and Other Reflections* (Oxford: Oxford University Press, 2007), p. 62 (§ 218).

29. 381 US 479 (1965).

30. 410 US 158 (1973).

31. 462 US 416 (1983).

32. 476 US 747 (1986).

33. 505 US 833 (1992).

34. An excellent synthesis of the Strasbourg's Court jurisprudence on the right to privacy may be found in Á. J. Gómez Montoro, "*Vida privada y autonomía personal o una interpretación passe-partout del artículo 8 CEDH*," in *La Constitución política de España. Estudios en homenaje a Manuel Aragón Reyes*, eds. F. Rubio Llorente et al. (Madrid: Centro de Estudios Políticos y Constitucionales, 2016), pp. 617–50.

35. ECtHR *Akdaş v. Turkey*, February 10, 2010.

36. ECtHR *Akdaş v. Turkey*, § 30.

37. ECtHR *Dickson and another v. United Kingdom*, December 15, 2007.

38. ECtHR *Stübing v. Germany*, April 12, 2012, § 55.

39. ECtHR *Stübing v. Germany*, § 59.

40. ECtHR *Stübing v. Germany*, § 60–61.

41. ECtHR *Paradiso Campanelli v. Italy*, January 27, 2015, §§ 22 and 31.

42. ECtHR *Paradiso Campanelli v. Italy*, § 80.

43. ECtHR *Paradiso Campanelli v. Italy*, § 77.

44. ECtHR *Paradiso Campanelli v. Italy* (Grand Chamber), January 24, 2017, § 197.

45. Decision *Pichon and Sajous v. France*, October 2, 2001. On the increase of cases regarding freedom of conscience in the field of bioethics, see C. Tollefsen, "Conscience, Religion and the State," in *Challenges to Religious Liberty in the Twenty-First Century*, ed. G. V. Bradley (New York: Cambridge University Press, 2012), pp. 122–35. It is also interesting to see the debate between John Corvino, on the one side, and Ryan T. Anderson and Sherif Girgis on the other: *Debating Religious Liberty and Discrimination* (Oxford: Oxford University Press, 2017).

46. Constitutional Court Judgment 145/2015, June 25, 2015.

47. Constitutional Court Judgment 161/1987, Ground 3.

48. See Alexy, *Theorie der Grundrechte*, pp. 90–92.

49. For a more detailed explanation of the concept of conscientious objection, as well as of its purpose and the meaning of its exceptionality, let me refer my own essay: "¿Exención de un *deber* de abortar? Sobre el registro navarro de objetores y el concepto de objeción de conciencia," *Revista Jurídica de Navarra* 58 (2014): 159–80.

50. In his recent book *Liberalism with Excellence*, Matthew Kramer has gathered some of the most significant arguments in this debate (pp. 49 ff.). In particular, he

discusses the arguments given by Jonathan Quong against Raz's position. See J. Quong, *Liberalism without Perfection* (Oxford: Oxford University Press, 2011), pp. 60 ff.

51. R. Nozick, "Coercion," in *Philosophy, Science, and Method: Essays in Honor of Ernest Nagel*, eds. S. Morgenbesser, P. Suppes, and M. White (New York: St Martin's Press, 1969), p. 449.

52. Kramer, *Liberalism with Excellence*, p. 54; see also Quong, *Liberalism without Perfection*, p. 65.

Chapter 7

Desireless life and undesirable life

1. INTRODUCTION

In this chapter, I will comment on two dehumanizing consequences that, in my view, are closely associated with an ateleological or antiperfectionist interpretation of rights: on the one hand, the widely accepted exclusion of unborn human beings from the right to life; on the other, the increasing tendency to deny the inviolability of the right to life to those human beings who do not want to continue living. The selection of these two problems does not arise from simple polemical zeal and nor has the preceding discussion been developed with them in mind. Moreover, I want to stress that *I do not* claim that one needs to be "an antiperfectionist" in order to diverge from my views on bioethical questions, but that an antiperfectionist approach to rights leads to a dehumanizing stance on those questions.

It means something that Ronald Dworkin dedicated an influential book to arguing in favor of a right to abortion and a right to euthanasia and that, together with John Rawls and other academics, he submitted an *amicus curiae* brief defending the creation of a right to assisted suicide to the Supreme Court of the United States. And as we have seen, Rawls himself has strongly supported the right to abortion, up to the point of suggesting that the denial of such a right in the first months of pregnancy is incompatible with public reason.

Having set out the basic tenets of legal and political antiperfectionist liberalism in part II of this book, part III is now devoted to a critical examination of some of its practical—and in my view dehumanizing—consequences. In this sense, I consider that the right to abortion and the right to euthanasia are closely linked to an interpretation of rights based on the desire principle. The understanding of human interests—and therefore of the substrate of rights—as experienceable desires leads to reducing the idea of an intrinsic and inalienable human life—what Dworkin calls "life in earnest"—to a mere function of the capacity to fulfill existing desires. From this perspective, the fact that a human being does not yet hold experienceable desires—"desireless life"—points toward their deprivation of rights, and the fact that a human being does not want to continue living—"undesirable life"—points toward their right to euthanasia.

Finally, I want to reiterate that, though this chapter deals with a more particular issue than the political questions analyzed in part II, it amounts to a critical revision of the application of the liberal-ateleological philosophical premises expounded there. The analysis of the problems is therefore not exhaustive but focuses on connecting the understanding of rights from the "desire principle" with the deprivation of the *nasciturus* of the right to life, on the one hand, and with the assertion of a right to assisted suicide, on the other. As has been stated, the selection of these cases arises from the simple fact that they are paradigmatic of the liberal-ateleological attitude, something that can easily be seen in the importance the liberal authors discussed—primarily Dworkin and Rawls—have given in their respective works to the defense of a right to abortion and of one to euthanasia.

2. DESIRELESS LIFE

First, we should consider the problem of the denial of human rights to the human being before birth. Not being capable of experiencing desires, the unborn baby is denied the possibility of having interests and is, in the end, left *hors la loi*, outside the protection of the law. This thesis has been widespread in the case law of constitutional courts and supranational human rights bodies since Harry Blackmun affirmed in *Roe v. Wade* (1973) that "the word 'person', as used in the Fourteenth Amendment, does not include the unborn."[1] On the basis of the denial of personhood to the unborn, the Strasbourg Court has declared that, generally, any limitation on abortion—also the prohibition of abortions exclusively performed for the sake of the mother's welfare or well-being—entails an interference in the right to privacy protected by Article 8 of the European Convention of Human Rights.[2] The German Federal Constitutional Court, whose jurisprudence has served as an example for several constitutional courts, has been reluctant to assert such constitutional right to abortion but has removed the barriers protecting the unborn's life on the same basis, namely that he or she is not a person.[3]

The underlying basis of this wide legal license of abortion is still questioned by many people. Wherever the courts recognize such a constitutional right to abortion, several objections are raised against the lack of necessary constitutional consensus to create this right. Notwithstanding the theoretical-political justification of these critiques, they do not address the substantial problem at stake but the lack of fairness in the decision-making process, a problem we will turn to in part IV of the book.

Beyond the lines of criticism based on the fair balance of powers and rule of law, in the following pages I wish to deal with the substantive question underlying the creation of a right to abortion, namely, the exclusion of the *nasciturus* from the *status personae*. In this context, I think that the liberal jurisprudential approach has found a paradigmatic development in Ronald Dworkin's work, whose construction will be critically examined. I will also contrast his conclusions with the ideas of another relevant intellectual who, though representing a minority view, has become increasingly influential: Princeton University professor, Peter Singer. Departing from the social standards of "political correctness," Singer has taken the desire principle in the interpretation of rights to its logical extremes.

2.1. Subjective intrinsic values: Dworkin on the *nasciturus*

In 1993, Ronald Dworkin dedicated a whole book, *Life's Dominion*, to developing his thesis on the appropriate constitutional treatment of abortion and euthanasia. The brilliance of Dworkin's prose, rich in examples and well-documented with regard to certain questions, is undeniable. He seems to be a knowledgeable writer on the secular and religious history of abortion. In his view, the disagreements on this issue ultimately respond to a lack of reflection on the content of the discussion itself. If we critically analyzed the presuppositions involved in our arguments, we would reach, says Dworkin, substantial agreement on the *pro-life* and *pro-choice* positions, following the self-denomination and self-understanding of the respective debating parties. Such an analysis is precisely the "ecumenical ambition"[4] of his work.

To carry out his project, Dworkin begins by asking himself what possible objections could inform rational opposition to the liberalization of abortion, and he arrives at two possible arguments: a "derivative" argument and an "independent" argument.[5] According to the "derivative argument," opposition to abortion "derives" from the fact that it violates the right to life of the unborn, which is an inherent right to their *status* as a person, to their being a person. This argument thus "presupposes and is derived from rights and interests that it assumes all human beings, including fetuses, have." The "independent argument," however, is based on the idea that "human life has an intrinsic, innate value; that human life is sacred just in itself, and that the sacred nature of a human life begins when its biological life begins, even before the creature whose life it is has movement or sensation or interests or rights of its own."

In Dworkin's opinion, the "derivative argument" is plainly untenable, given that the fetus is not a person. If the fetus were a person, he says, any form of decriminalization would be deplorable, for "no one can consistently hold that a fetus has a right not to be killed and at the same time hold it wrong for the government to protect that right by the criminal law."[6] At least in its initial stages of development, the unborn is not a person and, consequently, does not have rights. This is due to the simple fact that it lacks "interests of its own." In Dworkin's words, "It is very hard to make any sense of the idea that an early fetus has interests of its own, in particular an interest in not being destroyed, from the moment of its conception."[7] As "a caterpillar" has no interest in becoming "a butterfly," so the fetus has no interest in becoming a human adult. "It makes no sense to suppose that something has interests of *its own*—as distinct from its being important what happens to it—unless it has, or has had, some form of consciousness: some mental as well as physical life."[8]

Despite not developing these ideas as consistently as Peter Singer, Dworkin maintains a very similar conception of "interest" to the one held by him, one that is completely linked to the actual possession of consciously experienceable desires and preferences. "My interests are in play . . . not because of my capacity to feel pain but because of a different and more complex set of capacities: to enjoy or fail to enjoy, to form affections and emotions, to hope and expect, to suffer disappointment and frustration."[9] He confidently asserts that none of us who oppose abortion consistently holds that the fetus is a person. Even the standpoint of the Catholic Church is historically grounded in the "detached argument," which is based on the sacredness of life. For only in recent times has the church adopted the argument of "rights" as a powerful political weapon to defend the ban on abortion in the public forum.[10] Strictly speaking, however, this "derivative argument" would be untenable due to the lack of interests of the *nasciturus*.

That the unborn human being lacks personhood does not mean, according to Dworkin, that it lacks value and not just a relative value—be it "instrumental" or "subjective"—but genuinely intrinsic, sacred, or inviolable value.[11] This is really the *status* that we intuitively confer on the *nasciturus*, according to Dworkin. It is not a person but *res sacra*, that is, "something" whose "deliberate destruction would dishonor what ought to be honored."[12] At this point, Dworkin raises three closely related questions: (a) What makes for something to be sacred? (b) Are there degrees of sacredness? (c) Is it at times legitimate to destroy what is sacred?

(a) To the first question, Dworkin offers a "genetic" answer: "the nerve of the sacred lies in the value we attach to a process or enterprise or project rather than to its results considered independently from how they

were produced."[13] Thus, "recognizing the sanctity of life does not mean attempting to engineer fate so that the best possible lives are lived overall; it means, rather, not frustrating investments in life that have already been made."[14]
(b) To the second question, Dworkin gives a positive answer: there actually are degrees of sacredness. The scale of sacredness depends on the relative value that we associate with the different "creative investments" spent in a life's project. Such investments may have been the result either of individual effort and action (*personal investments*) or of nature itself (*natural investments*). Any attack against the sacred consists in unduly frustrating these investments.
(c) Finally, the third question is also positively answered by Dworkin: on certain occasions, the sacred may—or even should—be destroyed. When the different investments conferring due dignity on the sacred collide with each other, one must strike a balance in order to make a decision. In this balance, religious persons generally place a higher value on natural investments, while less religious persons tend to opt for their own investments.[15]

Under these assumptions, Dworkin traces both ethical and legal guidelines to issue a judgment on the legitimacy of abortion. From an ethical point of view, such a judgment is almost entirely subjective. The sacredness of life simply requires avoiding frivolity and behaving with integrity. Beyond this, the relative weight that someone confers on the life of the unborn may fluctuate. Thus, for example, the conflict between the prospects of personal fulfillment through a brilliant professional career and an incipient human life—which, according to Dworkin, cannot yet be called "life in earnest"[16]—may be ethically and without any egoism solved in favor of the personal professional project. Immoral abortion is presented by Dworkin as an extreme case, involving those who frivolously abort without any consideration of the value of the unborn human life.

From a legal viewpoint, Dworkin substantially endorses the conclusions of *Roe v. Wade*, adding a further argument in line with his own philosophical standpoint. Like the German Federal Constitutional Court, he thinks that the fetus is not a person but a value, *res sacra*. Yet he regards as contradictory the decision of the German Federal Constitutional Court to protect this "objective value" through the right to life enshrined in Article 2.2 of the German Basic Law—since this article protects *rights*, not mere values. *Roe's* judgment, leaving the decision in the hands of the mother's freedom, would seem to be more consistent. However, the main reason in favor of *Roe* would not be the right to privacy but the right to religious freedom. Both for believers, agnostics and atheists, the assessment of the sanctity of life is a matter of religious freedom.[17] Therefore, the state should give up any attempt at coercion in this matter and leave the decision in the hands of the individuals concerned. The strongest argument in favor of a right to abortion in the first stages of pregnancy would thus be religious freedom. This right could only disappear in advanced stages of pregnancy, once the woman has had time to make a responsible and free decision and has tacitly consented to a "natural increase of value" in the fetus's life. It is the task of the Supreme Court to draw reasonable boundaries determining the respective domains of the woman's ethical independence and the woman's legal responsibility. And in this sense, the parameters fixed by *Roe v. Wade* are considered by Dworkin to be reasonable.

2.2. Critical remarks on Dworkin's position

Thus far, I have presented a synthesis of Dworkin's line of argumentation. I have attempted to do so with the utmost possible fidelity to the author, without falling into distorting simplifications and avoiding rhetorical abuses that would obscure its inner logic. I would now like to formulate, with the same clarity, some critical remarks.

(a) *A misunderstanding?*

As has been explained, Dworkin's "ecumenical ambition" of finding a common framework for the debate among *pro-lifers* and *pro-choicers* lies in convincing those who defend the *status personae* of the *nasciturus* that their claim rests on a misunderstanding. I fear, though, that there is no such a misunderstanding. Dworkin denies the quality of personhood to the *nasciturus* on the basis that, having neither sentience nor self-consciousness, it lacks any interest. He therefore identifies the possession of interests with the possession of experienceable preferences and desires. This can easily be concluded from the way he randomly exchanges the expression "having interests" with the expression (which he himself emphasizes) "having interests of *its own*."[18] Even more clearly, it can be concluded from the fact that he associates "interests" with the "capacity to feel pain" and the capacities "to enjoy or fail to enjoy," "to form affections and emotions," "to hope and expect," or "to suffer disappointment and frustration."[19] The truth is, however, that those who maintain that the unborn is a *person* do not identify the *nasciturus* as a person by virtue of its having desires and preferences but for its belonging to a species with a rational nature, that is, a species whose individuals are persons by virtue of the dignity they possess *qua* individuals of that species. We will return to this question presently.

(b) A contradictory theory of value

The problematic aspects of Dworkin's approach are not confined, however, to his theory of personhood but also affect his theory of value. After distinguishing between instrumental, subjective, and intrinsic values, Dworkin completely relativizes intrinsic values up to the point of rendering them wholly subjective. It is not reasonable to say that the unborn is sacred, that it has intrinsic value—that is, value *in itself* and not just *for me*—and then, immediately afterward, to completely relativize its value to the subjective assessment made by each individual. "Something is intrinsically valuable," says Dworkin, "if its value is *independent* of what people happen to enjoy or want or need or what is good for them."[20] Yet, this intrinsic value becomes precarious and subjective the moment it is made dependent on the assessment of the individual called upon to decide that value. It is no longer an intrinsic value but a subjective value, no longer a value *in itself* but a value *for me*.

In the absence of an objective truth regarding the value of the unborn, we can only appeal to subjective responsibility. As he will later do in *Justice for Hedgehogs* with the whole of his moral theory, Dworkin begins to develop in *Life's Dominion* a theory of values that does not require any correspondence with reality (*adaequatio rei*): truth as commitment with reality, as responsibility (*res sponsio*). Inasmuch as the attitude of the person who has an abortion is not manifestly and radically inconsiderate, there can be no injustice at all in having that abortion. Now, where does the intrinsic—and not merely subjective—value of the *nasciturus* lie? Dworkin's thesis starts a process of dissolution of all intrinsic values that, if consistently maintained, leads to Peter Singer's views.

At the same time, however, Dworkin accepts the legitimacy of legally censuring an abortion that evinces manifest inconsiderateness. Yet, is this position not a contradiction of Dworkin's own previously held value-relativism? Does this legal censure not entail projecting one's own estimation of value and making it valid and enforceable onto others? If the woman considers that the life of the unborn is not sacred at all—a judgment as "religious," in Dworkin's terms, as its opposite—why should we force her to take it seriously? Wouldn't that be an impingement upon her religious freedom? I think Dworkin does not consistently follow his own theory of value, which leads to a strange admixture of moral dogmatism and subjectivism. While leaving the determination of the value of life up to individual arbitrariness, he cannot resist conferring on his own assessment of the value of life an intersubjective validity. Thus, for example, he has his whole argument rest on a value estimation stated without reserve, namely, that the life of a human being that cannot presently experience desires is not "life in earnest."[21]

On the other hand, the whole ordering of "values"—which falls under the responsibility of the individual making the value assessment—is made dependent on a purportedly objective assessment criterion, namely, that of the natural and personal investments spent on a being. Yet what validity can such a criterion claim to have if, immediately afterward, we are told that the balance between values is something strictly "personal"? If we deny intersubjective validity to value assessments, how is it possible to claim such validity for the assessment criterion itself?

(c) On the classical concept of person

Let us return to the theory of person on which Dworkin supports his claim that the *nasciturus* cannot be a right holder. Against the divorce of the argument of dignity from the argument of personhood, we should begin by highlighting that, in the tradition that has handed down to us the use of the term we are dealing with, dignity constitutes above all an attribute of personhood. It is a quality denoting superiority, greatness. Originally conceived of as a social attribute, the Latin *dignitas* began to be applied to human beings for their ontological nobility, and the *nomen dignitatis* that gave expression to such sacredness of the human being was precisely the term "person."[22] The Greek term is *hypostasis*—the underlying reality or substance—and the Latin one *persona*. The classical definition was proposed by Boethius in the sixth century: "individual substance of a rational nature" (*rationalis naturae individua substantia*).[23] Given that "substance" is an ambiguous term, identifiable with "nature," Richard of Saint Victor amended the definition in the twelfth century and stated that the person should not be called substance. He explicitly reserves this *nomen dignitatis* to the bearer of the substance, to the "incommunicable existence of a rational nature."[24] In the same sense, Thomas Aquinas declares that "this name *person* is not given to signify the individual on the part of the nature, but the subsistent reality in that nature."[25] It is the person ("someone") and not an impersonal life or human nature ("something"), the reality that receives an unparalleled tribute of dignity and excellence: "person signifies what is most perfect in all nature—that is, a subsistent individual of a rational nature."[26]

To link personhood to a currently possessed attribute of human nature—for example, the current capacity to harbor desires, aspirations, or preferences— is completely alien to the tradition to which we rightly owe the concept of person. And no less alien is the dissociation of the argument of personhood and the argument of sacredness: "the word *person* includes a reference to personal dignity."[27] Dworkin seems to fully overlook the genesis of this *nomen dignitatis*. He is certainly aware, by contrast, with the fact that Thomas Aquinas considered the fetus as lacking rational soul and, therefore, as deprived of personhood. However, if we take as an established premise the current state of embryology, which allows us to see in the embryo a fully identifiable individual of the human species, it is scarcely realistic to think that Aquinas would maintain his theory of successive animation.[28] In contrast to Dworkin's suggestion, Aquinas's denial of the *status personae* to the early fetus had nothing to do with the impossibility of subsuming the unborn in the category of those who do not experience desires or preferences.

What has been said should be enough to explain the standpoint of those who defend the right to life of the *nasciturus* regardless its capacity to harbor desires and preferences. This attribution of a right to life to the *nasciturus* appeals to the personal dignity of the *nasciturus*, and it is not as recent an argument as Dworkin claims it to be. Tracing the "rights argument" to Catholic doctrine of 1980s simply contradicts well-established facts.[29] The first driving forces of the pro-life movement were civic groups formed shortly after World War II, which appealed specifically to the *right to life*; and the first associations in defense of the right to life of the *nasciturus* were created in the 1960s. The focus on the *rights* of the unborn was due to the extraordinary expansion that rights discourse experienced after World War II as a vehicle to protect human dignity. Far from being a sectarian thesis, the "argument of rights" bound together persons of diverse religions and parties in the pro-life movement.

Finally, it should also be underlined that admitting—as Dworkin does—that a "sacred" life may deserve to be sacrificed for the sake of a brilliant professional career denotes a curious conception of the sacred. For would we dare to say that a brilliant professional career is something "sacred"? Has the life of someone whose professional career has been frustrated lost sacredness or value? The attribute of being conveyed by the term "dignity" cannot be made dependent on investments subjected to a free (or partially free) assessment.

2.3. The most consistent liberal: Singer on the *nasciturus*

The way Dworkin treats the concepts of value and personhood is extremely problematic. *On the one hand*, he takes for granted that the unborn is not a person because it does not have interests, for these presuppose the current capacity to experience preferences and desires. If the unborn now had such a capacity—that is, if it were a person in Dworkin's sense—that would in Dworkin's view rule out any possible form of decriminalization of abortion. *On the other hand*, Dworkin begins by defining the sacred as a matter of intrinsic value and, immediately afterward, makes that supposedly intrinsic value dependent on the right of the individual to freely determine it. This individual right is in turn rooted in the fact of being a person, that is, in the capacity of the right holder to harbor preferences and desires. The conjunction of these ideas generates a disturbing conclusion: what is truly sacred—what really deserves unconditional respect—is not one's ontological value or dignity, as the classical theory of personal dignity holds, but the possession of interests, which amounts to the possession of desires, preferences, or aspirations. This is, in my opinion, an impeccably consistent practical application of the theoretical model of antiperfectionist liberalism, as explained in part II.

Such has been the understanding of Peter Singer. After making his name in 1975 with his work *Animal Liberation*, Singer developed the practical consequences of "preference utilitarianism" in his *Practical Ethics* (1979). During most of his academic career—until 2014, when he announced his conversion to "hedonist utilitarianism"[30]—Singer has advocated "preference utilitarianism," an ethical theory to which I shall refer in this section. Despite the controversies raised by *Practical Ethics*, its influence continued to grow to the point where, in 2005, Singer was included by *Time Magazine* among the 100 most influential people in the world. In the following pages, I will be using the third edition of his *Practical Ethics* (2010), substantially revised and updated.

As already mentioned, Singer aligned himself in this work within the philosophical stream called "preference utilitarianism." In contrast with "hedonist utilitarianism," which sets itself the goal of maximizing pleasure and minimizing pain, preference utilitarianism "holds that we should do what, on balance, furthers the preferences of those affected"[31] by our action. What has to be favored, thus, is not the highest amount of pleasure but "the interests," conceived of as preferences or desires of those affected. The key principle of his moral theory is the "principle of equal consideration of interests."[32]

Nevertheless, how is it possible to weigh conflicting interests? "The preferences that should be counted, the preference utilitarians may say, are those that we would have if we were fully informed, in a calm frame of mind and thinking clearly."[33] After this preliminary consideration, Singer suggests seeking a "universal point of view"[34] to weigh interests. What seems to be decisive in this respect is impartiality. However, impartiality does not lead Singer to distinguish mere desires and preferences from a *rational will*, as Kant and the Aristotelian-Thomistic tradition do. The ultimate criterion never ceases to be desire or subjective preference. The impartiality of this criterion consists in not extrapolating our own subjective value judgments and in calibrating all preferences or desires in terms of the "intensity" with which they are experienced.

From this viewpoint, interests—and subsequently desires—arise with sentience. "The capacity for suffering and enjoying things is a prerequisite for having interests at all, a condition that must be satisfied before we can speak of interests in any meaningful way."[35] On the basis of sentience, Singer grounds his noble project of animal liberation: we have to keep "insisting that all sentient beings, whether self-aware or not, should have basic rights."[36] The interest that every sentient being *qua* sentient being has consists in not suffering without justification. Though I will come back later to this idea, I agree with Singer on this point. The problem does not lie in the interests he endorses but in the interests he denies. For Peter Singer, rights are exclusively grounded in subjective empirical experience, be it pain or pleasure (*sentience*) or be it the experience of one's own existence (*self-awareness* or *self-consciousness*).

What is the difference between a sentient being and a self-conscious being? The difference is that "a self-conscious being is aware of itself as a distinct entity, with past and future," and this makes it "capable of having desires about its own future":

> For most mature humans, these forward-looking desires are absolutely central to our lives, so to kill a normal human against his or her wishes is to thwart that person's most significant desires. Killing a snail does not thwart any desires of this kind, because snails are incapable of having such desires.[37]

In the context of preference utilitarianism, the term "person" no longer expresses the *nomen dignitatis* that a human being, as a member of the human species, holds due to his or her rational nature. Being a "person" is something much more prosaic, namely, having desires with regard to one's existence. This—and not the intrinsic dignity of the human being—is the basis of the right to life:

> According to preference utilitarianism, an action contrary to the preference of any being is wrong, unless this preference is outweighed by contrary preferences. Killing a person who prefers to continue living is therefore wrong, other things being equal. . . . The wrong is done when the preference is thwarted.[38]

Singer reiterates the foundation of the right to life in individual desires by quoting Michael Tooley, who explicitly declares the existence of "a conceptual connection between the desires that a being is capable of having and the rights that the being can be said to have."[39] This right to life is certainly not an absolute right: it may yield to other interests "if a person's desire to go on living is outweighed by the equally strong desires of others."[40] The only thing demanded of us is equal consideration for all desires. The practical consequences of Singer's theory are easily predictable, and in what follows I indicate only some of them:

(a) Arising and developing through self-awareness, personhood is a matter of *degree*, and the extent of its individual development corresponds to different degrees in its claim to be respected. Its foundation is therefore not "ontological" but depends on a scale of possible experiences according to a higher or lower mental life: "the more highly developed the mental life of the being, the greater the degree of self-awareness and rationality and the broader the range of possible experiences, the more one would prefer that kind of life, if one were choosing between it and a being at a lower level of awareness."[41]

(b) The interests—and therefore the rights—of a severely handicapped person with serious brain damage are lower and deserve less respect than those of a fully developed animal. If the handicapped person does not realize what is happening around them and is an orphan lacking people affectively attached to them, the act of killing them in order to perform experiments on their body would not violate anyone's rights and could improve the life of many.[42]

(c) Just as killing a severely handicapped person who lacks desires regarding their own existence is not wrong, neither is killing an unborn or an infant. Singer does not hesitate to question most of the liberal arguments usually given in favor of the right to have an abortion. Thus, for example, he challenges the criterion fixed in *Roe v. Wade* of the *incapability* of the fetus of living outside the mother's womb, for this is something that depends on technical development—and it would be nonsensical to make the moral *status* of the fetus dependent on something like technical development. Equally irrelevant is the criterion of the *dependence* of the fetus with respect to the mother, for dependence on others is common to many—not to say all—human beings. As for the idea of *privacy*, that cannot justify a right to abortion unless we have a prior argument depriving the fetus of the condition of "victim."[43] The only consistent criterion in which to ground a right to abortion is that *the right to life is based on the desire to be kept alive*, a desire that neither the unborn nor the recently born infant can harbor. Quoting a famous statement by Jeremy Bentham, Singer describes infanticide as "of a nature not to give the slightest inquietude to the most timid imagination."[44]

2.4. The background problem

(a) From ateleological liberalism to preference utilitarianism

The conclusions derived from Singer's reasoning have led many people to see his arguments a mere *reductio ad absurdum* that discredits the abstract premises on which it rests. Yet he considers that the difficulties we find in accepting his conclusions are due to our own unenlightened sensibility, which gets confused by trying to confer universal validity on our own estimations of what is sacred. While, for Dworkin, the freedom to assess the value of life is subject to certain restrictions derived from some previous objective estimations—substantially, the demand for a certain responsibility in the decision to have an abortion—Singer avoids falling into the inconsistency of universalizing *some* of his own value judgments and fearlessly draws the conclusions. If our assessment must be impartial, we have to see *all* our value judgments from an external point of view and consider them as mere *subjective impressions of a particular intensity*. Thus, he consistently concludes that (a) the supreme moral principle is the principle of equal consideration of all desires and interests; (b) rights correspond to desires, and they are therefore coextensive with sentience; (c) the right to life is linked to the possibility of having desires regarding one's own existence.

Obviously, the fact that Singer is consistent with the above-mentioned liberal premise does not mean that his theory lacks any inconsistency. As happens with Bentham's utilitarianism, we could argue against Singer that there are innumerable desires and interests that not only differ in intensity but, being mutually incommensurable, cannot be compared using the same unit of measurement.[45] Besides, we should also note that, strictly speaking, a radically impartial point of view, independent from any value judgment, would require us to deny intersubjective validity to the judgment we make about the conduct of those who consider they do not have to behave ethically. Under Singer's standards, those who behave ethically are simply following a preference, in exactly the same way as those who do not behave ethically. In condemning those who do not behave ethically, we are also just following a preference, and there is no reason why we could give it intersubjective validity. "We never advance a step beyond ourselves," as Hume said. If moral truth is just a negative criterion like impartiality toward any preference and value assessment, why not be impartial between one who behaves "ethically" and another who does not?

(b) An empiricist theory of the person

Finally, Singer's theses are profoundly counterintuitive not only in their conclusions but also in some of their premises. In particular, his theory of the person is taken from a counterintuitive thesis of empiricist philosopher John Locke, who reduces personality to actual self-consciousness, up to the point of exempting one from responsibility regarding unremembered actions.[46] Against Peter Singer, it has been noted that, since the embryo is a fully identifiable individual of the human species, it *eo ipso* has the rational nature which corresponds to this species. The fact that its nature requires time in order to actualize and that its powers are not exercisable from the moment of conception does not mean that it lacks a rational nature.[47] Its nature does not disappear in order to give rise to a new one but, from its initial embryonic stages, the human being actualizes "the minted form that lives and living grows"[48]—as Goethe defined the *entelecheia*, that is, the being that bears an imprinted *telos* toward which it tends.

According to Singer's view, it would be more suitable to our own perception of facts to say that the embryo does not have a rational nature but the potential to acquire a rational nature. That this idea is simply alien to our perception of reality may be proved by the first-person singular way in which we refer both to our infant unconscious past and our eventual senile future. Singer's position, however, seems to close itself off from the experience of the continuity of the subject through time, an exclusion based on an atomist conceptualization of reality that he also inherits from Locke's empiricism. In effect, Locke abandons the classical explanation of motion as the actualization of potentiality and mathematically interprets motion as an infinite succession of discrete events, identical with themselves.[49] But the truth is that we cannot reduce the idea of motion to this sequence of events. Being identical with themselves, those discrete events could not be in motion. The idea of "motion" requires introducing the concepts of anticipation and potentiality.[50]

To conclude, we should recognize in Singer's work a positive contribution to the concern that sentient beings deserve. The capacity of a being to experience pain certainly makes it a holder of interests and worthy of treatment according to its nature, and human beings bear some responsibility in this regard. As such, the development of a social consciousness toward the interests of animals is praiseworthy. However, the gap that we can appreciate between the basic self-consciousness shown by certain mammals and the human being's deep reflexivity seems to be more than a mere difference of degree. The departure from instinctive self-referentiality in the human being gives rise to freedom to judge about his ends and bestows a biographical and transcendent meaning on his existence. Biographical and transcendent consciousness leads the person to objectify his life from the outside, to confer a meaning upon his life that cannot be reduced—as in Singer—to the level of mere subjective desires. It is precisely this biographical meaning of existence that opens the horizon of the ethical perspective—that is, the perspective of life as a whole, of the right life, or the life that turns out well.

3. UNDESIRABLE LIFE

Having explained the "dehumanization" produced by the exclusion of human beings who lack the capacity to experience conscious desires from the protection of rights, in this section we will briefly comment on a "human right" that "antiperfectionist liberalism" has been trying to have recognized in recent years: the right to assisted suicide. In some Western legal systems, for example, the German, euthanasia has been taboo for some time due to the Nazi doctrine and practice of the "life unworthy of life" (*lebensunwertes Leben*). In several other Western legal systems, however, assisted suicide is already an established practice.[51] In the following pages, I will comment on the presence of this right in human rights case law, on the arguments raised in favor of this right, and on the serious risks that it creates.

3.1. Assisted suicide in rights jurisprudence

In the field of fundamental rights, the leading case of U.S. Supreme Court jurisprudence on euthanasia was *Cruzan v. Director, Missouri Department of Health* (1990), in which the majority of the court held that the requirement for clear and convincing evidence of the patient's will in order to withdraw his life support was legitimate.[52] Seven years later, in *Washington v. Glucksberg* and *Vacco v. Quill*,[53] the Supreme Court was directly confronted with the question of whether the due process clause of the Fifth Amendment included a right to assisted suicide. The decisions concerned statutes banning assisted suicide in the states of Washington and New York. Obviously, both cases had deep public repercussions and, among the opinions that accompanied the decisions, what came to be labeled *The Philosopher's Brief* had a very notable impact. Submitted to the Supreme Court by the *amici curiae* Ronald Dworkin, Thomas Nagel, Robert Nozick, John Rawls, Thomas Scanlon, and Judith Jarvis Thomson, the brief defended the existence of a fundamental right to assisted suicide.[54] In a unanimous decision, however, the court declared that such a right does not exist. Nonetheless, in 2006, in the important *Gonzales v. Oregon* case, the majority of the Supreme Court[55] held it as unconstitutional for the U.S. attorney general to invoke his powers upon controlled substances to impede the use of drugs for assisted suicide purposes when such drugs were not *per se* unlawful and their use had been approved by the state.

The European Court of Human Rights has gone beyond the U.S. Supreme Court in paving the way toward a right to assisted suicide. In a landmark decision in 2002,[56] the court explicitly held that the right to life enshrined in Article 2 of the Convention does not include a right to take one's own life. More recently still, in *Haas v. Switzerland* (January 20, 2011), the court advanced a clear step in the evolution toward a right to euthanasia. On the basis of the right to privacy (Article 8 of the European Convention of Human Rights), this decision considered the legitimacy of the denial by the Swiss authorities of a prescription necessary to obtain a substance that the appellant wanted to consume in order to commit assisted suicide. The Strasbourg Court held that, given the lack of consensus among the member states of the Convention with regard to assisted suicide, the right could not be considered violated. Nevertheless, it declared that "an individual's right to decide by what means and at what point his or her life will end, provided he or she is capable of freely reaching a decision on this question and acting in consequence, is one of the aspects of the right to respect for private life within the meaning of Article 8 of the Convention."[57]

In *Koch v. Germany* (July 19, 2012), the court issued a decision with respect to the request of a man whose spouse, suffering intense pain, had asked the public authority for permission to obtain a lethal dose of a substance. After several unfruitful attempts to obtain authorization in Germany, the couple went to Switzerland, where the woman was able to obtain the drug and committed suicide. Subsequently, the appellant tried to obtain a statement from the German administrative courts declaring the unlawfulness of the prior denial of permission to acquire the substance. After his lawsuit was declared inadmissible, and after unsuccessful appeals before the ordinary courts and the Federal Constitutional Court, the man filed an application before the Strasbourg Court alleging a violation of his right to private life. In this case, the European Court of Human Rights declared that assisted suicide is a legitimate interest covered by the right to privacy, and that his case should therefore had been examined by the national judicial organs. Strictly speaking, the European Court has not declared the existence of a human right to assisted suicide. For all that, it is important to note that the fact that the ECtHR considers assisted suicide to be a legitimate interest *prima facie* protected by Article 8 may be seen as the preamble to the creation of such a right.

A final case deserving our consideration is the *Gross v. Switzerland* decision of September 30, 2014. Again, the process began with the Swiss authorities' denial of permission to obtain a lethal substance to an old woman who—though not being seriously ill and not suffering severe pain—wanted to commit suicide. In line with its previous case law, the Court held that the mere wish to commit suicide falls within the *prima facie* content of the right to private life, and that the assistance to commit suicide constitutes part of the *prima facie* content of the positive obligations of the state concerning this right. In a close vote (4–3), the Court found a violation of the right to privacy due to the lack of a clear regulation on the matter.[58] The decision was appealed to the Great Chamber, and it was proved during the process that the woman had obtained her medical prescription in 2011 and committed suicide, a fact that had hitherto been hidden to the Court. Consequently, the Great Chamber declared the issue inadmissible for abuse of the right of an application.

3.2. The superfluous principle

The cases above show a progressive advancement toward the creation of a human right to suicide and assisted suicide. In the philosophical-political field, this right was promoted by liberal antiperfectionist thought, whose arguments I will examine in these pages. Nevertheless, first I would like to recall the framework with which this book opened.

That life has ceased to be ruled by a rationally recognizable mode of human fulfillment means that the desire principle and the reality principle—keeping the drives within the limits set by self-preservation—are no longer ruled by such rational *telos*. Thus, the reality principle has a function that is wholly subordinated to the desire principle. It is, as we have seen, the giving up of an immediate desire for the sake of satisfying future desires and aspirations.[59] Once life descends below a certain level of possible satisfactions—a level that has to be determined by the individual whose life is at issue—self-preservation cannot have any further normative value, and it thus ceases to have meaning, as Nietzsche pointedly saw:

> Physiologists should think twice before positioning the drive for self-preservation as the cardinal drive of an organic being. Above all, a living thing wants to *discharge* its strength—life itself is will to power—: self-preservation is only one of the indirect and most frequent *consequences* of this. —In short, here and elsewhere, watch out for *superfluous* teleological principles!—such as the drive for preservation.[60]

Once self-preservation ceases to contribute to a thriving biological state, a life rich in desires and satisfactions, it becomes meaningless. In the case of Nietzsche, the lack of meaning reaches the point of defending suicide as a sort of moral duty:

> A sick person is a parasite on society. Once one has reached a certain state it is indecent to live any longer. Vegetating on in cowardly dependence on physicians and their methods, once the meaning of life, the *right* to life has been lost, should be greeted with society's profound contempt.[61]

Fortunately, most of the people who defend the right to assisted suicide would oppose Nietzsche's words. They defend it only as a fundamental right not as a moral duty. I think, however, that we should take very seriously something I have been pointing out throughout this book with different arguments—namely, that political abstention with regard to the question of the good life is *indifferent* but not *neutral*. By endorsing assisted suicide as a right, the state would be lifting the barriers so that individuals and groups could struggle for the social recognition of their own preferences and judgments regarding which lives are worthy or unworthy.

3.3. Antiperfectionist liberalism and the defense of a right to assisted suicide

It is not necessary to give a detailed account of Dworkin's arguments in favor of a right to euthanasia, since they are the same as his arguments in favor of a right to abortion. The right to determine the value of life "before life in earnest has even begun" turns into a right to abortion (a right to kill); the right to determine the value of life "after life in earnest has ended" turns into a right to death (a right to be killed).[62] The state should abstain from imposing its own vision in this respect.

In fact, this thesis is based on a non-neutral proposal about what a "life in earnest" is and is not. Dworkin himself partially quotes Nietztsche's above-cited paragraph as a legitimate and respectable judgment on euthanasia: "in a certain state it is indecent to live longer."[63] Yet in doing so he omits the sentence with which Nietzsche opens his statement: "A sick person is a parasite on society" (*der Kranke ist ein Parasit der Gesellschaft*). If this view—considered by Dworkin's ateleological liberalism to be just one relative opinion among many—were to spread, an atmosphere of social pressure upon the terminally ill could be created, and such a pressure would jeopardize their legitimate belief in their own lives as something sacred.

As with abortion, Peter Singer has concluded the task begun by more orthodox ateleological liberalism of reducing value judgments to subjective preferences. Since the very meaning of a "dignified death" is under dispute, Singer refuses to use this term, which is colored with confusing moral implications. Instead, he proposes to leave behind the negative connotations of the strictly descriptive term "suicide."[64] From a strict application of the principle of equal consideration of desires and preferences—a principle that, in its abstract formulation, is also at the basis of Dworkin's political philosophy—opposing the right to freely commit suicide would be nonsensical.[65] Therefore, the true dilemma for Singer would not be voluntary euthanasia; it would be the nonvoluntary euthanasia of persons whose capacity to consent is restricted. In previous paragraphs, we have already seen that, from Singer's conception of the person, sentient beings lacking self-awareness also lack the right to life. We find here a new question: what happens with those sentient, non-self-conscious beings whose life is marked by pain? Is it possible to maintain that such a life is not worth living? Could this be maintained even in the absence of an express declaration of will by the subject whose life is at issue? Singer's answer is affirmative: a life marked by pain is not worth living, with the result that infanticide or euthanasia of severely handicapped human beings is not simply a right but a moral duty. "When the life of an infant will be so miserable as not be worth living, from the internal perspective of the being who will lead that life," utilitarianism entails "that if there are no 'extrinsic' reasons for keeping the infant alive—like the feelings of the parents—it is better that the child should be helped to die without further suffering."[66]

As I have been arguing, Singer's approach brings to a logical terminus liberal skepticism regarding human teleology and, at the same time, reveals with full clarity the dialectic implicit in this ideology. On the one hand, the reduction of all value judgments to subjective preferences leads him to exclude them, for the sake of consistency, from his discourse justifying euthanasia. Terms like "dignity" no longer represent a metaphysical requirement of reality, a transcendental quality of being demanding unconditional respect. Once these expressions cease to have anything to say about reality and only speak of the subjective preferences of the subject who uses them, it would be nonsensical to deploy them in order to justify an intersubjectively valid ethical discourse.

Once the objective validity of value judgments has been suppressed, Singer says, the justificatory discourse on euthanasia should search for an impersonal and impartial criterion. Such a role is played by the principle of equal consideration of all interests and preferences. Following this criterion, freely decided assisted suicide should be accepted. Yet, what are the preferences of those human beings who cannot express them? Here arises the true problem, for no one lacking an objective teleological criterion regarding what we ultimately want can answer this question. By setting himself up as a judge of which lives are worth living and which not, Singer simply extrapolates his own subjective preferences onto other people's lives. Again, the implicit dialectic of antiperfectionist liberalism is fulfilled: he who initially denied any validity to value judgments regarding the worthy and unworthy life ends up imposing his own value judgment that a life in pain is not worth living. It is, in the strictest and most rigorous sense, *lebensunwertes Leben*.

3.4. Conclusion: Euthanasia, dignified death, and therapeutic obstinacy

The scope of my analysis has been a supposed right to assisted suicide endorsed in different contexts during recent years. A more exhaustive treatment of the problem should also take into account so-called passive euthanasia, that is, the voluntary death produced as a consequence of the rejection of medical care that would keep the patient alive. Consequentialist authors like Peter Singer maintain the general irrelevance of the distinction between killing and letting die.[67] And in many cases, the difference is actually irrelevant. By way of example, denying a baby food and shelter is tantamount to killing it. Nevertheless, it seems that this omission cannot be equated to letting die a terminally ill person who would otherwise be kept alive in an irreversible vegetative state by a machine. Once more, the understanding of the teleological nature of life is indispensable to perceiving the difference between a life "whose time has come" and a life that must be maintained. In the words of Spaemann, "The nature of man, the impulse by which his 'ecological niche' is defined, grounds something like a basal normality of what we owe him, in such a way that denying him what we owe him is the same as causing him death."[68] It does not seem reasonable to understand life eschewing this perspective, and it does not seem possible to build a true ethical line of thought while ignoring the facts provided by biology. There are, of course, extreme cases where it is not clear whether leaving events to take their course is "killing" or "letting die." In such situations, the decision of the closest relatives and of the medical doctors should play a critical role, but creating a human right to suicide is a very different thing.

It also seems unreasonable to base a human right to assisted suicide on the traditional irrelevance of suicide. The legal irrelevance of attempted suicide was based on the private nature of this crime. With regard to the damages caused to third parties through this conduct, it was thought that the damage produced against oneself—the so-called *poena naturalis*—was enough punishment. Consistent with this approach, suicide has never generated public approval but quite the opposite. By contrast, legalizing assisted suicide entails a public statement on what constitutes or does not constitute "life in earnest," as Ronald Dworkin affirms. To the extent that this is a public judgment, it involves crosscutting implications for the whole of society, consequences that may reach every public domain, from public education to the practice of physicians and public servants. What was initially defended as a liberty may end up becoming an exercise of pressure on the "social parasites" that Nietzsche was talking about, who would be compelled to stop interfering in the "life in earnest" of their caregivers. Finally, the freedom of conscience of dissenters will also come under threat, especially if they hold positions from which they are called to cooperate in practices of assisted suicide.

NOTES

1. 410 US 158 (1973). See, from the same day, *Doe v. Bolton*, 410 US 179 (1973). See also the substantial confirmation of *Roe v. Wade* in *Planned Parenthood v. Casey*, 505 US 833 (1992). In *Stenberg v. Carhart*, 510 US 914 (2000), the Supreme Court declared contrary to the right to privacy the prohibition of the so-called partial-birth abortion, a method by which part of the fetus is extracted before killing it. In *Gonzalez v. Carhart*, 550 US 124 (2007), the court departed from this precedent and upheld the federal ban of partial-birth abortion.

2. See ECtHR *Open Door and Dublin Well Woman v. Ireland*, June 29, 1992; *Vo v. France*, July 8, 2004; *Tysiac v. Poland*, March 20, 2007; *A. B. C. v. Ireland*, December 16, 2010; and *P. and S. v. Poland*, 30 October 2012.

3. See FCC 39, 1 (*Abtreibung I*), February 25, 1975; FCC 88, 203 (*Abtreibung II*), May 28, 1993. See, in a similar vein, for example, the Spanish CCJ 53/1985, July 5, 1985.

4. Dworkin, *Life's Dominion*, p. xi.

5. Dworkin, *Life's Dominion*, p. 11.
6. Dworkin, *Life's Dominion*, p. 14.
7. Dworkin, *Life's Dominion*, p. 15.
8. Dworkin, *Life's Dominion*, p. 16 (emphasis in the original).
9. Dworkin, *Life's Dominion*, p. 17–18. This coincidence between Dworkin and Singer has also been noted, for example, by Kramer, *Liberalism with Excellence*, pp. 135 ff.
10. Dworkin, *Life's Dominion*, pp. 39–50.
11. Dworkin, *Life's Dominion*, pp. 71 ff.
12. Dworkin, *Life's Dominion*, p. 74.
13. Dworkin, *Life's Dominion*, p. 78.
14. Dworkin, *Life's Dominion*, p. 99.
15. Dworkin, *Life's Dominion*, pp. 89 ff.
16. Dworkin, *Life's Dominion*, p. 179.
17. On the detachment of the questions regarding value and sacredness—the proper scope of "religion," in Dworkin's opinion—from the idea of God, see Dworkin's posthumously published lectures: *Religion without God* (Cambridge, MA: Harvard University Press, 2013). See also R. Domingo's critique in "Religion for Hedgehogs? An Argument against the Dworkinian Approach of Religious Freedom," *Oxford Journal of Law and Religion* 2, 2 (2013): 371–92.
18. Dworkin, *Life's Dominion*, p. 16.
19. Dworkin, *Life's Dominion*, p. 17–18.
20. Dworkin, *Life's Dominion*, p. 71.
21. Dworkin, *Life's Dominion*, p. 179.
22. The term comes from the Etruscan *phersu* ("mask"), which in turn comes from the Greek *prosopon*. In the theater, *propopon* was the mask behind which the actor concealed his face. In the Latin language, the term *persona* ceased to refer to the actor's mask and began to identify his own role in the play: *dramatis personae*. The philologists from Alexandria employed the term to distinguish three forms of speech—first, second, and third person—and Roman jurisprudence for the first time applied the term to the human subject. With the development of Christian theology, the concept of person was refined and acquired its current common meaning. On the genesis and development of this concept, see Spaemann, *Persons*, pp. 17–33.
23. "Persona est naturae rationalis individua substantia" (Severinus Boetius, *Contra Eutychen et Nestorium*, III [*Differentiae naturae et personae*]).
24. "Naturae rationalis incommunicabilis existentia" (R. Saint Victor, *De Trinitate*, 4, 23).
25. "Hoc autem nomen 'persona' non est impositum ad significandum individuum ex parte naturae, sed ad significandum rem subsistentem in tali natura" (*S. Th.*, I, q. 30, a. 4).
26. "persona significat id quod est perfectissimum in tota natura, scilicet subsistens in rationali natura" (*S. Th.*, I, q. 29, a. 3).
27. "in nomine enim 'personae' intelligitur personae dignitas" (*S. Th.*, II-II, q. 63, a. 1).
28. The Thomistic explanation is developed in *S. Th.*, I, q. 118. It may be useful to compare the primitive embryology presupposed in the *Summa* with the facts provided,

for instance, by two contemporary Thomists as R. P. George and C. Tollefsen in *Embryo* (New York: Doubleday, 2008) pp. 27–56 ("The Facts of Embryology").

29. See, in this vein, the careful work by D. K. Williams, *Defenders of the Unborn. The Pro-Life Movement before* Roe v. Wade (New York: Oxford University Press, 2016), pp. 4 ff., 37 ff.

30. Katarzyna de Lazari-Radek and Peter Singer, *The Point of View of the Universe: Sidgwick and Contemporary Ethics* (Oxford: Oxford University Press, 2014).

31. Singer, *Practical Ethics*, 3rd ed. (Cambridge: Cambridge University Press, 2010), p. 13.

32. Singer, *Practical Ethics*, p. 20.
33. Singer, *Practical Ethics*, p. 14.
34. Singer, *Practical Ethics*, p. 21.
35. Singer, *Practical Ethics*, p. 50.
36. Singer, *Practical Ethics*, p. 67.
37. Singer, *Practical Ethics*, pp. 76–77.
38. Singer, *Practical Ethics*, p. 80.
39. Singer, *Practical Ethics*, p. 81.
40. Singer, *Practical Ethics*, p. 84.
41. Singer, *Practical Ethics*, p. 92.
42. Singer, *Practical Ethics*, p. 58.
43. Singer, *Practical Ethics*, pp. 126 ff.

44. Singer, *Practical Ethics*, p. 152. See also Jeremy Bentham, *Theory of Legislation* (London: Trübner, 1864), p. 265: "The offence is what is improperly called the death of an infant, who has ceased to be, before knowing what existence is—a result of a nature not to give the slightest inquietude to the most timid imagination; and which can cause no regrets but to the very person who, through a sentiment of shame and pity, has refused to prolong a life begun under the auspices of misery."

45. On utilitarianism and incommensurability, see Finnis, *Fundamentals of Ethics*, pp. 86–90.

46. J. Locke, *An Essay Concerning Human Understanding* (1690), Book II, chapter 27, pars. 6 ff. (ed. Wordsworth, Hertfordshire, 1998, pp. 211 ff.).

47. R. P. George and P. Lee, *Body-Self Dualism in Contemporary Ethics and Politic* (Cambridge: Cambridge University Press 2008), pp. 81–94.

48. "Geprägte Form, die lebend sich entwickelt" (Goethe, *Orphisch*, ΔAIMΩN, *Dämon*).

49. Locke, *An Essay Concerning Human Understanding*, Book II, chapter 27, pars. 9 ff.

50. See, in this vein, Spaemann, *Persons*, pp. 138–43.

51. For example, the Netherlands, Belgium, Luxembourg, Switzerland, or Colombia. In the United States, assisted suicide is legal, *v. gr.*, in California, Oregon, Vermont, Washington, and Montana.

52. 497 US 261 (1990).
53. 521 US 793 (1997).

54. *Amici curiae* Ronald Dworkin, Thomas Nagel, Robert Nozick, John Rawls, Thomas Scanlon, and Judith Jarvis Thomson, *State of Washington et al. v. Glucksberg et al.* and *Vacco et al. v. Quill et al.*, of January 8, 1997.

55. 546 US 243 (2006).
56. ECtHR *Pretty c. Reino Unido*, April 29, 2002.
57. ECtHR *Haas v. Switzerland*, January 20, 2011, § 51.
58. ECtHR *Gross v. Switzerland*, May 11, 2013, § 67.
59. Freud, "Formulations on the Two Principles of Mental Functioning," p. 223.
60. F. Nietzsche, *Jenseits von Gut und Böse. Vorspiel einer Philosophie der Zukunft*, in *Sämtliche Werke*, 9 (Berlin: Walter de Gruyter, 1988), pp. 27–28 (§ 13); *Beyond Good and Evil* (Cambridge: Cambridge University Press, 2002), p. 15.
61. F. Nietzsche, *Götzen-Dämerung oder Wie Man mit dem Hammer philosophirt*, in *Sämtliche Werke*, 9 (Berlin: Walter de Gruyter, 1988), p. 134 (IX § 36); *Twilight of the Idols or How to Philosophize with a Hammer* (Oxford: Oxford University Press, 1998).
62. Dworkin, *Life's Dominion*, p. 179.
63. Dworkin, *Life's Dominion*, p. 212.
64. Singer, *Practical Ethics*, p. 156.
65. Singer, *Practical Ethics*, pp. 169–76.
66. Singer, *Practical Ethics*, p. 162.
67. Singer, *Practical Ethics*, pp. 178–86.
68. R. Spaemann, "Die Euthanasiedebatte. Wir dürfen das Tabu nicht aufgeben," in *Die Zeit*, June 12, 1992.

Chapter 8

Playing God? Promethean desires

1. INTRODUCTION

To conclude part III, I shall refer to a practice proposed by ateleological liberalism that leads to unprecedented possibilities of expansion of the desire principle: so-called liberal eugenics.[1] Until less than two decades ago, the concept of eugenics—race improvement by favoring selective propagation—was taboo, associated with some of the darkest periods of modern history. It is no accident that in 1925 Hitler characterized planned and systematic sterilization of the disabled with eugenic purposes as "the most humane act of mankind."[2] Once in power, the German tyrant would implement his eugenic purposes through sterilization laws.

Nevertheless, modern eugenics did not begin with Hitler, already having close ties with the pragmatic mentality of certain Anglo-American circles of the late nineteenth and early twentieth centuries. The term was coined in 1883 by Francis Galton, and eugenics programs began to spread at the beginning of the twentieth century in the United States. In 1927, the celebrated Justice of the U.S. Supreme Court, Oliver Wendell Holmes, justified the sterilization of the disabled in *Buck v. Bell* by arguing that "three generations of imbeciles are enough."[3]

With these connotations of contempt for the less gifted, eugenics has enjoyed little favor among the intellectual elites until very recently. In recent years, the debate has intensified due to the progress of biotechnologies, which have opened new prospects with respect to the possibility of "designing" the features of progeny and augmenting their potentialities. This practice has been defended by the main proponents of liberal antiperfectionism—Rawls,[4] Dworkin[5]—and, as has been indicated, the term "liberal eugenics" has even been coined in order to distinguish eugenics as a "choice"—and therefore legitimate—from the old, coercively imposed eugenics:

> Nazi eugenicists would have used these technologies to dramatically curtail reproductive choice. Only a narrow range of human beings would have been deemed worthy of cloning; genetic engineering would have been imposed on couples whose reproductive efforts were deemed incapable of producing children sufficiently close to the Nazi ideal. But liberal eugenicists propose that these same technologies be used to dramatically enlarge reproductive choice. Prospective parents may ask genetic engineers to introduce into their embryos combinations of genes that correspond with their particular conception of good life.[6]

Far from being peacefully accepted, however, liberal eugenics has met opposition from prominent intellectuals, among them some sharp critics of liberal antiperfectionism such as Leon Kass,[7] Michael Sandel,[8] and Francis Fukuyama.[9] Finally, the renowned European philosopher Jürgen Habermas has also raised serious objections to nontherapeutic eugenics—that is, eugenics with the sole purpose of human enhancement.

In this chapter, I will critically assess the arguments of both sides of the debate. I think that this debate is particularly significant, since it clearly shows the consequences derived from two different ways of thinking. From the perspective of ateleological liberalism, the opinion is held that, from a strictly normative point of view, "nature—to put it in the words of Condorcet—has fixed no limits to our hopes" (desire principle):

> *In fine*, may it not be expected that the human race will be meliorated . . . by the real improvement of our faculties, moral intellectual and physical, which may be the result either of the improvement of the instruments which increase the power and direct the exercise of those faculties, or the improvement of our natural organization itself?[10]

In contrast with this view, the heirs of the classical, teleological tradition maintain that practical reason is able to immediately associate normative implications with nature. The reciprocal critiques and refutations of the arguments held by the different parties bring to light the difficulty in reconciling the competing positions in this debate. I will now try to faithfully reproduce the different arguments and defend the more humane character, also in this respect, of a political practice anchored in a teleological conception of the human being.

2. THE THESIS OF ANTIPERFECTIONIST LIBERALISM

The initial premise of antiperfectionist liberalism is that discrimination between better or worse ways of life cannot be politically established, and that the state's role therefore lies in ensuring for everybody what Rawls calls "primary goods," namely, useful goods capable of helping in the realization of whatever life project one wishes to pursue.[11] The enhancement of individual capacities would be an essential part of the state's mission in nonperfectionist liberal society. The increase of the individual's physical abilities constitutes a primary good, for it entails an empowerment to develop one's life project. Genetic design or manipulation constitutes an effective means of carrying out such an increase, so it is not only an unobjectionable but a beneficial action.

Thus, eugenics is—whenever freely chosen—a good. The role of the liberal state in this regard is nothing more than to foster research and development in this field—for it leads to an increase of primary goods—and to remain neutral with respect to individual eugenic choices, without either banning or imposing them. Eugenic choices must be guided by the particular conceptions of the parents regarding the good life, and they are directed at the enhancement of their children.[12] In Dworkin's words, it would be plausible to consider these choices an inherent faculty of the "fundamental human right" to "reproductive freedom."[13]

Finally, the fact that eugenics may have negative consequences would not entail a principled objection to it but a challenge and a call to make decisions about the right way to put it into practice. The quandary between a decision for or against eugenics would be sterile and should be therefore overcome. Instead, the community should focus its efforts on reflecting upon the best way to regulate eugenics in order to avoid damages to future generations.[14]

3. THE "INTERNAL CRITIQUE"

The first objection to liberal eugenics is an internal criticism, one "from within": namely, the already discussed lack of neutrality of antiperfectionist liberalism. Again in this case it fails to fulfill its promises. By considering eugenics as a primary good, and therefore desirable regardless of particular individual conceptions of the good life, the proponents of liberal eugenics—Rawls, Dworkin, Agar, Buchanan et al.—defend it as a collective enterprise and not simply as an individual decision. Only the decision to proceed to a specific eugenic practice is left to the parents, but the financial sources devoted to eugenic practices would, at least in part, come from the whole community. Rawls, for example, conceives of eugenics through genetic design not as a right but as an authentic obligation toward future generations. In *A Theory of Justice*, he affirms,

> In addition, it is possible to adopt eugenic policies, more or less explicit ... it is also in the interest of each to have greater natural assets. This enables him to

pursue a preferred plan of life. In the original position, then, the parties want to insure for their descendants the best genetic endowment (assuming their own to be fixed). The pursuit of reasonable policies in this regard is something that earlier generations owe to later ones, this being a question that arises between generations. Thus over time a society is to take steps at least to preserve the general level of natural abilities and to prevent the diffusion of serious defects.[15]

With this thesis, Rawls overlooks the possibility of a conflict between eugenic practices aiming at the maximization of primary goods, on the one hand, and the conception of the good life held by some citizens, on the other. In the above statement, we can again see something that we emphasized in our criticism to Rawls in the chapter 3, namely that the primary goods are not neutral, and that they may strongly conflict with many conceptions of the good life. Treating eugenics as a duty owed to future generations by preceding ones is the same as endorsing the increase of primary goods as a form of good life that the entire society should embrace, even at the expense of sacrificing alternative forms of the good life.

This lack of neutrality is equally clear in Ronald Dworkin's arguments. Dworkin insists that "the first principle of ethical individualism" commands "struggling to improve our species," and the "second principle forbids, in the absence of positive evidence of danger, hobbling the scientists and doctors who volunteer to lead it."[16] As in Rawls's *Theory of Justice*, liberal eugenics constitutes a collective enterprise that we must undertake, regardless of the existence of opposing visions.

In Dworkin's approach, an additional inconsistency is added, in part due to his own theory of equality. The value-neutrality that the state is bound to maintain while deciding whether a practice—in this case eugenics—may be banned does not prevent him from asserting a public duty to fund decisions that may conflict with the life projects of taxpayers. In his opinion, equality—the "sovereign virtue"—requires socializing, through a national health service, the cost of genetic engineering treatment, with the insurance being paid by all of the citizens, taking into account their present tastes and ambitions, the average wealth now found in that society, as well as full, state-of-the-art information about what benefits genetic engineering might bring them and what the cost of the insurance to provide it in those circumstances would be.[17]

On the one hand, liberal neutrality prevents the state from banning activities—in this case, eugenic activities—on the basis of a particular conception of the good life. *On the other hand*, equality demands that all citizens fund those activities if they are in fact extended social practices. The question must then inevitably be asked: if it is illicit to impinge upon a person's freedom to act or abstain from acting in accordance with a particular belief by an appeal to what the citizens think or do, how could it be legitimate to impinge upon this same freedom by demanding that person fund social benefits on the basis that the citizens are ready to cover them with an insurance? As anticipated in chapter 6, consistency should lead Dworkin to a more libertarian thesis, such as that of Robert Nozick, who—on this issue—advocated for a "genetic supermarket"[18] and not for publicly funded eugenics.

Finally, the public acceptance of eugenic practices is hardly compatible with the private freedom to criticize them as immoral. Little by little, such criticism would come to be considered discriminatory and irrational and would even be publicly condemned as a sort of "hate speech" against genetically manipulated individuals. Indeed, some of the staunchest proponents of liberal eugenics, such as Nicholas Agar or Allen Buchanan, do not hesitate to link the moral repugnance of those who oppose genetic manipulation to prejudice and discrimination.[19] Regardless of who is right in the background debate, it seems difficult to accept that, once the social acceptance of eugenics spread, liberal neutrality could allow its critics to peacefully defend their postulates. And the same would happen the other way around. The result, in any case, would not be neutral.

4. HABERMAS'S CRITIQUE AND THE LIBERAL RESPONSE

4.1. Habermas against the reification of the human being

The purpose of the "internal criticism" described above is to evince the lack of value-neutrality in liberal eugenics. In contrast to the classical teleology of the good life (which is denied), the increase of "primary goods" is endorsed as a sort of "ateleological teleology" that everybody should wish for, and eugenic enhancement constitutes the means by which such an increase in primary goods is attained.

One of the best-known criticisms of the liberal eugenics project has been formulated by Jürgen Habermas, whose discourse philosophy has already been examined in chapter 5. Habermas's criticism has a very special value given that it shows, on the one hand, how alien the design of human beings is to our simple moral intuitions; and on the other, how difficult it is to oppose eugenics with mere liberal-ateleological reasons.

First, Habermas gives great importance to the human reification involved in genetic manipulation. Faced with the progress made by biotechnology, he finds it "unsettling" that "the dividing line between the nature we are and the organic equipment we give ourselves is being blurred."[20] To a great extent, Habermas's concern is the same as that shown by eugenics critics in nonliberal traditions. The question lies in ascertaining whether the ban on eugenics—"the protection of the integrity of an unmanipulated genetic inheritance"—can be ethically and legally grounded in the inviolability and non-disposability of "the biological foundations of personal identity."[21] The background to these arguments stresses the reification involved in genetic manipulation and the harmful consequences that such reification would have for personal identity.

On the basis of these concerns, and starting from pure "liberal" and "postmetaphysical" premises as indicated, Habermas develops an argument against "liberal eugenics" with nontherapeutic ends. His argument is grounded in the conviction that the ethical self-understanding of the genetically designed or manipulated being could be damaged:

> When the adolescent learns about the design drawn up by another person for intervening in her genetic features in order to modify certain traits, the perspective of being a grown body may be superseded—in her objectivating self-perception—by the perspective of being something made. In this way, the dedifferentiation of the distinction between the grown and the made intrudes upon one's subjective mode of existence. It might usher in the vertiginous awareness that, as a consequence of a genetic intervention carried out before we were born, the subjective nature we experience as being something we cannot dispose over is actually the result of an instrumentalization of a part of our nature.[22]

Thus, the main objection set out by Habermas points out that canceling the difference between a human nature *spontaneously grown*—without external interference of third parties—and a genetic endowment *produced by others* would cause an irreversible damage to the "self-understanding" of the subject as author of their own biography. A harmful interference in the "self-perception" of the individual's identity would occur. "This is why the question of whether and how an act thus reified affects our capacity of being ourselves (*Selbstseinkönnen*), as well as our relation to others, is so disconcerting."[23]

4.2. Replies to Habermas's standpoint

Habermas's essay on genetic engineering was the object of an interesting discussion in the philosophy seminar directed by Ronald Dworkin and Thomas Nagel at New York University. Both the objections and counter-objections raised in the seminar, subsequently published in a *Postscript* to the English version of *The Future of Human Nature*, are worth our attention. In my view, they show the extent to which Habermas's arguments point toward a way of thinking that transcends the narrow framework of antiperfectionist liberalism. Unfortunately, however, he does not dare to break down the self-imposed restrictions of a "liberal" and "postmetaphysical" discourse.

The objection raised by Thomas Nagel and some other authors was basically that, from the point of view of the individual choosing their way of life, whether their genetic endowment comes from the "natural lottery" or the deliberate intervention of third parties is irrelevant. Confronting this objection, Habermas cautiously restricts the scope of his own claim: certainly, the act of genetically designing a person does not undermine her freedom "to give shape to her own life on an interpersonal level," but it does undermine the *self-understanding* of her autonomy. Insofar as someone has been genetically designed, he can stop perceiving himself as the author of his own life:

> There is no constraint of another's freedom to give shape to her own life on an interpersonal level—a level where one person could oppress another one. But as the designer makes himself the *co-author of the life of another*, he intrudes—from the interior, one could say—into the other's consciousness of her own autonomy. The programmed person, being no longer certain about the contingency of the natural roots of her life history may feel the lack of a mental precondition for coping with the moral expectation to take, even if only in retrospect, the *sole* responsibility for her own life.[24]

Based on deep considerations on the relevance of the distinction between *the produced* and *the naturally grown*, Habermas's claims ultimately come down to a negative impact on the moral self-perception of the subject as the sole author of their life. If, as in Buchanan's interpretation, Habermas's argument is exclusively confined to a "psychological fact,"[25] then it loses much of its strength and persuasiveness: the replacement of *the naturally grown* by *the produced* would only be ethically relevant for the psychological effects that could produce. However, such negative effects could also be the object of a further intervention. And the objection would vanish insofar as the information about the origins of their genetic endowment remained hidden to the person affected, as Dworkin pointed out.[26]

Habermas responds to this argument with a further question: is it permissible to withhold from someone the knowledge of such a biographically significant fact?[27] The answer is certainly negative, but the entire chain of arguments and counterarguments shows Habermas's reluctance to draw certain logical consequences that, though implicit in his premises, point far beyond the liberal self-restraint imposed on his own discourse. Despite rightly calling attention to the difference between *the natural* and *the made*, and despite rightly noting the *reification* involved in the genetic production and design of human beings, Habermas seems to admit that what is unacceptable in genetic intervention depends on whether the person affected is aware of that intervention and, consequently, their "self-perception" as a free being becomes undermined. The fact, rightly underscored by Habermas, that "we experience our own freedom with reference to something which, by its very nature, is not at our disposal,"[28] points—as Sandel has stressed—"*beyond the limits* of liberal, or 'postmetaphysical' considerations."[29] It points to the very inviolability of that human nature with respect to whose inviolability freedom is experienced. Liberal eugenics does not simply violate the possible "self-perception" of the subject: the self-perception of the subject signals a violation of his identity.

5. THE "EXTERNAL CRITIQUE" AND THE LIBERAL REPLY

In *The Future of Human Nature*, Habermas's liberal political argument is really built upon concerns and intuitions that do not fit with ateleological liberalism. Hence, the true arguments are to be found in Habermas's initial approach, in those moral reactions that he attempts to "disenchant" (*entzaubern*)—to use the term deployed by Max Weber[30]—and translate into a philosophical discourse made vulnerable by its self-imposed restraints.[31] It is precisely those moral intuitions that are challenged by liberalism, something that shows that we face a true "clash of orthodoxies,"[32] two radically different ways of thinking.

5.1. Begotten or made?

In the first place, one of the concerns expressed by Habermas points to the distinction between "the grown" (*das Gewachsene*) and "the made" (*das Gemachte*). Other authors have similarly set up a contrast between "the begotten" and "the made": *genitum non factum*. There are processes in life whose natural development has normative consequences affecting the very dignity of the human being. In this vein, the interpersonal union of love between man and woman may be more than a mere reproductive technique, *poiesis*; it may truly be the appropriate *praxis* for the worthy generation of a person who would arise from that *praxis* as a natural, foreseeable though in a certain sense unplanned consequence. Gottfried Benn beautifully expressed the distinctive features of this *praxis* through the words of a father to his son: "do not think that I was thinking about you when I joined your mother; but her eyes were so beautiful while we were making love."[33] In frank contrast to the reification produced in the act of designing humans, this way of coming into being, indirectly, through the interpersonal encounter of love, is for many critics of eugenics the genuinely worthy conception of a human being.

The most prominent advocates of liberal eugenics have scorned the distinction between *the begotten* and *the made*. Nicholas Agar, for instance, holds that there cannot be reification in the mode of procreation, for "it is hard to have non-instrumental motives in respect of a person who does not yet exist."[34] I think this objection is hardly persuasive, given that the act of generation is precisely what *gives existence* to the person who does not yet exist. To plan and determine their features through a mechanical act of production is to reify them in their very genesis. After such a procedure, the child could attribute their traits to the producer's planning. In the event they considered their life to be a misfortune, they could file a lawsuit and claim compensation for damages—as already happens with parents who, following a wrongly performed amniocentesis, file a lawsuit for damages against the medical professionals responsible for the birth of their child. In conclusion, the replacement of the natural act of begetting with a production process means that procreation is inevitably informed by the legal logic of planned production.[35]

Allen Buchanan's criticism is twofold. On the one hand, he says that, as a bare description of facts, to say that it is proper for a human being to be begotten in a loving, self-giving act of man and woman is false, for not every sexual act involves love.[36] Buchanan creates here a straw-man adversary, because the classical teleological tradition does not say that "the natural" is what each and every one does but what is consistent with human reason.

More significant is the objection that departing from the "natural context" of reproduction does not in itself mean that the connection between will and procreation through technique is wrong. To say otherwise would be, according to Buchanan, to fall into a "normative essentialism" and therefore into the naturalistic fallacy. However, I want to remark that "normative essentialism" and "naturalistic fallacy" are not the same thing, for the *being* cannot be reduced to an empirical *fact*.[37] Moreover, the very "value neutralization" of nature carried out by Buchanan entails at least one value judgment about the world, namely, that of "grasping it mechanistically and functionally as a domain of possible means."[38] Such an attitude is no less value-laden than its opposite, but this does not mean they are equally right. Neither those who oppose eugenics nor those who defend it can escape value judgment as the basis of their respective opposition or defense.

As happens with the important distinctions *grown/made* and *begotten/made*, several other analogous distinctions have been blurred by ateleological liberals, thus showing that we stand before two radically different ways of perceiving reality. Some advocates of liberal eugenics, for example, have traced the parallelism—duly criticized by Habermas—between genetic manipulation as an impact on the human being's "inner environment" and education as an impact in their "outer environment."[39] Once more, the utilitarian thought that equates human action (*praxis*) with the bare production of external outcomes (*poiesis*) overlooks how different both concepts are. In education, there is an interpersonal relationship between mentor and pupil that is fully absent in genetic manipulation. The *fruits* (1) arising from the *fertility* (2) of this *interpersonal relationship* (3)—in which, by interacting with each other, both educator and apprentice grow—cannot be equated to the *outputs* (1') produced by the *efficiency* (2') of a *mechanical and reifying process* (3'). It is no wonder that the abandonment of educational methods that fully repress the apprentice's freedom is considered a modern achievement.

5.2. Moral repugnance or physiological reaction?

In a well-known article, Leon Kass developed his own critique of eugenics by appealing to what he calls "the wisdom of repugnance." This expression, however, has given rise to some criticisms that also deserve comment. In Nicholas Agar's opinion, for example, Kass's repugnance is nothing but a mere physiological "yucky" feeling without any moral credibility.[40] Moreover, speaking of "repugnance" could lead to the fostering of unacceptable prejudices such as xenophobia, which was also originally based on an acritical, irrational repugnance. Speaking of repugnance in this context would only contribute to contempt for cloned human beings. To already existent discrimination, a new type would be added: discrimination due to genetic origin.

Agar's criticism does no justice, in my view, to the repugnance Kass is talking about. Kass's repugnance "revolts against the excesses of human willfulness, warning us not to transgress what is unspeakably profound."[41] Moral reactions of this kind are not comparable to mere physical nausea, as Charles Taylor pointedly argued several decades ago in a very pertinent paragraph:

> If you want to discriminate more finely what it is about human beings that makes them worthy of respect, you have to call to mind what it is to feel the claim of human suffering, or what is *repugnant* about injustice, or the awe you feel at the fact of human life.[42]

Hence, we are not dealing with a sort of mere physical discomfort but a reaction of moral repugnance whose genesis is a "framework" offering "background assumptions to our moral reactions" and providing "the context in which these reactions make sense." For "living within these frameworks" is not "an optional extra, something we might just as well do without," but provide "a kind of orientation essential to our identity." What seems "necessary to say all this" is, in Taylor's words,

> the resistance put up by the naturalist temper which permeates much of our philosophic thought, not only within the academy but in our society at large. The mode of thought which surfaces in contemporary sociobiology wants us to think of our moral reactions outside of any sense-making context, as on all fours with visceral reactions like nausea.[43]

In particular, that "unspeakably profound" thing that Leon Kass compels us to preserve is the very inviolability of the human being. In his practical philosophy, Kant bestowed on the feeling of respect a privileged *status*. It is not just any kind of reaction, he says in his *Critique of Practical Reason*, but "a feeling that is produced by an intellectual ground, and this feeling is the only one that we can cognize completely *a priori* and the necessity of which we can have insight into."[44] According to Kant, it serves the action "as an incentive to make this law [the objective moral law] its maxim"—that is, it confers on the objective moral reason a subjective motivating force and is "always directed only to persons."[45]

5.3. Gift or mastery?

The main objection against liberal eugenics emphasizes the risks inherent in "playing God." Dworkin himself has given expression to this objection, wondering to what extent the fears produced by the prospects of the large-scale design of human beings are justified. This possibility, Dworkin says, would radically alter the boundaries between chance and choice, boundaries that actually structure our values. Hence, displacing those limits could not only modify our values but also render them obsolete.[46] As has been mentioned, the very option to intervene or not in the genetic endowment of the embryo would come to be regarded as imputable, and it is not absurd to think that members of future generations might decide to sue their parents for letting them come into the world with "production defects." "The terror many of us feel at the thought of genetic engineering is not a fear of what is wrong; it is rather a fear of losing our grip on what is wrong," the fear of a "moral free-fall."

After this correct diagnosis of the situation, Dworkin adopts what I deem to be a remarkably unreasonable attitude. No matter how justified our fears are, he says, they do not involve a duty to refrain from genetically designing human beings. We would just be facing a challenge, not a reason to take a step back: "we play with fire and take the consequences, because the alternative is cowardice in the face of the unknown."[47]

But the alternative does not seem to be as simple as a straightforward quandary between courage and cowardice. Should we condemn the "precautionary principle," so important in the environmental sphere, as an attitude of sheer "cowardice" in the face of technological and industrial development? If there is something we have learned in the past decades with regard to human conduct, it is the destructive capacity of man when he gives free rein to his Promethean whims as well as the subsequent need to assess the impact of our interferences in nature before carrying them out.[48] Besides, the controversy about the genetic design of human beings cannot be encapsulated in the dilemma between cowardice and audacity but, as we are examining in this chapter, includes further dilemmas.

Indeed, a last important dilemma surrounding the possibilities and dangers ushered in with the genetic design of human beings is the alternative between conceiving of human life as an object of mastery and as a free gift, a *don gratuit*. Michael Sandel points out, for example, that applying the logic of mastery to our genetic endowment could erode the social bases of humility and prevent us from seeing our own abilities as gifts provided by nature or God.[49] In certain liberal circles, however, appealing to the reception of our natural properties as *gifts* sounds suspiciously like "murky rhetoric,"[50] not to say unscientific discourse that is diametrically opposed to what really matters in this debate: "human improvement."[51]

But what is the criterion to objectively speak of "human improvement" once we have rejected beforehand the existence of an objective human teleology? Once we have given up the idea of a universal rationality regarding the human ends, that is, the idea of a good human life, what kind of rationality could hold such "improvement" proposals? The rationality suggested by eugenicists is a technical rationality: they conceive of human "improvement" as if the human being were a machine whose perfection lies in its better "functioning" according to performance parameters determined by another human producer. Speaking of a technical rationality as the criterion of human improvement only makes sense, however, if we start from the premise that man is nothing but a complex machine. At this point, eugenicists cannot avoid the strong value judgments implicit in their proposals, no matter how they try to cover them with a false neutrality. They speak—to borrow Taylor's words—from more than questionable presuppositions regarding the idea of a "strong good":

> The rejection of the higher can be presented as a liberation, as a recovery of the true value of human life. Of course, the moral value attaching to this liberating move itself presupposes another context of strong good. But with that curious blindness to the assumptions behind their own moral attitudes, utilitarians and modern naturalists in general can just focus on the negation of the older distinctions and see themselves as freeing themselves altogether from distinctions as such.[52]

After "freeing themselves" from the dichotomy between *gift* and *mastery*, the supporters of liberal eugenics propose an idea of the strong good that is fully consistent with the whole mentality of ateleological liberalism. Among its components, we can count the following:

(a) *First*, the break with the classical idea of knowledge as an inner identification with the known object, well expressed in Aristotle's statement:

"knowledge in act is the same as the thing."[53] Instead, the idea of a purely objectifying knowledge as mastery of the world is assumed, an idea expanded by scientism and positivism: "human knowledge and human power are the same."[54] In the eugenic mentality, the exaltation of knowledge as power reaches the point of objectifying the human being. It is the consummation of the "dialectic of Enlightenment" referred to by Theodor Adorno and Max Horkheimer in the mid-twentieth century: initially aimed at realizing the emancipation of the human being from nature, technical reason ends up turning the human being itself—which is part of nature—into an object of its own mastery and exploitation.[55]

(b) *Second*, the desire principle takes the place of human teleology. The supporters of "liberal eugenics" speak of human improvement as a self-evident reality, but the desires of the parents are those that determine the meaning of their offspring's improvement—as Nicholas Agar admits and defends.[56]

(c) *Third*, the goods that we should all accept are reduced to the increase of what Rawls calls "primary goods" and which have been encapsulated in the eugenic ideal of "enhancement." Thus, all the goods that could be associated with our finitude, with human limitation, and the gifts of nature—and, among them, we should include the goods that are most esteemed by religious people, as Dworkin says in one of his writings[57]—lose any public relevance.

6. REFLECTIVE EQUILIBRIUM: TOWARD ANOTHER WAY OF THINKING

As I explained at the beginning of this chapter, the terms of our debate show a sharp disagreement ultimately rooted in two ways of thinking, in two ways of seeing and appreciating the same reality. The discussion takes place on two radically different axiological levels, so the contrary positions are not only refuted but also deplored and regretted: in one case as "repugnant," in the other as "ridiculous." In my view, the liberal thesis starts with the political advantage of presenting itself as unrelated to any particular conception of the good. Paradoxically, such self-understanding prevents the liberal view from critically perceiving its own shortcomings and limitations. Once we become aware of the value judgments underlying its conclusions, the only way to solve the controversy is to compare the value judgments held by both positions.

There are no value-neutral solutions for the moral conflict, for a "value-neutral" judgment is in reality a neutral kind of value judgment. Attempting to neutralize our moral reactions in order to solve the debate is already a moral option. In the words of Isaiah Berlin, "detachment is itself a moral position," and "neutrality is also a moral attitude."[58]

This raises the further problem regarding which impartial criterion could be used to decide upon the rational superiority of one position over the other. But the fact is that there does not exist such an impartial criterion—an "agreement on principle" between the parties, to put it in Plato's words.[59] Practical reason is not an "objectifying" reason but proceeds by comparing alternatives and recognizing in the first-person singular which of them is more reductive and, conversely, which entails an epistemic gain,[60] an "awakening to reality."[61]

As Rawls rightly pointed out, we need a moral and political theory that "yields principles which match our considered judgments duly pruned and adjusted," a theory that maintains a "reflective equilibrium" between the general principles and our (critically revised) moral judgments.[62] In this sense, I think that the liberal-ateleological perspective is more reductive and, as I have tried to show throughout the last three chapters, it sits uncomfortably with some of our most basic moral judgments. The identification of "human improvement" with "empowerment" or "enhancement"—with the supply of "primary goods" enabling the individual to satisfy his desires, no matter their content—is made in a very acritical way, after an emancipation of genuinely human distinctions—gift/mastery, reification/respect, begotten/made—which entails, in my view and that of many others, an authentic dehumanization.[63]

NOTES

1. The term was coined in 1998 by the Australian philosopher Nicholas Agar and is the title of a book in which he develops his positions: *Liberal Eugenics* (Oxford: Blackwell, 2004). See also, more recently, A. Buchanan's book, *Beyond Humanity* (Oxford: Oxford University Press, 2011).

2. Hitler, *Mein Kampf* (München: Eher, 1936), p. 279.

3. 274 US 207.

4. Rawls, *Theory of Justice*, pp. 92–93.

5. R. Dworkin, "Playing God: Genes, Clones, and Luck," in *Sovereign Virtue: The Theory and Practice of Equality* (Cambridge, MA: Harvard University Press, 2000), pp. 427–52.

6. Agar, *Liberal Eugenics*, p. 6.

7. See mainly L. Kass, "The Wisdom of Repugnance: Why We Should Ban the Cloning of Humans," *The New Republic* (June 2, 1997): 17–26; see also his book: *Life, Liberty and the Defense of Dignity: The Challenge for Bioethics* (San Francisco, CA: Encounter, 2002); *Human Cloning and Human Dignity: The Report of the President's Council of Bioethics* (New York: Public Affairs, 2002).

8. M. Sandel, *The Case against Perfection. Ethics in the Age of Genetic Engineering* (Cambridge, MA: Harvard University Press, 2007).

9. F. Fukuyama, *Our Posthuman Future: Consequences of the Biotechnology Revolution* (New York: Farrar, Strauss & Giroux, 2002).

10. N. Condorcet, *Outlines of an Historical View of the Progress of Human Mind* (Philadelphia, PA: Lang and Ustick, 1796), pp. 252–53.

11. See *supra* chapter 3, 2.2. See also Agar, *Liberal Eugenics*, p. 101.

12. Agar, *Liberal Eugenics*, p. 5.

13. Dworkin, "Playing God," p. 447. In the same vein, see J. Robertson, *Children of Choice: Freedom and the New Reproductive Technologies* (Princeton, NJ: Princeton University Press, 1994) p. 167.

14. Buchanan, *Beyond Humanity?*, pp. 13 ff.

15. Rawls, *Theory of Justice*, p. 92 (emphasis mine).

16. Dworkin, "Playing God," p. 452.

17. Dworkin, "Playing God," p. 437.

18. See Nozick, *Anarchy, State and Utopia*, p. 315.

19. Agar, *Liberal Eugenics*, p. 57; and Buchanan, *Beyond Humanity?*, p. 131.

20. Habermas, *Die Zukunft der menschlichen Natur*, p. 44; Engl. trans. *The Future of Human Nature* (Cambridge, MA: Polity Press, 2003), p. 22.

21. Habermas, *Die Zukunft der menschlichen Natur*, p. 50 (Eng. trans., p. 27).

22. Habermas, *Die Zukunft der menschlichen Natur*, pp. 94–95 (Eng. trans., pp. 53–54).

23. Habermas, *Die Zukunft der menschlichen Natur*, p. 123 (Eng. trans., p. 72).

24. Habermas, "Postscript," in *The Future of Human Nature*, pp. 81–82.

25. Buchanan, *Beyond Humanity?*, p. 5.

26. Habermas, "Postscript," p. 86.

27. Habermas, "Postscript," p. 87.

28. Habermas, *Die Zukunft der menschlichen Natur*, p. 101 (Eng. trans., p. 58).

29. Sandel, *Case against Perfection*, p. 81.

30. Weber, *Science as Vocation*, p. 30.

31. See, briefly, a similar criticism in Sandel, *Case against Perfection*, pp. 79–83.

32. I borrow the expression from Robert P. George, who has used it on several occasions, including in the title a book.

33. "Glaubt doch nicht, daß ich an euch dachte als ich mit eurer Mutter ging, ihre Augen wurden immer so schön bei der Liebe" (Gottfried Benn; *apud* Spaemann, "Wozu der Aufband? Solterdijk fehlt das Rüstzeug [1999]," in *Grenzen* [Stuttgart: Klett-Cotta, 2001], p. 409).

34. Agar, *Liberal Eugenics*, pp. 42–43.

35. See the same warning in Sandel, *Case against Perfection*, p. 87.

36. Buchanan, *Beyond Humanity?*, p. 127.

37. On the reduction of the concept of "fact" and "experience" to the empiricist concept of experience, see Alasdair MacIntyre, *After Virtue: A Study in Moral Theory*, 3rd ed. (Bloomington, IN: University of Notre Dame Press, 2007), pp. 79 ff.

38. Taylor, *Sources of the Self*, p. 149.

39. Robertson, *Children of Choice*, p. 167. The analogy is also made by Agar and by Buchanan. See, against the analogy, Habermas, *Die Zukunft der menschlichen Natur*, p. 89 (Eng. trans., pp. 49 ff.).

40. Agar, *Liberal Eugenics*, pp. 56–58.
41. Kass, *Wisdom of Repugnance*, p. 20.
42. Taylor, *Sources of the Self*, p. 8 (emphasis mine).
43. Taylor, *Sources of the Self*, p. 78.
44. *KpV*, p. 73 (*Cambridge Ed.*, pp. 199–200). See also the footnote in *Grundlegung*, p. 401 (*Cambridge Ed.*, p. 56), where Kant faces the objection of "seeking refuge" in "an obscure feeling" and not reason. It is—Kant insists—a feeling produced by reason.
45. *KpV*, p. 76.
46. Dworkin, "Playing God," p. 444.
47. Dworkin, "Playing God," p. 446.
48. For a synthetical explanation of the shift toward an ecological mentality, see F. Simón-Yarza, *Medio ambiente y derechos fundamentales* (Madrid: Tribunal Constitucional and Centro de Estudios Políticos y Constitucionales, 2012), pp. 13 ff.
49. Sandel, *Case against Perfection*, mainly pp. 85–100.
50. Buchanan, *Beyond Humanity?*, p. 2.
51. Agar, *Liberal Eugenics*, p. 46.
52. Taylor, *Sources of the Self*, p. 81.
53. "Idem autem est secundum actum scientia rei" *(S. Th.*, *I*, q. 79, a. 4; quoting Aristotle, *De Anima*, III, 430a).
54. "Scientia et potentia humana in idem coincidunt" (F. Bacon, *Novum Organum*, Aphorismi de interpretatione naturae et regno hominis, III, in *The Works of Lord Bacon, Collected and Edited by James Spedding, Robert Leslie Ellis and Douglas Denon Heath*, vol. I [London: Longman, 1858], p. 157). Identical thought is expressed by Hobbes: "the end of knowledge is power" (*Elementorum Philosophiae Sectio Prima De Corpore,* I, Ch. 1 [*De Philosophia*], in *Thomae Hobbes Malmesburiensis Opera philosophica quae latine scripsit omnia*, vol. I [London: John Bohm, 1839; repr. Aalen: Scientia Verlag, 1966], p. 6); as for Descartes, the end of knowledge is being "maîtres et possesseurs de la nature" (*Discourse de la Méthode*, VI [Paris: ed. Librairie Joseph Gibert, 1943], p. 56); and Comte's positivistic ideal is "savoir pour prévoir afin de pouvoir" (*Catéchisme positiviste*, Quatrième entretien [Paris: de Sandre, 2009], p. 141).
55. See M. Horkheimer and T. W. Adorno, *Dialektik der Aufklärung. Philosophische Fragmente* (Amsterdam: Querido, 1947), above all chapter 1 (*Begriff der Aufklärung*).
56. Agar, *Liberal Eugenics*, p. 5.
57. Dworkin, *Life's Dominion*, pp. 89 ff., where he admits that religious people tend to appreciate the gifts they have received from nature more than their own work. In another essay, Dworkin lets us glimpse his own conception of the good when he declares that "there is no value, aesthetic *or otherwise*—the emphasis is mine, though I think it is important—in the fact that some people are doomed to a disfigured and short life" (Dworkin, "Playing God," p. 441). Something that, seen from the point of view of the *don gratuit*, could receive a religious meaning, disregarding this perspective is emphatically deprived of value.
58. Berlin, "Five Essays on Liberty: Introduction," in *Liberty*, pp. 22–23.

59. *Crito*, 49d–e.
60. Taylor, *Sources of the Self*, pp. 71 ff.
61. Diels, *Die Fragmente der Vorsokratiker*, Heraclitus, § 89.
62. Rawls, *Theory of Justice*, § 4, p. 18. On "reflective equilibrium" as a justification method, see more extensively, Scanlon, "Rawls on Justification," in *The Cambridge Companion to Rawls*, pp. 139–67.
63. For a deep and readable argument regarding the main problems faced in this chapter—and underlying the whole book—I wish to refer the reader to one of the most brilliant essays on the subject: Lewis, *Abolition of Man*, especially chapter 3 (pp. 53 ff.).

Part IV

CONSTRUCTIVE PROPOSALS

Chapter 9

Teleology of civil liberties

1. INTRODUCTION

A purely conservative or over-communitarian reaction to the understanding of the rights of liberty as mere vehicles for the satisfaction of individual desires and preferences would be quite unsatisfactory. Faced with the whims of an exacerbated "left-wing" liberalism that unleashes the desire principle, a surrender to "right-wing" political messianisms that appeal to the self-preservation of collective identities and awaken tribal and nationalist instincts is a dangerous and recurring temptation. The anti-Semitism of Maurras's right-wing party in France—with its unworthy behavior in the *affaire Dreyfuss*[1]—or, above all, the political messianisms that emerged during the interwar period should make us aware of the risks of channeling the dissatisfaction produced by an excessive liberalism (*desire principle*) into an exacerbation of the conservative nationalist instinct (*reality principle*). Elevating one or other principle to the level of social goal means losing sight of the human good, which cannot be attained without liberty. The dehumanization of rights due to the lack of reference to human teleology is no less humane than the contempt for rights. Individual freedom deserves a central role in our political life. Suffocating the legitimate aspirations of the individual or diminishing their importance is as illegitimate as emancipating them from the common good. Moreover, it is contrary to the common good. In the light of contemporary populisms, I am convinced that this consideration is far from being superfluous.

In part IV of the book, I will sketch some proposals aimed at defining the position of individual liberties with respect to the common good in the context of our pluralistic society. To this end, I will draw on concepts that, when rightly understood, are extremely important for our pluralistic societies, such as John Rawls's idea of "public reason," Jürgen Habermas's "deliberative democracy," or Joseph Raz's "personal autonomy." As a starting point, I will devote this penultimate chapter to expounding the teleology that gives meaning to civil liberties. To articulate my discourse, I will largely draw on the work of John Finnis and on several essays published by Robert P. George in his book *Making Men Moral*. The rights of liberty are not ends in themselves but have a *telos* justifying them. In chapter 1, I have already explained the double dimension of the *telos* as "end" and "limit." Following this scheme, I will investigate below the end and limit of those rights.

2. THE *END* OF LIBERTIES: BASIC GOODS

Freedoms are not ends in themselves, in that they cannot be justified with a disregard for their right exercise. This is the sense of Joseph Raz's assertion: "wanting something is not a reason for doing it."[2] The fact of wanting something is not a sufficient reason to do it, in the sense that it is not justified by itself. What is the end, then, that justifies the exercise of freedom? In what sense may it be said that liberties are human goods? A first response must admit that civil liberties are *necessary conditions* for a full human life. Their justification lies in the development of the multiplicity of individual and social, material, and spiritual goods that give shape to human fulfillment. When the Universal Declaration of Human Rights was approved, people from cultures and traditions as diverse as Confucianism and Hinduism agreed that, though the idea of individual rights did not hold the central place that it does in our Western political culture, basic liberties were somehow present in their cultures as basic demands for a flourishing human life, suiting the needs of people in all circumstances,[3] or as "essential human freedoms and controls or virtues necessary for good life."[4] Therefore, it is not merely "individual choice" that justifies them, but—in the words formulated by Herbert L. A. Hart in one of his essays—"basic or fundamental individual needs."[5] According to John Finnis's terminology, the content of human rights and liberties are "basic aspects of human flourishing."[6] And though it does not play such a central role in his political philosophy, Rawls himself refers to the idea of certain basic human goods. In his view, "the things that are commonly thought of as human goods should turn out to be the ends and activities that have a major place in rational plans" of life.[7]

1. In the past decades, Finnis himself has attempted—together with other significant moral, political, and legal philosophers—to elucidate the content of a flourishing life through a list of basic "intrinsic goods," that is, through a list of self-evident and fundamental aspects of human development that, in

multiple ways, every rational human life seeks to instantiate.[8] Leaving aside the difficulties that the very idea of a list of incommensurable and distinct basic human goods—irreducible to each other—may have, I think it is hardly objectionable that "there are goods that are intrinsically valuable for human beings ('basic human goods') and, precisely as such, provide intelligible (non-instrumental) *reasons* for action, and not merely emotional motives."[9] Notwithstanding the possibility of irrational or merely emotional behavior, the justification for freedom lies in acting in accordance with reason, and acting in accordance with reason involves in the first place (if not only) pursuing human goods that reason identifies as purposes of our natural inclinations: life, knowledge, sociability, and so forth. As such, human natural inclinations are instinctively and nonrationally determined. However, practical reason grasps their orientation toward intelligible human goods that form the basis of our free action and human development.

Without being exhaustive, I would like to refer to some of these human goods as well as to their connection with the civil liberties traditionally protected:

(a) The first good I want to mention does not strictly speaking correspond to a civil "liberty" but to a right that is the presupposition of every liberty: *life*. The basic good of life is the primary support of the rest of human goods, and it corresponds to the instinct of self-preservation present in all beings. Also enshrined in some constitutional texts, *physical integrity* does not correspond to a good other than life. Strictly speaking, physical integrity is part of human vitality.[10] It belongs to the fundamental good of self-preservation that makes free development possible.

(b) Associated with several freedoms, *human interiority* deserves an explicit mention here. Self-determination and human flourishing are not possible without a sphere removed from the political realm. Nowadays, it is quite rightly accepted that the rupture with the total belonging of the individual to the *polis* constituted—as Larry Siedentop has underlined in an excellent work[11]—one of the great political liberations of the Christian age. In spite of being connected with several liberties, respect for human interiority has a particularly strong link with the modern *right to privacy*. Privacy or intimacy consists of a space removed from the public eye in which the individual can find himself alone or in which a small community may communicate with a degree of freedom and transparency that remains hidden to the general public. Hence, privacy is a relative concept, characterized not by its contraposition to the social but by its exclusion of public access. Indeed, privacy may have both an individual and a social dimension. There is a "shared privacy," for example, the family or other communitarian forms of intimacy.

Finally, privacy must be defined by reference to a space in which certain behaviors are safe from the risk of depersonalization that would occur if they were carried out in public. The need for a realm of intimacy is a consequence of the lack of reciprocal transparency among human beings, which opens the door to reification and manipulation of the other. Let us just think about numerous kinds of expressions of affection, advice, or rebuke. Only in the private domain are certain conducts and behaviors safe from public distortion or misrepresentation and can be enacted with personal authenticity. Likewise, only privacy allows us to share with full exclusivity certain things and thus create exclusive affective bonds.

Though a strict demand of human dignity, privacy does not entail that certain actions lack public relevance—and therefore legal consequences—solely because they are subjectively important for those who carry them out.[12] I fully share Robert P. George's opinion that this has been a source of extreme confusion in contemporary jurisprudence regarding the right to privacy. In truth, it is difficult to identify human actions—as opposed to mere thoughts—that, *ex natura rerum* and disregarding their effects and their circumstances, lack public relevance.

(c) Specifically protected by several civil liberties—freedom of speech and of the press, the right to peaceful assembly, religious freedom, and so forth—another basic good that deserves an explicit mention is *human sociability*. The human being is a *zoon politikon* and a *zoon logon echon*, a social animal and a language animal. His sociability starts in the bosom of the families that make up the political community. As the most basic social institution, *marriage*—"the deepest friendship" (*maxima amicitia*), as Aquinas characterized it[13]—constitutes a fundamental good both for the spouses and for the whole of society, since it is within marriage that new citizens are raised and educated. It is quite appropriate, therefore, that several legal orders have bestowed on marriage the rank of a constitutional right.

The political *vita activa*, in which most human beings realize themselves, cannot flourish without serious hindrance unless freedom of speech (*lexis*) and social cooperation (*praxis*) are recognized. Both *freedom of speech* and *freedom of assembly and association* make up essential attributes of the individual's citizenship *status* and preserve the community from tyranny. Especially in an open, democratic, and pluralistic society, letting the government decide which opinions may or may not be defended, and which doctrines may or may not be listened to, is completely contrary to reason. Yet, as a fundamental political good, *freedom of expression* should be defended and protected not only against state repression but also against the tyranny of public opinion and political correctness. In his classic *opuscule* on liberty, John Stuart Mill devoted several pages to criticizing the repression of thoughts and opinions by majorities. In a memorable paragraph that still remains pertinent, he said that "if all mankind minus one, were of one opinion, and only one person were of the contrary opinion, mankind would be no more justified in silencing that one person, than he, if he had the power, would be justified in silencing mankind."[14] It should be noted that Mill does not defend a supposed right to *insult, injure,* or *offend* but a right to peacefully defend one's own opinions. As a matter of fact, Mill admits that "even opinions lose their immunity, when the circumstances in which they are expressed are such as to constitute their expression a positive instigation to some mischievous act."[15] What Mill defends here is not a fundamental right to wrong one's neighbor but to peacefully express one's opinions, no matter how contrary to the majority's feelings and opinions they are. Both dimensions—freedom against the state and freedom against majority opinion—are essential aspects of freedom of speech; and freedom of speech preserves not only human sociability but also political *citizenship*.

As has been pointed out, freedom of *assembly* and freedom of *association* are also tightly linked to the goods of *human sociability* and *political citizenship*. Among classical political thinkers, Alexis de Tocqueville is perhaps the one who has left us the most fervent praise of these rights:

> After the liberty of acting alone, the liberty most natural to man is to combine his efforts with the efforts of his fellows and to act in common. So to me, the right of association seems almost as inalienable by nature as individual liberty. The legislator would not want to destroy it without attacking society itself.[16]

It is easy to see that cooperation for the sake of common action is a basic good, an inherent aspect of human sociability. Besides, there are further connections worth mentioning between freedom of assembly and association and other goods. In chapter 1, I emphasized the importance of intermediate communities in a pluralistic society in order to provide individuals with a moral environment that the state cannot.[17] It should be added that the proliferation of private associations is closely related to an active *citizenship*, as has been indicated. On this point, it is very appropriate to quote Tocqueville's remarks:

> Among democratic peoples, on the contrary, all citizens are independent and weak; they can hardly do anything by themselves, and no one among them can compel his fellows to lend him their help. So they all fall into impotence if they do not learn to help each other freely.[18]

Cooperation is an essential feature of efficient action in the public life of society, thus making it—as happens with free speech—an aspect of citizenship.

(d) *Knowledge of the truth* constitutes another basic human good, and it is protected through several civil liberties, paradigmatically *scientific freedom*. An additional explanation is not needed here.

(e) Closely related to the good of knowledge is the good of *religion*, understood as the right relationship of man with the transcendent origin and source of the world and of human existence.[19] To avoid misunderstanding, it must be stressed that keeping a right relationship with regard to the ultimate questions of our existence is not a mere option but a basic human good, and would be so *etsi Deus non daretur*, even if God did not exist. Practical reason does not initially identify the good of religion with a particular religion but with religion as such, a good deeply rooted in our inclination to the truth. In a very general sense, this good consists in standing and remaining in religious truth, wherever it may be. It is perhaps due to an unconscious reluctance to connect our religious search with the idea of truth that, quite frequently, legal scholars identify the content of religious freedom in a tautological way. They say, for example, that the good protected by religious freedom is "the rejection of any form of coercion on the grounds of one's beliefs, religious or non-religious."[20] However, the "non-coercion on the grounds of religious beliefs" is not the good protected by religious freedom but religious freedom itself. We cannot determine the *telos* (protected good) of religious freedom without reference to the good of religion; just as we cannot determine the good protected by freedom of expression, association, or science, without reference to the goods of expression, association, and science.

Indifference toward the ultimate source of meaning cannot constitute the good protected by religious freedom. The religious neutrality of the state should be conceived of as a lack of competence regarding the conclusions reached by its citizens with respect to religious issues. In a pluralistic society, where a general, communitarian spirit allowing for an institutionalized cooperation around a public cult does not exist, this neutrality becomes a true public good—closely related to the social peace, as has been discussed above.[21] Yet this neutrality should not be confused with the state's indifference toward the good of religion, with allowing the denigration of those beliefs and convictions legitimately held by citizens as a result of their religious search. Such denigration is an attack on the good of religion and has nothing to do with the so-called negative religious freedom.

It is also important to note that (self-proclaimed) "areligious" beliefs, however much they claim to be grounded in "negative" religious freedom—the freedom *not to* believe, *not to* confess, *not to* take part in a cult, and so forth—also find their value in the positive good of religion, namely in asserting a purportedly true relationship with the ultimate source of the universal order. If they reached the point of postulating indifference toward religious truth—that is, indifference toward the right relationship with the ultimate transcendent source of meaning—they would lack any value as positions regarding religion, and the state should not bestow on them the protection of religious freedom. The same must be said, of course, of those cults that do not seek any truth with regard to religious issues or that seek evil, as happens with satanic cults.

We could still refer to other liberties that are connected—as religious freedom is—with the good of knowledge: *freedom of thought and of conscience, freedom of information*, and so forth. However, I think that the examples above suffice to show how rights and liberties find their justification in human goods and not in freedom for the sake of freedom or anything of that sort.

2. It may still be appropriate to ask the following question: why do we speak of *freedoms* or *liberties* and not just proclaim a general right to human freedom? I do not mean a pointless general right to freedom, but a general right to freedom broadly oriented to human flourishing, instead of specific freedoms oriented to specific aspects of human flourishing. Indeed, in recent decades, some constitutional texts have included such a general right to freedom as a sort of residuary clause.[22] This practice is, however, far from being usual in comparative constitutionalism. The reason for the recognition of concrete freedoms lies in historical experience, which cannot be disregarded by law. The traditional enumeration of rights in constitutional and human-rights texts does not just respond to an exercise of philosophical inquiry. No matter how "human" or "universal" they are, their particular recognition is historically attached to specific reactions against particular experiences of unjust repression, as has been noted by—among others—the Spanish political theorist Manuel García Pelayo.[23] The explicit recognition of *religious freedom*, for example, is linked in its genesis to the covenants of some New England colonies drafted in the first half of the seventeenth century in a spirit of reaction against *religious intolerance*.[24] Also a consequence of particular historical oppressions are the first apologies and demands that gave rise to the recognition of *press freedom*, for example, John Milton's *Areopagitica* (1644). The same happens with the approval of a fundamental right to *privacy*, closely related to the emergence of specific new ways of invading intimacy arising from the implementation of new technical developments in the

field of journalism.[25] And to add a final and more recent example, the right to *physical integrity* did not appear in a constitutional text until its enshrinement in Article 2.2 of the German Basic Law, that is, until the aftermath of the horrors experienced during the Nazi regime.[26]

3. Before concluding this section, I want to mention an additional implication of what has been explained and one that is necessary in order to avoid a common misunderstanding. An abstract catalogue of liberties grounded in basic human goods is certainly beautiful, but we should not expect more than that. In their *abstract formulation*, human rights do not offer any indication regarding specific moral and legal implications. Hence, the widely extended appeal to a "human rights morality" is plainly wrong, since *a mere juxtaposition of basic human goods does not make up a morality*. Human rights simply indicate intelligible goods that coincide with what Thomas Aquinas called the "most common principles" (*communissima*) of practical reasoning. In the best-case scenario, a positive human rights catalogue could offer no more than a list of self-evident (*per se nota*)[27] principles. These principles do not constitute in themselves any particular moral conclusion, and any rational agent—including the criminal—may act for the sake of a human good. They are just "pre-moral"[28] principles. This means that "one's understanding of those most basic first principles is not itself an understanding of the moral principles needed to give guidance in the various 'fields and circumstances' of one's actual life."[29]

3. THE *LIMIT* OF LIBERTIES: A "RIGHT TO DO WRONG"?

Having enumerated—nonexhaustively, as has been said—some of the main goods for the sake of which rights are recognized and preserved, a reference to the other side of the *telos*—namely, the *limit* of rights—becomes necessary. This, in turn, leads us to an old problem that has gained currency in the last years: the debate on a supposed "right to do wrong." This problem transcended the academic debate and drew the attention of many public intellectuals, and even of society at large, in the aftermath of the attacks on the French satirical weekly magazine *Charlie Hebdo*, on January 7, 2015. The condemnation of such crimes was accompanied by public reflections and debates on the limits of rights and, in particular, on whether freedom of speech includes a right to insult.[30]

3.1. The Dworkin/Waldron thesis

Does it make sense to speak of a freedom to offend or, more generally, of a right to do wrong? The question is not just whether positive legislation may in fact confer this right but whether there is a *moral* freedom, that is, an authentic human right to do wrong. The discussion of this issue goes back in time. In *Taking Rights Seriously*, Ronald Dworkin articulated an unequivocal defense of this right. He understood the right as a duty not to interfere in one's freedom: "in most cases when we say that someone has the 'right' to do something, we imply that it would be wrong to interfere with his doing it, or at least that some special grounds are needed for justifying any interference." Thus, he continues, "There is a clear difference between saying that someone has a right to do something in this sense and saying that it is the 'right' thing for him to do, or that he does not 'wrong' in doing it. Someone may have the right to do something that is the wrong thing for him to do."[31]

Jeremy Waldron's opinion is similar, but he offers a more extensive argument. In fact, Waldron is the one who really provoked a wide debate on the "right to do wrong" through an article published in the early 1980s.[32] In that paper, he insisted,

> The cutting edge of the claim that P has a right to do A is the correlative claim that other people are morally required to refrain from interfering with P's performance of A. If P has a right to do A, then it follows that it is wrong for anyone to try to stop P from doing A.[33]

Shortly thereafter, Waldron lists a number of good reasons that may induce someone to assert a right to do wrong. For instance, the act of interfering with the wrongdoer may have harmful collateral effects such as risking the life of third parties, or may reduce public expenditure, or may diminish the reputation of the police. Several further reasons could certainly be added to those provided by Waldron. However, it is interesting that he himself concludes his article on "the right to do wrong" by admitting that, "in real life," the expression "I have a right to do A" "is most often uttered by someone who intends to do A and is responding to moves by other people to prevent his carrying out that intention." And, as he pointedly notes, "There is something odd about having the intention to do A and sincerely believing that A is wrong."[34]

3.2. Finnis/George's critique: "Claim-rights" versus "liberty-rights"

Waldron's remark on the oddity of intending to do something wrong on the grounds of a right to do it remains unintegrated in his theory and leaves the reader in a state of confusion. This confusion is due to a mistake that has been rightly pointed out by Robert P. George.[35] On the one hand, Waldron seems to suggest that there is a true moral freedom to do wrong; on the other hand, he defines the right to do wrong in such terms that his thesis is finally deprived of the provocative force suggested by the title of the article. To understand the problem of a right to do wrong, George—who is inspired by a brief and intelligent essay of John Finnis[36]—draws on the triadic analysis of fundamental legal positions developed by Wesley N. Hohfeld.[37] More precisely, he draws on the crucial difference between what Hohfeld calls "rights" or "claim-rights" and "privileges" or "liberty-rights."

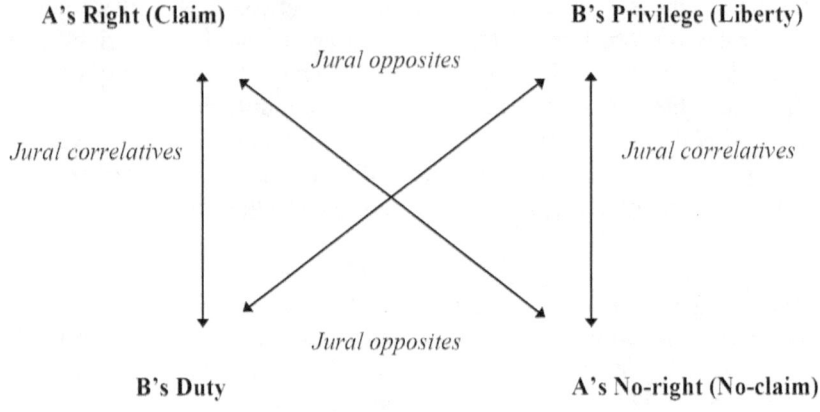

The two Hohfeldian "active" positions—right or claim, on the one hand, and privilege or liberty, on the other—are related to their correlatives and opposites in the following way:

(a) A's having a right or *claim* to X against B *entails* B's having the corresponding duty to X against A (*correlatives*).
(b) A's having a right or *claim* to X against B *opposes* to A's not having a right or *claim* to X against B (*opposites*).
(c) B's having a privilege or *liberty* to X against A *entails* A's not having a right or *claim* not-to-X against B (*correlatives*).
(d) B's having a privilege or *liberty* to X against A *opposes* to B's having a *duty* not-to-X against A (*opposites*).[38]

If we analyze the scheme with rigor, we may notice something that was pointedly emphasized by John Finnis and that turns out to be decisive with regard to the supposed right to do wrong: understood as a *claim*, Hohfeld's subjective right does not consist in doing or refraining from doing something, but its content is always someone else's action or omission: "A's claim-right is always to B's action or omission, never to A's."[39] Strictly speaking, *there does not exist, nor can there ever exist, a moral "right to do wrong."* This is not a trivial issue. The analysis of legal positions is useful to refine the language and avoid misunderstandings, a task of whose importance Hohfeld was quite aware. Quoting Holland, he pointed out that "the identity of the terms seems irresistibly to suggest an identity between the ideas expressed by them:"[40]

(a) If, by the term right, we mean a privilege or liberty-right, it is obvious that *there does not exist* a right to do wrong: B cannot have a moral liberty to X against A and simultaneously have its opposite, namely, a moral duty not-to-X against A.[41]
(b) If, by the term right, we mean a claim-right, then the so-called right to do wrong has an imprecise sense, because no claim has as content an action or omission of the claim-holder.[42] The content (X) of A's right-claim cannot therefore be "doing wrong" but coincides with the content of B's duty: "not preventing A from doing wrong." The object of A's claim-right is never A's action or omission.

The erroneous idea of a "right to do wrong" is suggested by a subtle admixture of the idea of claim (the "right") with a content that could only belong to a liberty (one's action or omission). The mistake is produced because the claim's content can in fact be refraining from hindering a wrong action. At the same time, however, the suspicion that we are before a misunderstanding persists, for it is clear that a person's moral freedom is not compatible with an opposing moral duty. The confusion is clarified through the analysis.

3.3. Other contributions to the debate

More recently, other authors have continued this debate. Among them, David Enoch has defended the existence of a liberty-right to violate one's duty, and his approach will enable me to clarify a final point. Enoch maintains that, given that the Hohfeldian positions refer to triadic relations between two subjects (A and B) and an object (X), nothing prevents us from speaking of a liberty-right to violate one's duty, at least in two cases:

(a) First, it is perfectly plausible to assert A's liberty-right to X against C and a simultaneous duty of A not-to-X against B.
(b) Second, it is also plausible to assert A's liberty-right against B, C, D . . . , and a simultaneous duty of A not-to-X lacking any addressee.

In my view, Enoch's assertions are simply trivial, for the terms of the comparison in which he supports his purported "right to violate one's duty" are not homogeneous. He does not compare a liberty against C with a duty against C but *against B*, in the first case, and *non-directional* (the so-called victimless immoralities) in the second one. Given that the comparison lacks homogeneous terms, we do not gain any understanding of the relationship between the concepts of *liberty* and *duty*. It is obvious that the relationship between A and C is not included *per se* in the relationship between A and B; and equally heterogeneous is the second comparison between a triadic relationship—like those analyzed by Hohfeld—and a binary one.

Finally, it is possible to abandon Hohfeld's triadic positions while maintaining the concept of liberty as "non-duty." In this case, however, the appropriate correlate for a *nondirectional* moral liberty-right (i.e., a moral liberty-right lacking any specific addressee) would be a *nondirectional* moral non-duty. And neither in this case can we affirm that a right to do wrong exists: A cannot have a moral liberty to X and, at the same time, a moral duty not-to-X. Consequently, A cannot have a moral liberty-right to do a moral wrong.

3.4. Three kinds of claim-rights to do wrong

A liberty-right to do wrong, therefore, does not exist. What may and does in fact exist—and, moreover, fittingly so—is a claim-right against the state and other citizens, under certain conditions, preventing one from doing wrong. Authors such as Galston and George have grounded this claim-right in terms I overall deem to be correct, with an important caveat I will set forth immediately. I want to propose here, in any case, my own classification of the different kinds of reasons that could ground a duty to tolerate evil:

(a) Prudential reasons

In the first place, there are frequent cases where, *even though the conduct is unjust and directly or indirectly harmful to society*, there are compelling public-interest reasons to tolerate it. Let us think, for example, about the risk of excessive oppression resulting from a wrong application of a prohibition—due to excess zeal in pulling up the weeds, the crop is damaged—or about the difficulty of defining the prohibition in terms that do not hinder other legitimate conducts; and so on. In such cases, prudence may recommend tolerating a particular harm in order to avoid a worse one. Nevertheless, the *claim-right* in these cases has a purely derivative character. It is justified neither in the moral *status* (*status* as a moral subject) nor in the political *status* (*status* as a political subject) of the acting individual but in a duty on the side of the authority based on considerations regarding the common good. It is, strictly speaking, what German jurisprudence has labeled a "reflex right" (*Rechtsreflex*).

(b) Strictly private questions

Second, there exists a claim-right to do wrong that is based on the *political irrelevance of the immoral conduct at issue*, in its strict non-affecting of society. It is indeed necessary to distinguish between purely moral and political issues.[43] Private immoralities in the proper sense—namely, immoralities that do not affect third parties either directly or indirectly—remain beyond the scope of what may be prohibited. In this case, the *claim-right* is not purely derivative but strictly primary or "originary," since it is the very *status* of the individual as a moral subject that hinders society from compelling them to fulfill moral obligations that neither directly nor indirectly affect justice. In the words of Thomas Aquinas, "Human law makes precepts only about acts of justice, and if it commands acts of other virtues, this is only in so far as they assume the nature of justice";[44] and "since justice is directed to others," it is "only about external actions and things, . . . in so far as one man is related to another through them."[45] By contrast, "in those matters that relate to himself it would seem at a glance that man is master of himself, and that he may do as he likes."[46]

At least in its abstract formulation, this thesis seems not to be too far from the modern "harm principle" proposed by John Stuart Mill. Firmly established as a basic tenet of classical liberalism, the harm principle prevents the coercive banning of actions with no other purpose than the moral good of the addressees of the prohibition, that is, without those actions harming other people—be they an identifiable third party or society at large. Mill devoted the whole of his seminal essay *On liberty* to the harm principle, as he announced in the very first pages of that work:

> The object of this Essay is to assert one very simple principle, as entitled to govern absolutely the dealings of society with the individual in the way of compulsion and control, whether the means used be physical force in the form of legal penalties, or the moral coercion of public opinion. That principle is, that the sole end for which mankind are warranted, individually or collectively, in interfering with the liberty of action of any of their number, is self-protection. That the only purpose for which power can be rightfully exercised over any member of a civilized community, against his will, is to prevent harm to others. His own good, either physical or moral, is not a sufficient warrant. He cannot rightfully be compelled to do or forbear because it will be better for him to do so, because it will make him happier, because, in the opinions of others, to do so would be wise, or even right. These are good reasons for remonstrating with him, or reasoning with him, or persuading him, or entreating him, but not for compelling him, or visiting him with any evil in case he do otherwise. To justify that, the conduct from which it is desired to deter him, must be calculated to produce evil to someone else. The only part of the conduct of any one, for

which he is amenable to society, is that which concerns others. In the part which merely concerns himself, his independence is, of right, absolute. Over himself, over his own body and mind, the individual is sovereign.[47]

Notwithstanding a certain excess in Mill's rhetoric, as well as his references to public opinion—which are to a great extent justified due to the context in which he lived—this paragraph contains, in my view, an important political truth, provided that it is strictly and rigorously interpreted. As such, the harm principle does not exclude defining the scope of rights on the basis of what is morally good for society. It merely precludes placing the foundations of a coercive regulation in the sole good of the particular addressee of such coercion. Let us imagine, for example, a citizen who, in full use of his mental faculties, decides to go on a hunger strike that threatens his life. The state should not coercively feed him for the sake of his own physical or moral well-being; it could only do so on the ground of other political reasons concerning third parties.

(c) Absence of "public reasons"

Finally, there are cases in which, though a conduct is harmful for society, *there is not enough public consensus to coercively ban it*.[48] This argument is not alien to the Thomistic tradition,[49] though it did not find in that tradition an emphasis comparable with that of modernity. It is ultimately the problem faced by John Rawls's concept of public reason. Without identifying themselves with the Rawlsian conception, major philosophers close to the classical tradition have underlined the importance of the concept of public reason in political decision making.[50]

Public reason means publicly justifiable reason, that is, an exercise of reason that can be publicly justified. In his classical version, natural law is nothing but practical reason, and a task of practical reason—especially of the virtues of prudence and justice—is precisely to distinguish between what someone may impose on himself and what he may claim to be publicly imposed. Public acceptability and justification constitutes a requirement in the process of rational *determination* of the common good, and disregarding such a condition would go against the common good. As Martin Rhonheimer has rightly noted, "For natural-law reasons to be valid reasons in the sphere of the political and public reason they must be a political *application, restriction, or concretization* of natural law, according to the logic of the political."[51]

Having said this, it is fair to add that, once public reasons acquire the force of customs and, even more, of constitutional law, they take on, so to speak, a life of their own. They become legal *topoi*, commonplaces of public legal discourse. If we consider the actual terms of the classical doctrine of natural law, we can also speak here of determinations (*determinationes*) of practical reason, provided that the principles at issue are just. Otherwise, they would not be public reasons but public "unreasons," and we would need to put our energies into trying to eradicate them. Once more, however, practical reason would require such eradication to be publicly justified, which brings us back to the starting point.

Here, it may be asked again whether the right to be treated in accordance with public reason is an originary or derivative claim-right, a primary one, or a mere "reflex right" derived from someone else's duty. In my view, we are not just dealing with a "weak" or "purely derivative" right. In the absence of public reasons to prohibit a harmful conduct, anyone affected by the prohibition could invoke their own political *status* as a citizen. Certainly, the individual does not act here under the protection of a moral liberty-right to do wrong, which—as has been said—would be a contradiction in terms. Moreover, he may not even justify his *agere licere* in his own moral autonomy regarding what he is only concerned about, for we assume that his action affects society. The claim he could assert, however, is not just a "weak" or "derivative" one,[52] for it is linked to his political *status*, which grounds the legitimate expectation of a legal treatment based on public reasons.

Like the moral realm, the political realm belongs to the domain of practical reason. There is, however, a relative autonomy of the political with respect to the moral, an autonomy that lies precisely in the need to provide a public justification for any exercise of power. This public justification cannot be simply identified with a factual consensus—as frequently happens, manifestly abusing the concept—since that would mean depriving such a consensus of the need for justification: it would be the surrender of reason. Social practices against practical reason are not public reasons but *public unreasons*. That said, the argument opposing a public unreason may only be imposed as law insofar as society has been convinced about the reasonableness of such an argument. And the process by which this occurs is what Ihering called "the struggle for law":

> It is the language which the wounded feeling of legal right will speak, at all times and in all places; the power, the firmness of the conviction, that law must remain law, the lofty feeling and *pathos* of a man who is conscious that, in what he claims, there is question not only of his person but of the law.[53]

This remark, in which Ihering glosses the defense of a private cause—and one of such a questionable justice as Shylock's in *The Merchant of Venice*—reaches a supreme level of validity when it refers to those committed to the defense of the common good.

NOTES

1. On Maurras's ateleological "right-wing" political thought, see further Spaemann, *Der Ursprung der Soziologie aus dem Geist der Restauration: Studien über L. G. A. De Bonald* (München: Kösel, 1959), especially pp. 181 ff.
2. J. Raz, *The Morality of Freedom* (Oxford: Oxford University Press, 1986), p. 389.
3. Chung-Shu Lo, "Human Rights in the Chinese Tradition," in *Human Rights: Comments and Interpretations; a Symposium Edited by UNESCO* (UNESCO, 1949), p. 187.
4. S. V. Puntambekar, "Human Freedoms and Hindu Thinking," in *Human Rights: Comments and Interpretations; a Symposium Edited by UNESCO*, p. 200. Regarding the globalization of human rights in a multicultural context, see F. Simón-Yarza, "Individual Rights," in *Max Planck Encyclopedia of Comparative Constitutional Law* (Oxford: Oxford University Press, February 2017).
5. "Bentham on Legal Rights," in A. W. B. Simpson, ed., *Oxford Essays in Jurisprudence*, Second Series (Oxford: Clarendon Press, 1973) p. 201.
6. Finnis, *Natural Law and Natural Rights*, p. 205.
7. Rawls, *Theory of Justice*, § 65, p. 379; see also pp. 373–74.
8. Finnis, *Natural Law and Natural Rights*, pp. 59 ff.
9. R. P. George, *In Defense of Natural Law* (Oxford: Oxford University Press, 1999), p. 24.
10. *Cfr.* Finnis, *Natural Law and Natural Rights*, p. 86.
11. Siedentop, *Inventing the Individual*, p. 28, pp. 115 ff.
12. George, *Making Men Moral*, p. 210.
13. *Summa contra Gentiles*, III, 123.
14. J. S. Mill, *On Liberty*, ed. D. Bromwich and G. Kateb (New Haven, CT: Yale University Press, 2003) p. 87.
15. Mill, *On Liberty*, p. 121.
16. Tocqueville, *De la démocratie en Amérique I, II, 4* (Bib. Pléiade), p. 217 (Eng. trans. of the historical-critical ed. by E. Nolla, vol. II, Indianapolis: Liberty Fund, 2009), p. 309.
17. See *supra* chapter 1, 3.2.a.
18. *De la démocratie en Amérique II, II, 5*, p. 622 (Eng. trans. of the historical-critical ed. by E. Nolla, vol. III, Indianapolis, IN: Liberty Fund, 2009), p. 898.
19. See, in this regard, Finnis, *Natural Law and Natural Rights*, pp. 89–90. See also, in a similar vein and with an explicit reference to civil liberties, George, *Making Men Moral*, pp. 219–28.
20. See, as an illustrative example, the Spanish work of reference in the field by L. M. Díez-Picazo, *Sistema de derechos fundamentales*, 4th ed. (Madrid: Civitas, 2013), p. 227.
21. See *supra* chapter 3, 3.2.a.
22. See more extensively, with a reference to nearly all the constitutional texts recognizing such a right, F. Simón-Yarza, "Right to Freedom," in *Max Planck Encyclopedia of Comparative Constitutional Law* (Oxford: Oxford University Press, August 2016).

23. M. García Pelayo, *Derecho Constitucional Comparado*, in *Obras completas*, I, 2nd ed. (Madrid: Centro de Estudios Políticos y Constitucionales, 2009), p. 352.

24. See in this respect, the classical study by G. Jellinek, *Die Erklärung der Menschen- und Bürgerrechte* (Leipzig: Duncker & Humblot, 1895).

25. See the classical work by S. Warren and L. Brandeis, "The Right to Privacy," *Harvard Law Review* 4 (Dec. 15, 1890), 193.

26. See U. Di Fabio, "Art. 2, Abs. 2," in *Grundgesetz Kommentar*, eds. T. Maunz and G. Dürig (München: Beck, Sep. 43 [2004]), pp. 12, 54 ff. (§§ 4 and 51 ff.).

27. See *supra* chapter 1, 2.3.

28. Finnis, *Natural Law and Natural Rights*, p. 34.

29. Finnis, *Fundamentals of Ethics*, p. 69.

30. See, for example, the article by Paolo Flores d'Arcais, *Plaidoyer pour la liberté d'offenser*, published in *Philosophie magazine* on February 2015. Right after the attack, a massive display of solidarity was expressed through the slogan, initially posted on Twitter, *Je suis Charlie*. Meanwhile, as the offensive and repugnant cartoons were spread across the world, many people lost their sympathy for the magazine and, without ceasing to condemn the horrible attacks, emphatically asserted: *Je ne suis pas Charlie*. See, among the most notable opinions, D. Brooks, "I Am Not Charlie Hebdo," *New York Times*, January 8, 2015; T. Cole, "Unmournable Bodies," *New Yorker*, January 9, 2015; B. Klug, "The Moral Hysteria of *Je suis Charlie*," *Mondoweiss.net*, January 11, 2015. As time passed, the debate took some distance from the issue at stake, and several papers reflecting on the meaning and limits of religious freedom and of freedom of speech appeared in academic and cultural reviews.

31. Dworkin, *Taking Rights Seriously*, p. 188. See also, incidentally and in very broad terms, the assertion of a possible right to do wrong in J. Raz, *The Authority of Law*, 2nd ed. (Oxford: Oxford University Press, 2009), p. 274.

32. See J. Waldron, "A Right to Do Wrong," *Ethics* 92 (1981): 21–39. The article was replied to by W. Galston, "On the Alleged Right to Do Wrong: A Response to Waldron," *Ethics* 93 (1983): 320–24, and some time later, by R. P. George, "Taking Rights Seriously. Waldron on 'The Right to Do Wrong,'" in *Making Men Moral*, pp. 110–28. More recently, other authors have participated in the discussion, *v. gr.*, D. Enoch, "A Right to Violate One's Duty," *Law and Philosophy* 21 (2002): 355–84; and O. J. Herstein, "Defending the Right to Do Wrong," *Cornell Law Faculty Publications*, Paper 339 (2012), pp. 1–23.

33. Waldron, "A Right to Do Wrong," p. 29.

34. Waldron, "A Right to Do Wrong," p. 39.

35. George, *Making Men Moral*, pp. 115 ff.

36. J. Finnis, "Rights: Their Logic Restated," in *Collected Essays IV* (Oxford: Oxford University Press, 2011), pp. 375–88.

37. See W. N. Hohfeld, "Some Fundamental Legal Conceptions as Applied in Judicial Reasoning," *Yale Law Journal* 23 (1913): 16; repr. in Hohfeld, *Fundamental Legal Conceptions as Applied in Judicial Reasoning and Other Legal Essays* (New Haven, CT: Yale University Press, 1920), pp. 23–64.

38. "Always, when it is said that a given privilege is the mere negation of a duty, what is meant, of course, is a duty having a content or tenor precisely opposite to that of the privilege in question" (Hohfeld, "Some Fundamental Legal Conceptions," p. 39).

39. Finnis, "Rights," p. 378.

40. Hohfeld, "Some Fundamental Legal Conceptions," p. 40.

41. This is the central thesis maintained by Galston, "On the Alleged Right to Do Wrong," p. 321.

42. George, *Making Men Moral*, p. 119.

43. See, for example, M. Rhonheimer, "The Liberal Image of Man and the Concept of Autonomy," in *The Common Good of Constitutional Democracy* (Washington, DC: CUA, 2013), p. 69; "Rawls's '*Political Liberalism*' Revisited," pp. 239–48; and Finnis, "Limited Government," in *Collected Essays: Vol. III*, pp. 87 ff. George seems to hold a stricter position in *Making Men Moral*, pp. 32–33.

44. *S. Th.*, I-II, q. 100, a. 2; see also Finnis, *Aquinas*, pp. 222 ff.

45. *S. Th.*, II-II, q. 58, a. 8.

46. *S. Th.*, II-II, q. 122, a. 1: "Manifestissime autem ratio debiti, quae requiritur ad praeceptum, apparet in iustitia, quae est ad alterum, quia in his quae spectant ad seipsum, videtur primo aspectui quod homo sit sui dominus, et quod liceat ei facere quodlibet; sed in his quae sunt ad alterum, manifeste apparet quod homo est alteri obligatus ad reddendum ei quod debet."

47. Mill, *On Liberty*, p. 80.

48. This argument is also developed by Galston, "On the Alleged Right to Do Wrong," p. 323.

49. *S. Th.*, I-II, q. 91, a. 4; and q. 96, a. 1c and a. 2. See *supra*, chapter 1, 3.2.a.

50. See in particular the considerations—accompanied with abundant historical references—of Rhonheimer, "Rawls's '*Political Liberalism*' Revisited" and "Rawlsian Public Reason, Natural Law, and the Foundation of Justice," in *The Common Good of Constitutional Democracy*, pp. 190–291. See also, in a slightly different sense, the essays by R. P. George and C. Wolfe ("Natural Law and Public Reason") and by J. Finnis ("Abortion, Natural Law and Public Reason"), in George and Wolfe, eds., *Natural Law and Public Reason* (Washington, DC: Georgetown University Press, 2000), pp. 51–107; and, also by Finnis, "'Public Reason' and Moral Debate," in *Collected Essays*, I (Oxford: Oxford University Press, 2011), especially pp. 258–59.

51. Rhonheimer, "Rawls's '*Political Liberalism*' Revisited," p. 200 (emphasis mine). It is not right, however, the way Rhonheimer expresses himself when he affirms that "natural law, as such, does not distinguish moral actions generally from the specifically political," or that "natural-law reasons do not distinguish between the moral norms a person is obliged to impose on her own actions and what she legitimately may impose on the actions of others" ("Rawls's '*Political Liberalism*' Revisited," p. 199; the same idea is reiterated, e.g., in pp. 239 ff.). The distinction between what someone can impose on his action and what someone can impose on the actions of others is a distinction of practical reason and therefore of natural law.

52. See in a different sense, George, *Making Men Moral*, p. 122.

53. R. von Ihering, *Der Kampf um's Recht* (1872), ed. F. Ermacora (Berlin: Propyläen Verlag, 1992), p. 116; Eng. trans.: *The Struggle for Law* (Chicago, IL: Callaghan, 1915), p. 86.

Chapter 10

Perfectionist liberalism and restriction of the rights discourse

1. INTRODUCTION

In this last chapter of the book, I will revisit two important concepts that may prove helpful to understanding the meaning of rights in a pluralistic society: "personal autonomy" and "deliberative democracy." The first of these categories was developed by Joseph Raz to describe a positive defining feature of liberal modernity without falling into skepticism regarding the moral good. The second idea—Habermas's "deliberative democracy"—constitutes a demand for fairness in the process of determination of intersubjectively valid norms regarding fundamental moral questions in a pluralistic society. As I will defend below, deliberative democracy offers a good starting point for downgrading rights discourse in favor of a wider social dialogue around the common good and a more respectful attitude toward the rule of law.

2. "PERFECTIONIST LIBERALISM" AND "PERSONAL AUTONOMY" IN JOSEPH RAZ

In part II, I have attempted to underline some inconsistencies that, in my opinion, characterize the work of the two most important representatives of legal and political "antiperfectionist" liberalism. I would now like to discuss a line of liberal thought that is largely compatible with the classical teleological tradition and, in my view, much more fruitful than that followed by Rawls and Dworkin. I speak of "liberal perfectionism," whose main exponent has been the legal philosopher Joseph Raz.

In his notable work *The Morality of Freedom* (1986), Raz tried to find the essence of liberalism by distancing himself from ateleological proposals and exploring the importance that autonomy and pluralism have for modern political society. Desires and goals are subordinated, as Raz says, to reasons, and "one does not wish one's desire satisfied if one's reason for the desire is mistaken even if one continues, through ignorance, to entertain the desire. One does not wish merely not to have mistaken desires; one also does not wish to have them satisfied." This shows that "want-satisfaction as such cannot be an intrinsic good." For "not wishing that what one desires will happen if one's belief in a reason for it is mistaken is no more than an acknowledgment of the reason-dependent character of desire." Hence, "want-satisfaction *qua* want-satisfaction is not intrinsically valuable, at least not if there are valid ideal-regarding principles." In the end, "the only reason for satisfying other people's desires is to help them, i.e., help them get what is good for them or what they want." And "one does not help people to lead the lives they want to have by satisfying their false desires," because "people do not wish to have a life based on falsehood."[1]

In this last sentence, Raz has found the key that, at a deeper level, inexorably links teleology with desire: that which is truly good constitutes what we really and ultimately desire. Precisely because he does not fall prey to the degradation of freedom resulting from overlooking human teleology, Raz has been able to polish up certain genuinely liberal values that—for several reasons—played but a peripheral or marginal role in past centuries. For this reason, he includes proposals with which the classical tradition should engage and from which it could learn without giving up its identity.

In contrast to the "antiperfectionism" postulated by Rawls, Dworkin, and so many other authors, the final chapters of *The Morality of Freedom* propose a "perfectionist" or teleological liberalism whose distinctive feature is the preeminent role conferred on *personal autonomy* and *plurality of values*. It is undoubtedly a fruitful approach that avoids the evils of dropping teleology and allows for an authentic dialogue with the classical, teleological tradition—a dialogue from which, as I have just said, this tradition can benefit.

Above all, Raz develops the ideal of *autonomy* as characteristic of Western postindustrial societies. The issue is not simply *moral* autonomy, the capacity to choose the good as an attribute of the rational being. Raz has in mind what he labels *personal* autonomy, a particular ideal of modern life that lies in the capacity to write one's own biography by choosing from among a plurality of diverse goods. To summarize, this ideal affirms that "people should make their own lives" by "controlling, to some degree, their own destiny, fashioning it through successive decisions throughout their lives."[2] Consequently, autonomy is opposed both to coercion and to the lack of integrity of those whose existence oscillates without a unifying thread of meaning.[3] "The autonomous life is discerned not by what there is in it but by how it came to be."[4] This ideal of autonomy presupposes three conditions of real relevance for the exercise of political power:[5]

(a) The possession of "appropriate mental abilities," meaning of a minimum of practical rationality in order to understand the means required for the ends one has set and to make a coherent plan of life.
(b) Second, the autonomous life needs an "adequate range of options." This is what distinguishes the modern ideal of personal autonomy from the *homme situé* of past ages. Moral autonomy exists in both cases, but the ability to build a personal life project only exists when there is a range of options to choose from.
(c) Third, autonomy requires a certain "independence," understood as the absence of coercion and manipulation in the choice of one's life. Coercion and manipulation reduce the options and distort the processes of choice and formation of preferences, thus eliminating personal autonomy.

It is important to stress that, for Raz, "autonomy is valuable only if exercised in pursuit of the good," though it demands the individual be the author of their life by choosing from among diverse goods. Given that the possibility of choosing evil cannot be completely suppressed—especially in a modern, open society—personal autonomy requires "the availability of morally acceptable options."[6]

A highly relevant aspect from the political point of view is that, as happens with other political goods, personal autonomy requires a favorable and nurturing environment. It is certainly not possible to make someone autonomous, just as it is not possible to make them virtuous. Instability of character or hedonist depravation makes people incapable of writing a minimally coherent biography and put them at the mercy of their momentary whims. In this regard, however, the state's mission consists, as happens with the promotion of virtue, in creating an environment favorable to autonomy.[7] Moral ecology is an important part, in my view, of an atmosphere favorable to personal autonomy. Personal autonomy is not possible without a degree of integrity and personal stability that allows for keeping a consistent and committed life. How is it possible, we should ask ourselves, to achieve this integrity without a favorable ethical environment? Paradoxically, the virtues of autonomy are inextricably linked—as Alasdair MacIntyre has shown—with the virtues of dependence.[8]

Yet Raz considers that the pursuit of immoral options cannot be coercively restrained, for "the means used, coercive interference, violates the autonomy of its victim." In his view, "it violates the condition of independence and expresses a relation of domination and an attitude of disrespect for the coerced individual."[9] It would therefore be permissible to promote moral ecology through several incentives but never through state coercion. Robert P. George has criticized this thesis with a solid argument, namely, that punishing behavior against public morality does not *per se* imply a higher infraction of autonomy than punishing other harms and offenses.[10] Provided that we do not fall into superficial prudery or stifling moralism, restraining a behavior for the fact that it morally degrades society could be, of course, a service to the personal autonomy of citizens.

There remains here very little to add with regard to *value pluralism* that is not implicit in what has already been said. Without renouncing the existence of boundaries imposed by human teleology, Raz expressly affirms that there are many ways of flourishing. Even more, he says there exists a plurality of virtuous characters incompatible with each other, in the sense that they cannot be possessed by the same person at the same time. "Whichever form of life one is pursuing there are virtues which elude one because they are available only to people pursuing alternative and incompatible forms of life."[11] Not only is the pluralism of characters not wrong, but it constitutes an unquestionable richness for society. As has been indicated in the previous section, the aim of civil liberties is the pursuit of human goods. The particular way of exercising civil liberties and of pursuing those goods depends on each individual, and what fits with a healthy liberalism is that the range of options has a certain extension, meaning that the place occupied by someone in society is not be rigidly determined.

3. DELIBERATIVE DEMOCRACY AND RESTRICTION OF THE RIGHTS DISCOURSE

Raz's liberalism results in a plural political way of life in which people are confronted with a relatively wide range of noble life opportunities. This political doctrine implies no skepticism concerning the good life, nor does it make the mistake of justifying freedom with a disregard for the human goals it is aimed at. In my opinion, we are dealing with a fruitful and modern liberalism, free from the dehumanizing consequences that ateleological antiperfectionism carries within.

In this section, I would like to revisit an equally fruitful idea, proposed by Jürgen Habermas: "deliberative democracy." It has already been explained that the most fertile ground for discourse theory is the domain of law, and in particular the adequate design of the legislative process. The "intersubjective" point of view is not—*pace* Habermas—the moral point of view, though it is the political decision-making point of view. The moral determination of the *bonum* is monological, though the public verification of generally valid rules is dialogical. As I will maintain in the following pages, Habermas's discourse theory should lead us to revise a *praxis* that involves a serious obstacle for rational political deliberation: the misdirection of the difficult moral discussions splitting society to rights discourse and the interruption of that discourse through the constitutional courts.

3.1. The meaning of constitutional rights in the context of discourse theory

In his work *Between Facts and Norms*, Habermas developed the meaning of fundamental constitutional liberties from the point of view of his discourse theory. Liberties guarantee spaces of "private autonomy," that is, areas characterized by the "liberation from the obligations" of what Habermas calls "communicative freedom." These are, in other words, spaces removed from discourse, where one acts without the need to rationally verify one's conduct in accordance with the rules of discourse. "Private autonomy extends as far as the legal subject does *not* have to give others an account or give publicly acceptable reasons for her action plans." Or expressed differently, "legally granted liberties entitle one to *drop out of* communicative action, to refuse illocutionary obligations; they ground a privacy freed from the burden of reciprocally acknowledged and mutually expected communicative freedoms."[12]

It is difficult to offer a clearer and more accurate account of the political meaning of legal-positive fundamental freedoms than the one described by Habermas. When we recognize a fundamental right, a more or less specific issue—the content of that right—is removed from public deliberation and decision and an individual space of "self-government"—as it has been called by Attracta Ingram[13]—is created with regard to that issue. The political significance of characterizing a conduct as the content of a constitutional liberty is hence extraordinary. It is with good reason that the definition of constitutional liberties requires a constitutional consensus. It is an indispensable requirement in a democracy, for the definition of constitutional liberties involves a sharp political cut that will restrain the limits of discourse: whoever acts under the protection of fundamental liberties does not need to politically justify himself.

A democracy cannot exist without fundamental liberties, especially without freedom of speech. If communicative freedoms constitute a true "transcendental-pragmatic" presupposition of discourse, and if the aspiration to public deliberation constitutes a genuine aspiration of a democratic system, communicative freedoms become a basic premise of democracy. Here, Habermas follows the trail of the classical modern liberal political thinkers from Tocqueville to John Stuart Mill. However, an undue expansion of fundamental liberties puts at risk the very premise of democracy, for it tends to remove issues from political debate and limits the right to intervene. Once a behavior is included under the umbrella of civil liberties, whoever seeks to question such behavior faces the objections of an individual claiming to be exempt from the need for public justification. To the extent that the law legally acknowledges the legitimacy of such an autonomous space, the person who questions the behavior acts with a reduced freedom of speech, for they are *standing against rights*, that is, against spaces legally removed from discourse. Thus, given that every right involves a restriction of free speech, the undue expansion of rights illegitimately undermines freedom of speech and thus diminishes democracy.

3.2. The expansion of rights: An approach to the problem

As has just been indicated, fundamental freedoms play an essential role in a democracy, while at the same time, their undue expansion constitutes a threat for democracy and even for freedom itself. The two perennial questions, ever-present in political theory, are the following:

(a) What is the just measure of liberties ("substantive justice")? The answer can only come from practical reason. Without a discourse open to the integral human good, liberties lack any point or meaning.
(b) Who is competent to make intersubjectively valid decisions regarding the just measure of liberties ("procedural justice")? Or, to put it in classical terms: *Quis iudicabit?* Here, it seems fully appropriate to recall Habermas's proposal regarding the right *point of view* for the rational verification of normative contents with general validity. The political point of view—not the moral one—is the *intersubjective* point of view, and the exclusion of a substantive issue from future political discourses is the first act of political discourse. In other words, it is an act of the *constituent* discourse.

The answer just given to the second question raises serious doubts concerning an extended *praxis* of current jurisprudence, namely the expansion of rights *in the absence of a true constituent consensus*, the transformation of the great moral controversies into rights controversies and the subsequent restriction of public discourse. Originally, the criticism of the so-called jurisdictional state—in which the Supreme Court replaces the democratic legislator—was raised in Germany due to the transition from the liberal understanding of rights to their broader understanding as "principles" or "values."[14] This transition, to which I have devoted special attention in a long essay,[15] was criticized by some scholars in Germany, the most prominent among them perhaps being the legal theorist and constitutional lawyer Ernst-Wolfgang Böckenförde.[16]

However, the main problem of the expansion of the rights discourse and the replacement of the legislator—not the only problem but probably the deepest—has to do with judicial activism on morally controversial questions. This problem has been strongly debated in the United States. Yet, in contrast to the German controversy over value jurisprudence, the American debate has not taken place in the field of legal dogmatics but in those of political theory and constitutional interpretation theory.

In his work *Between Facts and Norms*, Habermas shows a deep knowledge of the American debate and, in some passages, he seems to favor dialogue and political compromise rather than a battle over "rights as trumps":

> Compromises make up the bulk of political decision-making processes in any case. Under conditions of cultural and societal pluralism, politically relevant goals often embody interests and value orientations that are by no means constitutive for the identity of the community at large, and hence are not constitutive for the whole of an intersubjectively shared form of life.[17]

Similarly, Cass Sunstein has maintained that "incompletely theorized agreements are well-suited to a system of adjudication, containing diverse people who disagree on first principles."[18]

3.3. The debate upon the expansion of rights: Revision of the arguments in favor of judicial activism

Before stating a definitive opinion with regard to solving the moral conflicts in the field of rights, I would like to point out some illusions or false approaches that frequently distort the discussion and tend to obscure political reasoning.

First, some advocates of judicial activism—chief among them Ronald Dworkin—have described their proposal as a "moral reading of the Constitution,"[19] which appears to confer upon it an ethical superiority over more restrictive theories. Frankly, this type of label does not contribute to clarifying the debate. By creating a solid consensus, the prescription of a restrictive canon is an attempt to restrict *externally* ("preinterpretively," to use Dworkin's own terminology) the judge's interpretive options, not to curtail his *internal* moral reasoning. In fact, restrictive theories do not exclude the "interpretive optimization" of the constitutional clauses by the judge, but rather suggest the need for the creation of a restrictive "preinterpretive consensus" that would *externally* restrain the judge's competence, and therefore would be prior to his *internal* optimization of the clauses. In other words, judicial minimalism is not an answer to the hard cases but rather an attempt to reduce the number of hard cases by creating a preinterpretive consensus favorable to a restrictive vision of judicial review. When a "paradigm" or a "preinterpretive consensus" exists, as Dworkin says, "a variety of forces . . . conspires toward convergence."[20] For the judicial minimalist, this convergence advances democratic values and fits better with the rule of law.[21]

The question is also often wrongly addressed in the *natural law tradition*. It is not uncommon to hear that, given the *natural law origins of rights*, judges should never defer to the legislature where such rights are at issue. The difficulty with this argument is that it does not address the question of which branch of government should have the power to authoritatively determine the content of natural law. Thus, for example, John Locke, who was perhaps the most influential proponent of the view that the legitimacy of power depends upon the protection of the natural rights of individuals, simultaneously argued for the supremacy of the Parliament and also contended that any effort by Parliament to transfer its power to others would itself be illegitimate.[22] In other words, "to govern, on Locke's account, is to make a public judgment as to what natural law requires—both in general and in detail and to set that judgment up as a basis for social coordination and enforcement. And that is what the Lockean legislature does."[23]

Similarly, nothing in the classical natural law tradition suggests that the courts rather than the legislature should have the final authority to determine the content of natural law. According to the main proponents of this theory, natural law neither dictates the appropriate means for its "implementation" nor prescribes any particular authority to implement it.[24] Therefore, there is no substantive requirement of justice that is inconsistent with the idea that primary responsibility for determining the content of justice and natural law rests with the legislative branch; on the contrary, considerations of fairness suggest that the legislature should have that power in a pluralistic society. *Quod omnes tangit ab omnibus approbari debet*.

Turning to the liberal arguments in favor of an expansive interpretation, Ronald Dworkin has suggested that judicial review can provide a superior republican deliberation, a *forum of principles* in which the judges are in a better position to make decisions on principle. This argument appeals to the justice of the outcomes and the quality of public debate in the context of a wide moral reading of the Constitution. According to Dworkin,

> There is no necessary connection between a citizen's political impact or influence and the ethical benefit he secures through participating in public discussion or deliberation. The quality of the discussion might be better, and his own contribution more genuinely deliberative and public spirited, in a general public *debate* preceding or following a judicial decision than in a political *battle* culminating in a legislative vote or even a referendum.[25]

This opinion of Ronald Dworkin is open to several objections. While it is true that the deliberation of the legislature does not guarantee results that are consistent with the definition of the primary principles of justice, there is no reason to believe that the deliberation of a high court will produce such results either. Dworkin's thesis lacks sufficient empirical support, as is shown by the very history of judicial review concerning the cases around which there was no consensus at the time they were decided. Let us think, for example, of the interpretive activism of the U.S. Supreme Court in *Dred Scott v. Sandford* (1857), the decision that created a constitutional right to own slaves; or *Lochner v. New York* (1905), the decision denying public authorities the power to limit working hours—which clearly contrasts with, for example, the beneficial activism displayed in *Brown v. Board of Education* (1954), the decision ordering desegregation. Even if we consider current controversial issues, it is not possible to demonstrate conclusively, as Waldron has explained, that the discussion has been superior in those countries where a high court has removed the controversy from the political sphere.[26]

Moreover, the very nature of judicial review appears to demonstrate the contrary. Dworkin calls our attention to the deliberation that follows the decision when, ironically, such deliberation is curtailed by the decision itself, which fixes at the level of constitutional consensus highly controversial issues upon which such consensus does not exist.[27] The definition of a *fundamental right* creates a *disability*—to follow W. Hohfeld's typology of legal positions—for the legislator.[28] In the absence of a constitutional consensus, the binding force of precedent is, in fact, a defect, even though it does confer authority on the judge's decision. When a constitutional consensus is lacking, the decision must have the provisional status typical of a deliberative democracy, that is, it must continue to be subjected to legislative discussion and to majority rule. A decision concerning highly controversial moral issues cannot set a constitutional precedent without offending dissenters.[29] Thus, referring to the "expansive" interpretation of the *Bill of Rights* by the Supreme Court of Ireland, Judge John Kenny observed, "Judges have become legislators and have the advantage that they do not have to face an opposition."[30]

Furthermore, it is important to add that decisions on questions of principle are precisely the main object of constitutional and ordinary legislation in a democracy, since they are the ones carried out in accordance with *natural moral reason* and not with the *artificial reason* of legal technique.[31] All profound moral questions not settled by the Constitution raise ethical considerations concerning public goods that transcend the individual. Restricting these discussions to the discourse of legal rights may distort and impair natural moral reason instead of enriching it. The artificial reason of law is a great servant but a terrible master. Taken in its proper role, it is essential to the rule of a stable and predictable order of law, but it fails when it attempts to supplant natural reason. If we burden the court with the task of solving the moral questions that split society on the sole grounds of an abstract positive basis that is in fact eclipsed by metapositive reasons, we cannot say that the court is behaving as an enforcer of positive law. Ironically, this criticism of the abuse of constitutional jurisdiction through the moral enforcement of abstract clauses of rights had already been made by the main inspiration behind the European system of judicial review: Hans Kelsen.[32] In any case, one does not need to be a positivist to defend the rule of law and the legal predetermination of judicial decisions. Drawing on arguments based on the ideal of rule of law, natural law scholar John Finnis has reached very similar conclusions to those defended by Kelsen.[33] The criticism of an excessive judicial arbitrariness constitutes a classical theme, already present in Aristotle's *Rhetoric*.[34]

Finally, we have to consider the problem of the *risk of error*. Certainly, this risk is run both when the decision is made by representative popular institutions and when it is made by a court. Nevertheless, to the extent that both political opponents defend their views as fundamental rights before a high court, the error on the part of the latter may bring with it a special moral degradation to society. The right defended by one party (e.g., the right to life of the unborn) is considered by the other party a violation of a right (e.g., the right to privacy of the mother) and vice versa. In the absence of a moral consensus, a purely accidental majority in the court would turn the violation of a fundamental right into a fundamental right. The most repugnant thing about *Dred Scott* is that, by abusing the text of the U.S. Constitution, it consecrated slavery as a right by asserting that "the right of property in a slave is distinctly and expressly affirmed in the Constitution."[35] In his debates with Douglas, Lincoln stated,

> I believe that no fault can be pointed out in that argument; assuming the truth of the premises, the conclusion, so far as I have capacity at all to understand it, follows inevitably. There is a fault in it as I think, but the fault is not in the reasoning; the falsehood in fact is a fault of the premises. I believe that the right of property in a slave is not distinctly and expressly affirmed in the Constitution, and Judge Douglas thinks it is.[36]

This characterization of slavery was the premise on which Justice Taney based his decision and which Lincoln refuted. If we reflect that the main moral controversies have been decided in the past decades by the courts, we have serious reasons to ask ourselves: are we not in some cases converting the violations of rights into rights? Precisely for ethical considerations, it is preferable for the controversial decisions to be adopted on the level of ordinary legislation: let the successes be legislative successes and the errors be legislative errors. Otherwise, we run the risk of trivializing human rights. This argument—which was advanced by John Finnis in his Maccabean Lecture in Jurisprudence at the British Academy (1985)[37]—is perhaps the strongest *moral* argument in favor of judicial restraint.

3.4. CONCLUSION

For all the above-mentioned reasons, I deem it necessary to remove the moral controversies splitting society from the jurisdictional field of human, fundamental, or constitutional rights. In the United States, liberal interpretivism has faced the strong opposition of originalism, a judicial philosophy that proposes a return to the original public understanding of the text to unfold its meaning.[38] Notwithstanding the complexity of this debate and the criticisms that originalism may deserve, to a great extent it has emerged as a reaction against the persistent abuse of the constitutional text since the early 1960s. Considering the abuse of the text and the consequent reaction of originalism, I cannot help citing Socrates's wise words in the *Phaedrus*:

> You know, Phaedrus, that's the strange thing about writing, which makes it truly analogous to painting. The painter's products stand before us as though they were alive, but if you question them, they maintain a most majestic silence. It is the same with written words; they seem to talk to you as though they were intelligent, but if you ask them anything about what they say, from a desire to be instructed, they go on telling you just the same thing forever. And once a thing is put in writing, the composition, whatever it may be, drifts all over the place, getting into the hands not only of those who understand it, but equally of those who have no business with it; it doesn't know how to address the right people, and not address the wrong. *And when it is ill-treated and unfairly abused it always needs its parent to come to its help*, being unable to defend or help itself.
> —PHAEDRUS: Once again you are perfectly right.[39]

Without undertaking here an in-depth analysis of the ideal method of constitutional interpretation, it suffices to conclude that rational deliberation upon the great political questions dividing society is not possible if those questions are settled in the battlefield of "rights as trumps." In this sense, it may be appropriate to finish the book by briefly recalling the framework of understanding with which it opened. I suggested in the Preface that, due to the influence of "antiperfectionist" or "ateleological" liberalism, the desire principle now often replaces practical reason in the interpretation and definition of the content of rights. At the crossroads between reason (see part I) and desire (see part II), the option in favor of reason requires honest and peaceful deliberation. Facing "reasonable pluralism" by removing the question of the human good from the discussion about the scope of rights is neither just nor fair. It entails conferring constitutional *status* on a particular "comprehensive doctrine" whose consequences are, as I have attempted to show in part III, dehumanizing. What reasonable pluralism demands is to recognize the plurality of paths for human fulfillment and, wherever there are discrepancies, to envisage and design the political institutions called to solve them in a fair manner (part IV). The genuine idea of "public reason" does not require neutrality with regard to the human good. What it requires is to adjust the force of the different decisions to the actual degree of consensus that has produced them. Consequently, the meaning of constitutional rights can only be the outcome of a constituent public reason.

NOTES

1. Raz, *Morality of Freedom*, pp. 139–44.
2. Raz, *Morality of Freedom*, p. 369.
3. Raz, *Morality of Freedom*, pp. 381–85.
4. Raz, *Morality of Freedom*, p. 371 (emphasis mine).
5. Raz, *Morality of Freedom*, pp. 372–78.
6. Raz, *Morality of Freedom*, p. 381.
7. Raz, *Morality of Freedom*, p. 407.
8. MacIntyre, *Dependent Rational Animals*, p. 5.
9. Raz, *The Morality of Freedom*, p. 418.
10. George, *Making Men Moral*, pp. 182–88.
11. Raz, *Morality of Freedom*, p. 396. Rightly understood, this thesis does not contradict, in my view, the classical doctrine of the interconnection of virtues. According to Aristotle, all virtues are present in the virtue of prudence, for the prudent person lives in accordance with reason *(Nich. Eth.*, VI, 1144b). When he speaks of incompatible virtues, Raz understands virtue as a mere positive inclination of character, what Thomas Aquinas calls "matter of virtue" *(S. Th.*, I-II, q. 66, a. 2) or "imperfect moral virtue" (q. 65, a. 1). In this sense, virtues are not interconnected.
12. Habermas, *Between Facts and Norms*, pp. 119–20.
13. A. Ingram, *A Political Theory of Rights* (Oxford: Oxford University Press, 1994), pp. 17 ff., 168 ff., 214 ff.
14. The origins of this interpretation may be found in Rudolf Smend's constitutional theory, developed in *Verfassung und Verfassungsrecht* (München and Leipzig: Duncker & Humblot, 1928). Smend conceived of the catalog of fundamental rights as the social "system of values" (*Wertsystem*) (p. 163). On the historical development of this doctrine, see the documented work by K. Stern, *Das Staatsrecht der Bundesrepublik Deutschland*, III/1 (München: Beck, 1988), pp. 890–907. In contemporary constitutional theory, the most important defense of fundamental rights as principles or "optimization requirements" may be found in Robert Alexy's theory of fundamental rights. For a sharp criticism of Robert Alexy's theory of rights, see F. J. Urbina,

"A Critique of Proportionality," *American Journal of Jurisprudence* 57 (2012): 52 ff.; and *A Critique of Proportionality and Balancing* (Cambridge: Cambridge University Press, 2017).

15. Simón-Yarza, *Medio ambiente y derechos fundamentales*, pp. 99–205.

16. E.-W. Böckenförde, "Grundrechte als Grundsatznormen. Zur gegenwärtigen Lage der Grundrechtsdogmatik," *Der Staat* 29 (1990): 1 ff.

17. Habermas, *Between Facts and Norms*, pp. 282–83.

18. C. Sunstein, *Legal Reasoning and Political Conflict* (New York; Oxford: Oxford University Press, 1996), p. 192. See also A. Gutmann and D. Thompson, *Democracy and Disagreement: Why Moral Conflict Cannot Be Avoided in Politics, and What Should Be Done about It* (Cambridge, MA: Harvard University Press, 1996); and R. P. George, "Law, Democracy and Moral Disagreement," in *In Defense of Natural Law* (Oxford: Oxford University Press, 1999), pp. 315 ff.

19. See R. Dworkin, "The Moral Reading and the Majoritarian Premise," in *Freedom's Law* (Cambridge: Harvard University Press, 1996), pp. 1–38.

20. Dworkin, *Law's Empire*, p. 88.

21. See C. Sunstein, *A Constitution of Many Minds* (Princeton, NJ: Princeton University Press, 2009), p. 23.

22. See J. Locke, *Two Treatises of Government*, II, 2nd ed. 24 repr. (Cambridge: Cambridge University Press, 2013), especially paragraph 212 (p. 407).

23. J. Waldron, *Law and Disagreement* (New York: Oxford University Press, 2001), p. 308. Waldron's distinction between *moral rights* and *legal rights* runs in a similar direction (see "Between Rights and the Bill of Rights," in Waldron, *Law and Disagreement*, p. 211).

24. See *supra*, chapter 1, 3.2.b.

25. See R. Dworkin, "The Forum of Principle," in *Matter of Principle*, pp. 69 ff.; and *Freedom's Law*, p. 30 (emphasis mine). In subsequent writings, Dworkin has introduced an interesting distinction between what he labels *partnership conception of democracy* and *majoritarian conception of democracy* (see *v. gr., Justice in Robes* [Cambridge, MA: Belknap Press of Harvard University Press, 2006], pp. 132 ff.; *Is Democracy Possible Here?* [Princeton, NJ: Princeton University Press, 2006], pp. 131 ff.; and, above all, his comprehensive work, *Justice for Hedgehogs*, pp. 382 ff.). Dworkin admits deviations from the principle of equal impact if, without discrimination, the legitimacy of the decisions is improved, and the results are more consistent with the dignity of the citizens. Despite the appropriateness of this distinction, the harms of an expansive judicial interpretation of rights on moral issues outbalance the eventual benefits.

26. See *v. gr.* Waldron, *Law and Disagreement*, p. 290.

27. In this sense, Rawls's opinion in favor of judicial activism and the extraparliamentary decision of the main moral issues dividing society—an opinion that is close to the one defended by Dworkin—stands in striking contrast to his defense of a "pure procedural justice" in *A Theory of Justice*. See, in this vein, Rawls, *Political Liberalism*, pp. 231 ff.: "The Supreme Court as Exemplar of Public Reason." See also the *Amici curiae* brief submitted before the U.S. Supreme Court on January 8, 1997, by Ronald Dworkin, Thomas Nagel, Robert Nozick, John Rawls, Thomas Scanlon, and

Judith Jarvis Thomson, defending the enshrinement of a right to euthanasia in the cases *State of Washington et al. v. Glucksberg et al.* and *Vacco et al. v. Quill et al.*

28. *Cfr.* Hart, *Concept of Law*, p. 69; and Waldron, *Law and Disagreement*, p. 221.

29. In a similar sense, see Sunstein, *Constitution of Many Minds*, p. 42.

30. J. Kenny, "The Advantages of a Written Constitution Incorporating a Bill of Rights," *North Ireland Legal Quarterly* 30 (1979): 196; *apud* Finnis, *Collected Essays III*, p. 43.

31. The distinction between the *artificial reason* of law and *natural reason* is stated succinctly by Sir Edward Coke in his famous passage of the *Commentary Upon Littleton:* "'Nihil quo est contra rationem est licitum'; for reason is the life of the law, nay the common law itselfe is nothing else but reason; which is to be understood of an artificiall perfection of reason; gotten by long study, observation and experience, and not of every man's naturall reason; for, Nemo nascitur artifex" (The first part of the Institutes of the Law of England, or, *A commentary upon Littleton* [1628], 97b [Philadelphia: 1st American, from the 16th European Edition, Johnson and Warner and Samuel L. Fisher, vol. I, 1812], p. 337).

32. See in this vein his sharp remarks in "Wesen und Entwicklung der Staatsgerichtsbarkeit," in *Veröffentlichungen der Vereinigung der Deutschen Staatsrechtslehrer*, 5 (Berlin and Leipzig: Walter de Gruyter, 1929), pp. 68–70.

33. See his *Maccabean Lecture* before the British Academy, "Human Rights and Their Enforcement," in *Collected Essays III*, pp. 19 ff.

34. *Rhetoric*, 1354a.

35. *Dred Scott v. Sandford*, 60 US 393 (1856).

36. A. Lincoln and S. Douglas, *The Lincoln-Douglas Debates* (Mineola, NY: Dover, 2004), p. 234.

37. J. Finnis, "Human Rights and Their Enforcement," p. 43: "Here, perhaps, is the special insult added to the injury done when courts, in the name of rights, have overturned statutes and thereby sustained, abetted, or even imposed child labour, widespread pornography, and abortion. It is not so much that the constitutional status of the bill of rights impedes prompt remedies for these injustices. Rather, it is the inauthenticity of the appearances which the courts in these cases kept up—the appearance of doing what courts characteristically do when doing justice according to law." See several contributions to this topic in A. Sajó, ed., *Abuse: The Dark Side of Fundamental Rights* (Utrecht: Eleven International Publish, 2006); M. Cartabia, "L'universalità dei diritti umani nell'età dei nuovi diritti," *Quaderni costituzionali* 3 (2009): 537–68; and K. Lohmus, *Caring Autonomy: European Court of Human Rights and the Challenge of Individualism* (New York: Cambridge University Press, 2015).

38. See mainly R. Bork, *The Tempting of America. The Political Seduction of the Law* (New York: Free Press, 1990); and A. Scalia, *A Matter of Interpretation* (Princeton, NJ: Princeton University Press, 1998).

39. Plato, *Phaedrus*, 275d–e (emphasis mine).

Bibliography

Agar, N., *Liberal Eugenics* (Oxford: Blackwell, 2004).
Alexy, R., *Der Theorie des rationalen Diskurses als Theorie der juristische Begründung* (Frankfurt am Main: Suhrkamp, 1983).
———, *Theorie der Grundrechte* (Frankfurt am Main: Suhrkamp, 1986).
Annas, J., *The Morality of Happiness* (Oxford: Oxford University Press, 1994).
Aquinas, T., *Opera omnia*, ed. Enrique Alarcón (www.corpusthomisticum.org); for the *Summa Theologiae*: Engl. trans. *The Summa Theologica of S. Thomas Aquinas*, 5 vols. (Westminster, MD: Christian Classics, 1981).
Aristotle, *The Complete Works of Aristotle* (The Revised Oxford Translation, ed. Jonathan Barnes, 2 vols., Princeton, NJ: Princeton University Press—Bollingen Series, 1984, repr. 1995).
Augustine, St., *De civitate Dei*, in *Corpus Christianorum Series Latina*, XLVII–XVIII (Turnhout: Brepols, 1955).
———, *De Libero Arbitrio*, in *Corpus Christianorum Series Latina*, XXIX (Turnhout: Brepols, 1970).
———, *De Ordine*, in *Corpus Christianorum Series Latina*, XXIX (Turnhout: Brepols, 1970).
Bacon, F., *Novum Organum*, in *The Works of Lord Bacon, Collected and Edited by James Spedding, Robert Leslie Ellis and Douglas Denon Heath*, vol. I (London: Longman, 1858).
Bentham, J., *Theory of Legislation* (London: Trübner, 1864).
Berlin, I., "Five Essays on Liberty: Introduction," in Isaiah Berlin, *Liberty* (Oxford: Oxford University Press, 2002).
———, "Historical Inevitability," in Isaiah Berlin, *Liberty* (Oxford: Oxford University Press, 2002).
———, "Two Concepts of Liberty," in Isaiah Berlin, *Liberty* (Oxford: Oxford University Press, 2002).
———, *The Crooked Timber of Humanity: Chapter in the History of Ideas*, 2nd ed. (Princeton, NJ; Oxford: Princeton University Press, 2013).

Berti, E., "L'uso 'scientifico' della dialettica in Aristotele," in *Nuovi studi aristotelici* (Brescia: Morcelliana, 2014), pp. 265–82.

Böckenförde, E.-W., "Die Entstehung des Staates als Vorgang der Säkularisation," in *Staat—Gesellschaft—Freiheit. Studien zur Staatstheorie und zum Verfassungsrecht* (Frankfurt am Main: Suhrkamp, 1976).

———, "Grundrechte als Grundsatznormen. Zur gegenwärtigen Lage der Grundrechtsdogmatik," *Der Staat* 29 (1990): 1–31.

Bork, R., *The Tempting of America: The Political Seduction of the Law* (New York: Free Press, 1990).

Buchanan, A., *Beyond Humanity?* (Oxford: Oxford University Press, 2011).

Budziszewski, J., *Commentary on Thomas Aquinas's Treatise on Law* (Cambridge: University Press, 2014).

Byrd, S., and Hruschka, J., *Kant's Doctrine of Right* (Cambridge: Cambridge University Press, 2010).

Cartabia, M., "L'universalità dei diritti umani nell'età dei nuovi diritti," *Quaderni costituzionali* 3 (2009): 537–68.

Coke, E., *The First Part of the Institutes of the Law of England, or, A Commentary upon Littleton* (1st American, from the 16th European Edition, Philadelphia: Johnson and Warner and Samuel L. Fisher, 1812).

Comte, A., *Catéchisme positiviste* (Paris: de Sandre, 2009).

Condorcet, N., *Outlines of an Historical View of the Progress of Human Mind* (Philadelphia, PA: Lang and Ustick, 1796).

Corvino, J., Anderson, R. T., and Girgis, S., *Debating Religious Liberty and Discrimination* (Oxford: Oxford University Press, 2017).

De Lazari-Radek, K., and Singer, P., *The Point of View of the Universe: Sidgwick and Contemporary Ethics* (Oxford: Oxford University Press, 2014).

Descartes, R., *Discourse de la Méthode* (Paris: Librairie Joseph Gibert, 1943).

Devlin, P., *The Enforcement of Morals* (Oxford: Oxford University Press, 1965).

Di Fabio, U., "Art. 2, Abs. 2," in *Grundgesetz Kommentar*, eds. T. Maunz and G. Dürig (München: Beck, 2004).

Diels, H. A., *Die Fragmente der Vorsokratiker* (Berlin: August Raabe, 1897). Eng. trans. *Kathleen Freeman* (Cambridge, MA: Harvard University Press, 1948).

Díez-Picazo, L. M., *Sistema de derechos fundamentales*, 4th ed. (Madrid: Civitas, 2013).

Domingo, R., "Religion for Hedgehogs? An Argument against the Dworkinian Approach of Religious Freedom," *Oxford Journal of Law and Religion* 2, 2 (2013): 371–92.

Dworkin, R., "Lord Devlin and the Enforcement of Morals," *Yale Law Review* 75 (1965–1966): 986–1005.

———, *Taking Rights Seriously* (Cambridge, MA: Harvard University Press, 1977).

———, "Rights as Trumps," in *Theories of Rights*, ed. Jeremy Waldron (New York: Oxford University Press, 1984), pp. 153–67.

———, "The Forum of Principle," in *A Matter of Principle* (Oxford: Oxford University Press, 1985), pp. 33–71.

———, "Liberalism," in *A Matter of Principle* (Oxford: Oxford University Press, 1985), pp. 181–204.

———, "Do We Have a Right to Pornography," in *A Matter of Principle* (Oxford: Oxford University Press, 1985), pp. 335–72.
———, *Law's Empire* (Cambridge, MA: Belknap Press of Harvard University Press, 1986).
———, "The Original Position" (1973), in *Reading Rawls*, ed. N. Daniels (Oxford: Blackwell, 1989), pp. 17–53.
———, *Foundations of Liberal Equality* (Salt Lake City: University of Utah Press, 1990).
———, *Life's Dominion: An Argument about Abortion, Euthanasia and Individual Freedom* (New York: Random House, 1993).
———, "The Moral Reading and the Majoritarian Premise," in *Freedom's Law* (Cambridge, MA: Harvard University Press, 1996), pp. 1–38.
———, "Playing God: Genes, Clones, and Luck," in *Sovereign Virtue: The Theory and Practice of Equality* (Cambridge, MA: Harvard University Press, 2000), pp. 427–52.
———, "Equality and the Good Life," in *Sovereign Virtue: The Theory and Practice of Equality* (Cambridge, MA: Harvard University Press, 2002), pp. 237–84.
———, *Is Democracy Possible Here?* (Princeton, NJ: Princeton University Press, 2006).
———, *Justice in Robes* (Cambridge, MA: Belknap Press of Harvard University Press, 2006).
———, *Justice for Hedgehogs* (Cambridge, MA: Belknap Press of Harvard University Press, 2011).
———, *Religion without God* (Cambridge, MA: Harvard University Press, 2013).
Dworkin et al., *Amici curiae* Ronald Dworkin, Thomas Nagel, Robert Nozick, John Rawls, Thomas Scanlon, and Judith Jarvis Thomson, *State of Washington et al. v. Glucksberg et al.* and *Vacco et al. v. Quill et al.*, January 8, 1997.
Ely, J., *Democracy and Distrust. A Theory of Judicial Review* (Cambridge, MA: Harvard University Press, 1981).
Enoch, D., "A Right to Violate One's Duty," *Law and Philosophy* 21 (2002): 355–84.
Faggion, A., Pinzani, A., and Sánchez Madrid, N., eds., *Kant and Social Policies* (London: Palgrave Macmillan, 2016).
Ferguson, J., *Moral Virtues in the Ancient World* (London: Methuen, 1958).
Finnis, J., *Fundamentals of Ethics* (Washington, DC: Georgetown University Press, 1983).
———, *Aquinas: Moral, Political, and Legal Theory* (Oxford: Oxford University Press, 1998, repr. 2004).
———, *Natural Law and Natural Rights*, 2nd ed. (Oxford: Oxford University Press, 2011).
———, "Discourse, Truth, and Friendship," in *Collected Essays*, I (Oxford: Oxford University Press, 2011), pp. 41–61.
———, "'Public Reason' and Moral Debate," in *Collected Essays*, I (Oxford: Oxford University Press, 2011), pp. 256–76.
———, "Human Rights and Their Enforcement," in *Collected Essays*, III (Oxford: Oxford University Press, 2011), pp. 19–46.

———, "Duties to Oneself in Kant," in *Collected Essays*, III (Oxford: Oxford University Press, 2011), pp. 47–71.
———, "Rawls's A Theory of Justice," in *Collected Essays*, III (Oxford: Oxford University Press, 2011), pp. 72–75.
———, "Limited Government," in *Collected Essays*, III (Oxford: Oxford University Press, 2011), pp. 83–106.
———, "Rights: Their Logic Restated," in *Collected Essays*, IV (Oxford: Oxford University Press, 2011), pp. 375–88.
Flores d'Arcais, P., "Plaidoyer pour la liberté d'offenser," *Philosophie magazine* (Feb. 2015).
Frankfurt, H., "Freedom of the Will and the Concept of a Person," *Journal of Philosophy* LXVIII (1971): 5–20.
Freud, S., "Formulations on the Two Principles of Mental Functioning" (1911), in *The Standard Edition of the Complete Works of Sigmund Freud*, XII (London: Hoghart Press, 1953).
———, *Jenseits des Lustprinzips* (1920), in *Gesammelte Werke*, XIII, 8th ed. (Frankfurt am Main: Fischer, 1976).
Fukuyama, F., *Our Posthuman Future: Consequences of the Biotechnology Revolution* (New York: Farrar, Strauss & Giroux, 2002).
Fuller, L., "Positivism and Fidelity to Law: A Reply to Professor Hart," *Harvard Law Review* 71–74 (1958): 630–72.
Gadamer, H.-G., *Wahrheit und Methode. Grundzüge einer philosphische Hermeneutik*, in *Gesammelte Werke*, vol. I (Tubingen: Mohr Siebeck, 1990).
Gagarin, M., *Antiphon the Athenian: Oratory, Law and Justice in the Age of the Sophists* (Austin: University of Texas Press, 2002).
Galston, W., "On the Alleged Right to Do Wrong. A Response to Waldron," *Ethics* 93 (1983): 320–24.
García Pelayo, M., *Derecho Constitucional Comparado*, en *Obras completas*, I, 2nd ed. (Madrid: Centro de Estudios Políticos y Constitucionales, 2009).
Gentili, A., *De iure belli* (Oxford: Clarendon Press, 1933, repr. ed. 1612).
George, R. P., *Making Men Moral* (Oxford: Oxford University Press, 1993).
———, *In Defense of Natural Law* (Oxford: Oxford University Press, 1999).
George, R. P., and Lee, P., *Body-Self Dualism in Contemporary Ethics and Politics* (Cambridge: Cambridge University Press, 2008).
George, R. P., and Tollefsen, C., *Embryo* (New York: Doubleday, 2008).
George, R. P., and Wolfe, C., eds., *Natural Law and Public Reason* (Washington, DC: Georgetown University Press, 2000).
Glendon, M. A., *Rights Talk: The Impoverishment of Political Discourse* (New York: Free Press, 1991).
Goethe, J. W., *Orphisch*, ΔAIMΩN, *Dämon*.
Gómez Montoro, Á. J., "*Vida privada y autonomía personal o una interpretación passe-partout del artículo 8 CEDH*," in VV.AA., *La Constitución política de España. Estudios en homenaje a Manuel Aragón Reyes* (Madrid: Centro de Estudios Políticos y Constitucionales, 2016), pp. 617–50.
Gray, J., *Enlightenment's Wake: Politics and Culture at the Close of the Modern Age* (London; New York: Routledge, 2007).

Gutmann, A., and Thomson, D., *Democracy and Disagreement: Why Moral Conflict Cannot Be Avoided in Politics, and What Should Be Done about It* (Cambridge, MA: Harvard University Press, 1996).

Habermas, J., "Die Utopie des guten Herrschers," *Merkur* 26 (1972): 1266 ff.

———, *Moralbewußtsein und kommunikatives Handeln* (Frankfurt am Main: Suhrkamp, 1983). Eng. trans.: *Moral Consciousness and Communicative Action* (Cambridge: MIT Press, 1990).

———, *Erläuterungen zur Diskursethik* (Frankfurt am Main: Suhrkamp, 1991). Eng. trans.: *Justification and Application. Remarks on Discourse Ethics* (Cambridge: MIT Press, 1993).

———, *Faktizität und Geltung. Beiträge zur Diskurstheorie des Rechts und des demokratischen Rechtsstaats* (Frankfurt am Main: Suhrkamp, 1992). Eng. trans.: *Between Facts and Norms: Contributions to a Discourse Theory of Democracy* (Cambridge: MIT Press, 1996).

———, *Die Zukunft der menschlicher Natur. Auf den Weg zu einer liberalen Eugenik?* (Frankfurt am Main: Suhrkamp, 2001). Eng. trans. (with an additional "postscript"): *The Future of Human Nature* (Cambridge, MA: Polity Press, 2003).

———, "Religion in der Öffentlichkeit: Kognitive Voraussetzungen für den 'öffentlichen Vernunftgebrauch' religiöser und säkularer Bürger,' " in *Zwischen Naturalismus und Religion: Philosophische Aufsätze* (Frankfurt am Main: Suhrkamp, 2005), pp. 119–54.

Habermas, J., and Ratzinger, J., *Dialektik der Säkularisierung. Über Vernunft und Religion* (Freiburg-Basel-Vienna: Herder, 2005).

Hart, H. L. A., "Separation of Law and Morals," *Harvard Law Review* 71, 4 (1958): 593–629.

———, "Bentham on Legal Rights," in *Oxford Essays in Jurisprudence*, Second Series, ed. A. W. B. Simpson (Oxford: Clarendon Press, 1973).

———, "Rawls on Liberty and Its Priority" (1973), in *Reading Rawls*, ed. N. Daniels (Oxford: Blackwell, 1989), pp. 230–52.

———, *The Concept of Law*, 2nd ed. (Oxford: Oxford University Press, 1994).

Herstein, O. J., "Defending the Right to Do Wrong," *Cornell Law Faculty Publications*, Paper 339 (2012): 1–23.

Hitler, A., *Mein Kampf* (München: Eher, 1936).

Hobbes, T., *Leviathan sive de materia, forma et potestate civitatis ecclesiasticae et civilis*, en *Thomae Hobbes Malmesburiensis Opera philosophica quae latine scripsit omnia*, vol. III (London: John Bohn, 1841; repr. Aalen: Scientia Verlag, 1966).

———, *Leviathan, or The Matter, Form, and Power of a Commonwealth Ecclesiastical and Civil* (Oxford: Oxford University Press, 1998).

———, *Elementorum Philosophiae Sectio Prima De Corpore*, en *Thomae Hobbes Malmesburiensis Opera philosophica quae latine scripsit omnia*, vol. I (London: John Bohm, 1839; repr. Aalen: Scientia Verlag, 1966).

Hohfeld, W. N., "Some Fundamental Legal Conceptions as Applied in Judicial Reasoning," 23 *Yale Law Journal* 23 (1913): 16; repr. Hohfeld, *Fundamental Legal Conceptions as Applied in Judicial Reasoning and Other Legal Essays* (New Haven, CT: Yale University Press, 1920), pp. 23–64.

Holmes, O. W., *Holmes-Laski Letters*, vol. 1 (Cambridge, MA: Harvard University Press, 1953).

Horkheimer, M., and Adorno, T. W., *Dialektik der Aufklärung* (Amsterdam: Querido, 1947). Eng. trans.: W. Adorno, *Dialectic of Enlightenment: Philosophical Fragments* (Stanford, CA: Stanford University Press, 2002).

Hume, D., *A Treatise of Human Nature* (1740), ed. L. A. Selby-Bigge (Oxford: Clarendon Press, 1888).

Ihering, R. von, *Geist des römischen Rechts auf verschiedenen Stufen seiner Entwicklung*, III-1 (Leipzig: Breitkopf und Härtel, 1865).

———, *Der Kampf um's Recht* (1872) (Berlin: Propyläen Verlag, 1992). Eng. trans.: *The Struggle for Law* (Chicago, IL: Callaghan, 1915).

Ingram, A., *A Political Theory of Rights* (Oxford: Oxford University Press, 1994).

Jellinek, G., *Die Erklärung der Menschen- und Bürgerrechte* (Leipzig: Duncker & Humblot, 1895).

———, *Allgemeine Staatslehre*, 3rd ed. (Berlin: Springer, 1921).

Justinian, *Digestum Vetus Pandectarum Iuris Civilis* (Lyon: Hugo a Porta, 1558–1560).

Kant, I., *Gesammelte Werke* (Akademieausgabe von Immanuel Kants Gesammelten Werken: https://korpora.zim.uni-duisburg-essen.de/Kant/). Eng. trans.: *The Cambridge Edition of the Works of Immanuel Kant—Practical Philosophy* (Cambridge: Cambridge University Press, 1999); Eng. trans.: *Cambridge Edition of the Works of Immanuel Kant: Religion and Rational Theology* (Cambridge: Cambridge University Press, 1996).

———,*Eine Vorlesung Kants über Ethik*, ed, P. Menzer (Berlin: Pan Verlag Rolf Heise, 1924). Eng. trans.: *Cambridge Edition of the Works of Immanuel Kant: Lectures on Ethics* (Cambridge: Cambridge University Press, 1997).

Kass, L., "The Wisdom of Repugnance. Why We Should Ban the Cloning of Humans," *New Republic* (June 2, 1997), pp. 17–26.

———, *Life, Liberty and the Defense of Dignity: The Challenge for Bioethics* (San Francisco, CA: Encounter, 2002).

Kass, L., et al., *Human Cloning and Human Dignity: The Report of the President's Council of Bioethics* (New York: Public Affairs, 2002).

Kelsen, H., *Allgemeine Staatslehre* (Berlin: Julius Springer, 1925).

———, *Vom Wesen und Wert der Demokratie*, 2nd ed. (Tubingen: J. C. B. Mohr, 1929).

———, "Wesen und Entwicklung der Staatsgerichtsbarkeit. Mitbericht von Professor Dr. Hans Kelsen in Wien," in *Veröffentlichungen der Vereinigung der Deutschen Staatsrechtslehrer*, 5 (Berlin and Leipzig: Walter de Gruyter, 1929), pp. 30–89.

Kenny, J., "The Advantages of a Written Constitution Incorporating a Bill of Rights," *North Ireland Legal Quarterly* 30 (1979): 189–206.

Korsgaard, C. M., "From Duty and for the Sake of the Noble: Kant and Aristotle on Morally Good Action" (1996), in *Kant on Emotion and Value* (Oxford: Oxford University Press, 2008), pp. 174–206.

Kramer, M. A., *Liberalism with Excellence* (Oxford: Oxford University Press, 2017).

Kriele, M., *Recht und praktische Vernunft* (Göttingen: Vandenhoek & Ruprecht, 1979).

———, *Einführung in die Staatslehre: Die geschichtlichen Legitimitätsgrundlagen des demokratischen Verfassungsstaates*, 5th ed. (Opladen: Westdeutscher Verlag, 1994).
La Rochefoucauld, F., *Collected Maxims and Other Reflections* (Oxford: Oxford University Press, 2007).
Lewis, C. S., *The Abolition of Man* (New York: Harper Collins, 2001).
Lincoln, A., and Douglas, S., *The Lincoln-Douglas Debates* (Mineola, NY: Dover, 2004).
Lo, C.-S., "Human Rights in the Chinese Tradition," in *Human Rights: Comments and Interpretations; a Symposium Edited by UNESCO* (UNESCO, 1949).
Locke, J., *Two Treatises of Government*, 2nd ed., 24th repr. (Cambridge: Cambridge University Press, 2013).
———, *An Essay Concerning Human Understanding* (Hertfordshire: Wordsworth, 1998).
Lohmus, K., *Caring Autonomy: European Court of Human Rights and the Challenge of Individualism* (New York: Cambridge University Press, 2015).
MacIntyre, A., *Whose Justice? Which Rationality?* (Notre Dame, IN: University of Notre Dame Press, 1988).
———, *Dependent Rational Animals: Why Human Beings Need the Virtues* (Chicago, IL; La Salle, PA: Open Court, 1999).
———, *After Virtue: A Study in Moral Theory*, 3rd ed. (Notre Dame, IN: University of Notre Dame Press, 2007).
Mill, J. S., *On Liberty*, ed. D. Bromwich and G. Kateb (New Haven, CT: Yale University Press, 2003).
Nagel, T., "Rawls on Justice" (1973), in *Reading Rawls*, ed. N. Daniels (Oxford: Blackwell, 1989), pp. 1–16.
Nietzsche, F., *Götzen-Dämerung oder Wie Man mit dem Hammer philosophirt*, en *Sämtliche Werke*, 9 (Berlin: Walter de Gruyter, 1988); Eng. trans.: *Twilight of the Idols or How to Philosophize with a Hammer* (Oxford: Oxford University Press, 1998).
———, *Jenseits von Gut und Böse. Vorspiel einer Philosophie der Zukunft*, en *Sämtliche Werke*, 9 (Berlin: Walter de Gruyter, 1988); Eng. trans.: *Beyond Good and Evil* (Cambridge: Cambridge University Press, 2002).
Nozick, R., "Coercion," in *Philosophy, Science, and Method: Essays in honor of Ernest Nagel*, eds. S. Morgenbesser, P. Suppes, and M. White (New York: St Martin's Press, 1969), pp. 440–72.
———, *Anarchy, State and Utopia* (New York: Basic, 1974, repr. 2013).
O'Neill, O., "Constructivism in Rawls and Kant," in *The Cambridge Companion to Rawls*, ed. S. Freeman (Cambridge: Cambridge University Press, 2003), pp. 347–64.
Ors, Á. d', *Nueva introducción al estudio del Derecho* (Madrid: Civitas, 1999).
Ortega y Gasset, J., *La rebelión de las masas* (Madrid: Espasa Calpe, 2005).
Owen, G. L. E., "Logic and Metaphysics in Some Earlier Works of Aristotle," in *Aristotle and Plato in the Mid-Fourth Century: Papers of the Symposium Aristotelicum Held at Oxford in August 1957*, eds. I. Düring and G. E. L. Owen (Göteborg: Elanders Boktryckeri, 1960), pp. 180–99.

Placencia, L., "Kant y la voluntad como 'razón práctica,'" *Tópicos* 41 (2011): 63–104.

Plato, *Collected Dialogues*, eds. Edith Hamilton and Huntington Cairns (Princeton, NJ: Princeton University Press—*Bollingen Series*, 2009).

Puntambekar, S. V., "Human Freedoms and Hindu Thinking," in *Human Rights: Comments and Interpretations; a Symposium edited by UNESCO* (UNESCO, 1949).

Quong, J., *Liberalism without Perfection* (Oxford: Oxford University Press, 2011).

Radbruch, G., "Gesetzliches Unrecht und Übergesetzliches Recht," *Süddeutsche Juristen-Zeitung* 1, 5 (1946): 105–08.

———, "Die Erneuerung des Rechts," *Die Wandlung* 2, 1 (1947): 8–16.

Rawls, J., "Kantian Constructivism in Moral Theory," *Journal of Philosophy* 77 (1980).

———, "Justice as Fairness: Political Not Metaphysical," *Philosophy and Public Affairs* 4, 3 (1985).

———, "Themes in Kant's Moral Philosophy," in *Kant's Transcendental Deductions*, ed. Eckart Förster (Stanford, CA: Stanford University Press, 1989).

———, *A Theory of Justice*, rev. ed. (Cambridge, MA: Belknap Press of Harvard University Press, 1999).

———, *Justice as Fairness: A Restatement*, ed. Erin Kelly (Cambridge MA: Belknap Press of Harvard University Press, 2001).

———, *Political Liberalism*, ex. ed. (New York: Columbia University Press, 2005).

———, *Lessons on the History of Political Philosophy* (Cambridge MA: Belknap Press of Harvard University Press, 2007).

Raz, J., *The Morality of Freedom* (Oxford: Oxford University Press, 1986).

———, *The Authority of Law*, 2nd ed. (Oxford: Oxford University Press, 2009).

Rhonheimer, M., *The Perspective of Morality* (Washington, DC: Catholic University of America Press, 2011).

———, "The Liberal Image of Man and the Concept of Autonomy," in *The Common Good of Constitutional Democracy* (Washington, DC: Catholic University of America Press, 2013), pp. 36–71.

———, "The Democratic Constitutional State and the Common Good," in *The Common Good of Constitutional Democracy* (Washington, DC: Catholic University of America Press, 2013), pp. 72–141.

———, "The Political Ethos of Constitutional Democracy and the Place of Natural Law in Public Reason: Rawls's '*Political Liberalism*' Revisited," in *The Common Good of Constitutional Democracy* (Washington, DC: Catholic University of America Press, 2013), pp. 191–264.

———, "Rawlsian Public Reason, Natural Law, and the Foundation of Justice: A Response to David Crawford," in *The Common Good of Constitutional Democracy* (Washington, DC: Catholic University of America Press, 2013), pp. 265–91.

Robertson, J., *Children of Choice: Freedom and the New Reproductive Technologies* (Princeton, NJ: Princeton University Press, 1994).

Rousseau, J.-J., *Confessions*, in *Oeuvres complètes*, vol. I (Paris: Gallimard, Bibliothèque de la Pléiade, 1959).

———, *Contrat social*, in *Oeuvres complètes*, vol. III (Paris: Gallimard, Bibliothèque de la Pléiade, 1964).
———, *Émile*, in *Oeuvres complètes*, vol. IV (Paris: Gallimard, Bibliothèque de la Pléiade, 1964).
———, *The Political Writings of Jean-Jacques Rousseau*, ed. Vaughan, vols. I and II (Cambridge: Cambridge University Press, 1915).
Sajó, A., ed., *Abuse: The Dark Side of Fundamental Rights* (Utrecht: Eleven International Publish, 2006).
Sandel, M., *Liberalism and the Limits of Justice*, 2nd ed. (Cambridge: Cambridge University Press, 1998).
———, *The Case against Perfection. Ethics in the Age of Genetic Engineering* (Cambridge, MA: Harvard University Press, 2007).
Scalia, A., *A Matter of Interpretation* (Princeton, NJ: Princeton University Press, 1998).
Scanlon, T. M., "Rawls on Justification," in *The Cambridge Companion to Rawls*, ed. S. Freeman (Cambridge: Cambridge University Press, 2003), pp. 347–64.
Schmitt, C., "Die Tyrannei der Werte," in VV.AA., *Säkularisation und Utopie. Ebracher Studien. Ernst Forsthoff zum 65. Geburtstag* (Stuttgart-Berlin-Cologne-Mainz: W. Kohlhammer, 1967), pp. 37–62.
Schwember, F., *El giro kantiano del contractualismo* (Pamplona: Universidad de Navarra, 2007).
Siedentop, L., *Inventing the Individual. The Origins of Western Liberalism* (Cambridge, MA: Harvard University Press, 2014).
Simón-Yarza, F., *Medio ambiente y derechos fundamentales* (Madrid: Centro de Estudios Políticos y Constitucionales, 2012).
———, "De la igualdad como *límite* a la igualdad como *tarea* del Estado: Evolución histórica de un principio," *Revista Española de Derecho Constitucional* 97 (2013): 76–113.
———, "¿Exención de un *deber* de abortar? Sobre el registro navarro de objetores y el concepto de objeción de conciencia," *Revista Jurídica de Navarra* 58 (2014): 159–80.
———, "La interpretación de los derechos en perspectiva teórica y práctica," in VV.AA., *La Constitución política de España. Estudios en Homenaje a Manuel Aragón Reyes* (Madrid: Centro de Estudios Políticos y Constitucionales, 2016), pp. 895–918.
———, "Right to Freedom," in *Max Planck Encyclopedia of Comparative Constitutional Law* (Oxford: Oxford University Press, August 2016).
———, "Individual Rights," in *Max Planck Encyclopedia of Comparative Constitutional Law* (Oxford: Oxford University Press, February 2017).
———, "Natural Law Theories and Constitutionalism," in *Max Planck Encyclopedia of Comparative Constitutional Law* (Oxford: Oxford University Press, September 2018).
Singer, P., *Practical Ethics*, 3rd ed. (Cambridge: Cambridge University Press, Cambridge, 2010).
Smend, R., *Verfassung und Verfassungsrecht* (München and Leipzig: Duncker & Humblot, 1928).

Solzhenitsyn, A., "The Exhausted West," *Harvard Magazine* (July–August 1978).
Spaemann, R., *Der Ursprung der Soziologie aus dem Geist der Restauration: Studien über L. G. A. De Bonald* (München: Kösel, 1959).
——, "Die Utopie der Herrschaftsfreiheit," *Merkur* 26 (1972): 735–52.
——, "Zur Ontologie der Begriffe 'Rechts' und 'Links,'" in *Was die Wirklichkeit lehrt: Golo Mann zum 70. Geburtstag*, eds. H. Hentig and A. Nitschke (Frankfurt am Main: Fischer, 1979).
——, *Rousseau—Bürger ohne Vaterland* (Piper: München, 1980).
——, "Die Euthanasiedebatte. Wir dürfen das Tabu nicht aufgeben," in *Die Zeit* (June 12, 1992).
——, "Sittliche Normen und Rechtsordnung," in *Das christliche Freiheitsverständnis in seiner Bedeutung für die staatliche Rechtsordnung*, eds. H. Marré, D. Schümmelfeder, and B. Kämper (Münster: Aschendorff, 1996), pp. 5 ff.
——, "Wozu der Aufband? Solterdijk fehlt das Rüstzeug (1999)," in *Grenzen* (Stuttgart: Klett-Cotta, 2001).
——, *Natürliche Ziele. Geschichte und Wiederentdeckung des teleologischen Denkens* (Stuttgart: Klett-Cotta, 2005).
——, *Happiness and Benevolence* (Edinburgh: T & T Clark, 2005).
——, *Persons: The Difference between "Someone" and "Something"* (Oxford: Oxford University Press, 2012).
Starobinski, J., *Jean-Jacques Rousseau: la transparence et l'obstacle* (Paris: Gallimard, 1971).
Stern, K., *Das Staatsrecht der Bundesrepublik Deutschland*, III/1 (München: Beck, 1988).
Strauss, L., *Natural Right and History* (Chicago, IL: University of Chicago Press, 1953).
Sunstein, C., *Legal Reasoning and Political Conflict* (New York; Oxford: Oxford University Press, 1996).
——, *A Constitution of Many Minds* (Princeton, NJ: Princeton University Press, 2009).
Taylor, C., *Sources of the Self: The Making of Modern Identity* (Cambridge, MA: Harvard University Press, 1989).
Tierney, B., *Religion, Law and the Growth of Constitutional Thought 1150–1650* (Cambridge: Cambridge University Press, 1982).
Tocqueville, A., *De la démocratie en Amérique*, en *Oeuvres*, vol. II (Paris: Gallimard, Bibliothèque de la Pléiade, 1992). Eng. trans.: *Historical-Critical*, ed. E. Nolla, 4 vols. (Indianapolis, IN: Liberty Fund, 2009).
Tollefsen, C., "Conscience, Religion and the State," in G. V. Bradley, *Challenges to Religious Liberty in the Twenty-First Century* (New York: Cambridge University Press, 2012), pp. 122–35.
Urbina, F. J., "A Critique of Proportionality," *American Journal of Jurisprudence* 57 (2012): 49–80.
——, *A Critique of Proportionality and Balancing* (Cambridge: Cambridge University Press, 2017).
Vigo, A., "Kant: liberal y anti-relativista," *Estudios públicos* 93 (2004): 29–49.
Waldron, J., "A Right to Do Wrong," *Ethics* 92 (1981): 21–39.

———, *Law and Disagreement* (New York: Oxford University Press, 2001).
Warren, S., and Brandeis, L., "The Right to Privacy," *Harvard Law Review* 4 (December 15, 1890): 193.
Weber, M., "Die 'Objektivität' sozialwissenschaftlicher und sozialpolitischer Erkenntnis," *Archiv für Sozialwissenschaft und Sozialpolitik* 19, 1 (1904): 22–87.
———, "Science as Vocation," in *The Vocation Lectures: Politics as a Vocation—Science as Vocation* (Indianapolis, IN: Hackett, 2004).
Williams, D. K., *Defenders of the Unborn: The Pro-Life Movement Before* Roe v. Wade (New York: Oxford University Press, 2016).
Zambrano, P., "De la imparcialidad al pluralismo razonable y del pluralismo razonable a la circularidad semántica," in *John Rawls. Justicia, liberalismo y razón pública*, ed. I. Garzón Vallejo (Mexico: UNAM, 2016) pp. 205–239.

Index of names

Adorno, Theodor L. W., 2, 7, 165, 168
Agar, Nicholas, 155, 157, 160, 162, 165, 166, 167, 168
Alexy, Robert, 92, 104, 122, 126, 202
Anderson, Ryan T., 126
Annas, Julia, 16, 30, 125
Antiphon, 28
Apel, Karl-Otto, 93
Apollinaire, Guillaume, 117
Aquinas, St Thomas, 2, 5, 7, 12–13, 15, 18–19, 21–24, 28–33, 35, 38–39, 42–43, 46, 49–51, 55, 64, 70, 72, 80, 85, 89–90, 96, 105, 111–12, 125, 136–38, 149–50, 168, 176, 185–86, 188, 190, 202
Aristotle, 3, 5, 7, 11–12, 14–20, 24, 28–33, 35, 38–39, 42, 46, 48, 51, 55, 76, 80–81, 85–86, 89, 90, 138, 164, 168, 200, 202, 204
Augustine, St, 24, 32, 49
Austin, John, 33

Bacon, Francis, 168
Benn, Gottfried, 160, 167
Bentham, Jeremy, 33, 116, 140–41, 150, 188
Berlin, Isaiah, 12, 28, 31, 33, 48, 51, 166, 168
Berti, Enrico, 30

Blackmun, Harry, 130
Böckenförde, Ernst-Wolfgang, 71, 196, 203
Bodin, Jean, 63, 71
Boethius, Anicius Manlius Severinus, 136, 149
Bohm, John, 33, 168
Bork, Robert, 204
Bradley, Gerard V., 126
Brandeis, Louis, 189
Bromwich, David, 188
Brooks, David, 189
Buchanan, Allen, 155, 157, 159, 161, 166, 167, 168
Budziszewski, Jay, 31, 105
Burian, Peter, 32
Byrd, B. Sharon, 42, 49–50

Callicles, 28, 31, 102
Cartabia, Marta, 204
Cicero, Marcus Tullius, 32
Coke, Sir Edward, 204
Cole, Teju, 189
Comte, Auguste, 168
Condorcet, M. J. A., Marquis de, 154, 167
Corvino, John F., 126
Crito of Alopece, 86
Cronin, Ciaran P., 104

Daniels, Norman, 71–72, 87
De Lazari-Radek, Katarzyna, 150
Descartes, René, 168
Devlin, Patrick, 4, 7
DeWolfe Howe Mark, 125
Diels, Hermann Alexander, 105, 169
Díez-Picazo, Luis María, 188
Di Fabio, Udo, 189
Domingo, Rafael, 149
Douglas, Stephen, 200, 204
Dreyfus, Alfred, 173
Dürig, Günter, 189
Düring, Ingemar, 33
Dworkin, Ronald, 4, 6, 7, 33, 73–89,
 91, 109, 110, 114–16, 121, 125,
 129–37, 141, 143, 145–46, 148–51,
 153, 155–59, 163, 165–68, 180–81,
 189, 191–92, 197–99, 203

Enoch, David, 183, 189
Ermacora, Felix, 190

Faggion, Andrea, 51
Finnis, John, 23, 31–33, 49–50,
 72, 106, 125, 150, 174, 181–82,
 188–90, 200–201, 204
Flores d'Arcais, Paolo, 189
Förster, Eckart, 71
Forsthoff, Ernst, 105
Frankfurt, Harry, 72
Freeman, Samuel, 71
Freud, Anna, 7
Freud, Sigmund, 2–3, 7, 151
Fukuyama, Francis, 154, 167
Fuller, Lon, 33

Gadamer, Hans-Georg, 16–17, 30–31
Gagarin, Michael, 28
Galston, William A., 184, 189, 190
Galton, Sir Francis, 153
García Pelayo, Manuel, 179, 189
Gentili, Alberico, 63, 72
George, Robert P., 28, 58, 70, 150, 167,
 174, 176, 181–82, 184, 188–90,
 194, 202–3

Girgis, Sherif, 126
Glaucon, 26–27
Glendon, Mary Ann, 115–16, 121,
 125, 126
Goethe, J. W., 142, 150
Gómez Montoro, Ángel J., 126
Gutmann, Amy, 203

Habermas, Jürgen, 6, 35, 56, 91–106,
 109, 154, 157–61, 167, 174, 191,
 194–97, 202–3
Hart, H. L. A., 5, 24–25, 32–33, 65, 72,
 174, 204
Hegel, G. W. F., 94
Hentig, Harmut, 7
Heraclitus of Ephesus, 96, 169
Herstein, Ori J., 189
Hippias of Elis, 28
Hitler, Adolf, 80, 153, 166
Hobbes, Thomas, 25–27, 33–34,
 90–91, 168
Hohfeld, Wesley Newcomb, 182–84,
 189, 190, 199
Holland, Thomas Erskine, 183
Holmes, Oliver Wendell, 111, 125, 153
Horkheimer, Max, 2, 7, 165, 168
Hruschka, Joachim, 42, 49–50
Hume, David, 59–60, 70, 84, 112, 141

Ihering, Rudolf von, 109, 124, 187, 190
Ingram, Attracta, 195, 202
Isidore of Seville, St, 25, 33

Jellinek, Georg, 22, 25, 32, 189
John, St, 100
Julius Caesar, 32, 96, 105

Kämper, Burkhard, 105
Kant, Immanuel, 5, 35–51, 55, 57,
 59, 64, 70–72, 75–76, 88, 92–94,
 98–99, 101, 103, 106, 114, 125, 138,
 163, 168
Kass, Leon, 154, 162–63, 166, 168
Kateb, George, 188
Kelly, Erin L., 70

Index of names

Kelsen, Hans, 25, 32, 100, 105, 200, 204
Kenny, John, 199, 204
Klein, Joel Thiago, 50
Klug, Brian, 189
Koons, Robert C., 30
Korsgaard, Christine M., 48
Kramer, Matthew, 114, 125, 126, 127, 149
Kriele, Martin, 71, 98, 101, 105, 106

La Rochefoucauld, François de, 117, 126
Lee, Patrick, 150
Lewis, Clive Staples, 105, 169
Lincoln, Abraham, 200, 204
Lo, Chung-Shu, 188
Locke, John, 141–42, 150, 198, 203
Lohmus, Katri, 204

MacIntyre, Alasdair, 18, 28, 30–31, 86, 90, 125, 167, 193, 202
Mann, Golo, 1, 7
Mann, Thomas, 1
Marré, Heiner, 105
Maunz, Theodor, 189
Maurras, Charles, 173, 188
McCarthy, Thomas, 104, 105
Menzer, Paul, 44, 50
Mill, James, 116
Mill, John Stuart, 22, 79, 116, 177, 185–86, 188, 190, 195
Milton, John, 179
Morgenbesser, Sidney, 127

Nagel, Thomas, 60–61, 71, 143, 150, 158–59, 203
Nietzsche, F. W., 96, 145–46, 148, 151
Nitschke, August, 7
Nozick, Robert, 88, 113, 123, 125, 127, 143, 150, 157, 167, 203

O'Neill, Onora, 71
Ors, Álvaro d', 30
Ortega y Gasset, José, 4, 7
Owen, Gwilym E. L., 33

Paul, St, 41
Phaedrus of Myrrhinus, 201
Pilate, Pontius, 100
Pinzani, Alessandro, 51
Placencia, Luis, 49
Plato, 11, 18, 22, 24, 25, 27–29, 31–33, 51, 85, 89, 90, 102, 105, 106, 166, 169, 204
Protagoras of Abdera, 85
Puntambekar, Shrikrishna Venkatesh, 188

Quong, Jonathan, 127

Radbruch, Gustav, 33
Ratzinger, Joseph, 104
Rawls, John, 5–7, 35, 55–75, 83–84, 87–88, 91, 94, 96, 100, 109, 110, 111, 112, 113, 125, 129–30, 143, 150, 153, 155–56, 165–67, 169, 174, 186, 188, 191–92, 203
Raz, Joseph, 6, 61, 71, 82, 89, 124, 127, 174, 188–89, 191–94, 202
Rehg, William, 104
Rhonheimer, Martin, 29, 72, 98, 105, 186, 190
Richard of St Victor, 136, 149
Robertson, John, 167
Rousseau, Jean-Jacques, 19, 25–28, 34, 45, 57, 90
Rubio Llorente, Francisco, 126

Sajó, Andras, 204
Sánchez Madrid, Nuria, 51
Sandel, Michael, 60, 67, 71–72, 112, 125, 154, 160, 164, 166, 167, 168
Scalia, Antonin, 204
Scanlon, Thomas Michael, 87, 88, 143, 150, 169, 203
Schmitt, Carl, 97, 101, 105
Schümmelfeder, Dieter, 105
Schwember, Felipe, 49
Shapiro, Alan, 32
Siedentop, Larry, 33, 175, 188

Simmias of Thebes, 86
Simón-Yarza, Fernando, 88, 126, 168, 188, 203
Simpson, A. W. Brian, 188
Singer, Peter, 131–32, 135, 137, 138, 139, 140, 141, 142, 146–47, 149–51
Smend, Rudolf, 202
Socrates, 17–18, 25–26, 28–29, 31, 85, 86, 95, 102, 201
Sophocles, 32
Spaemann, Robert, 1, 2, 7, 29, 34, 55, 68, 72, 88–90, 96, 98, 100, 105, 125, 147, 149–51, 167, 188
Starobinski, Jean, 90
Stern, Klaus, 202
Strachey, James, 7
Strauss, Leo, 15, 28, 30, 33
Sunstein, Cass R., 197, 203–4
Suppes, Patrick, 127

Taney, Roger B., 200
Taylor, Charles, 31, 68, 72, 96–97, 105, 162, 164, 167–68, 169
Thompson, Dennis, 203

Thomson, Judith Jarvis, 143, 150, 204
Thrasymachus of Chalcedon, 31
Tierney, Brian, 33
Tocqueville, Alexis de, 95, 103, 105, 106, 177, 188, 195
Tollefsen, Christopher O., 126, 150
Tooley, Michael, 139
Tribe, Laurence, 87
Tugendhat, Ernst, 101

Ulpian, G. Domitius A., 13, 23, 29, 32, 44
Urbina, Francisco Javier, 202

Vigo, Alejandro G., 48, 50

Waldron, Jeremy, 89, 180–81, 189, 199, 203–4
Warren, Samuel, 189
Weber, Max, 33, 87, 90, 160, 167
White, Morton, 127
Williams, Daniel K., 150
Wolfe, Christopher, 190

About the author

Fernando Simón-Yarza is associate professor of constitutional law at the University of Navarra (Spain). He graduated in law with an academic award for the best grades. His doctoral thesis was awarded with the prestigious "Tomás y Valiente Prize 2011," given every two years by the Center for Political and Constitutional Studies and the Constitutional Court of Spain to the best work on constitutional law written in Spanish (see Article 2 Rules of the Prize).

He has completed research stays in the Westfälische Wilhelms-Universität Münster (2008–2009), Boston University (2012), and Princeton University, where he was a visiting fellow at the James Madison Program of American Ideals and Institutions (2014–2015). He has delivered lectures and participated in conferences in several universities and academic centers of different countries: Autonomous University of Madrid, University of Barcelona, Spanish Center for Political and Constitutional Studies, Princeton University, University of Oxford, University of Massachusetts, Scuola Superiore Sant'Anna (Pisa, Italy), University of the Andes (Chile), University of Parma (Italy), Catholic Portuguese University (Lisbon, Portugal), Cardinal Stefan Wyszyński University in Warsaw (Poland), Université Paris I—Panthéon Sorbonne, Autonomous University of Tlaxcala (Mexico), and so forth. He has widely published on issues related to constitutional law and constitutional theory, and he has collaborated regularly as a peer reviewer with the main Spanish constitutional law reviews.

He is a member of the Constitutionalists Association of Spain and of the James Madison Society (Princeton University).